PSYCHOLOGY OF EATING

Neil Rowland
University of Florida

Emily Crews Splane
Flagler College

PEARSON

Boston   Columbus   Indianapolis   New York   San Francisco   Upper Saddle River
Amsterdam   Cape Town   Dubai   London   Madrid   Milan   Munich   Paris   Montréal   Toronto
Delhi   Mexico City   São Paulo   Sydney   Hong Kong   Seoul   Singapore   Taipei   Tokyo

Editor in Chief: Ashley Dodge
Acquisitions Editor: Susan Hartman
Editorial Assistant: Amandria Guadalupe
Vice President/Director of Marketing: Brandy Dawson
Executive Marketing Manager: Kelly May
Senior Marketing Coordinator: Courtney Stewart
Managing Editor: Denise Forlow
Program Manager: Reena Dalal
Senior Operations Supervisor: Mary Fischer
Operations Specialist: Diane Peirano

Art Director: Jayne Conte
Cover Designer: Bruce Keselaar
Cover Image: © Mikhail hoboton Popov/Shutterstock
Director of Digital Media: Brian Hyland
Digital Media Project Manager: Tina Gagliostro
Full-Service Project Management and Composition: Abinaya Rajendran/Integra Software Services Pvt. Ltd.
Printer/Binder: R R Donnelley/Harrisonburg
Cover Printer: R R Donnelley/Harrisonburg
Text Font: 10/12, Minion Pro

Credits and acknowledgments borrowed from other sources and reproduced, with permission, in this textbook appear on appropriate page within text.

Library of Congress Cataloging-in-Publication Data
Rowland, Neil.
    Psychology of eating/Neil Rowland, University of Florida, Emily Splane,
Flagler College.—First Edition.
        pages cm
    Includes bibliographical references.
    ISBN-13: 978-0-205-85263-5 (alk. paper)
    ISBN-10: 0-205-85263-7 (alk. paper)
    1. Food habits—Psychological aspects.   2. Nutrition—Psychological aspects.   3. Nutrition policy.
    I. Splane, Emily.   II. Title.
    TX357.R795 2013
    394.1'2—dc23
                                                                                2013018169

10 9 8 7 6 5 4 3 2 1

ISBN-10:   0-205-85263-7
ISBN-13: 978-0-205-85263-5

BRIEF CONTENTS

CONTENTS

PREFACE

People are obsessed with food. If you do not have enough food, which was almost always the case for our distant ancestors, your thoughts and actions are directed toward obtaining food. Even in today's world in which many of us have plenty of "mouth-ready" food available, people spend large amounts of time thinking about food or rituals in which food plays a prominent role. Huge for-profit industries have been built on these human proclivities, ranging from advertising, production or retailing of an increasing array of tasty foods, to weight management or loss and medical treatment of obesity-related diseases.

Have you ever stopped to ask why humans are so attracted to food, or whether it is unique to humans? This book attempts to pose these questions, and explore answers. We firmly believe that psychological science is the only academic discipline that is capable of spanning and integrating the vast range of subdisciplines that are relevant to the topic. In this text, we focus on "normal" eating: How did it evolve, how does it develop and become manifest in modern society, and what functions does it fulfill? We also address contemporary problems associated with eating. We have a chapter devoted to diagnosable eating disorders including anorexia and bulimia nervosa; however, from a perspective of sheer numbers and adverse economic impact, eating too much and becoming obese is by far the biggest problem. Thus, much of the book is focused on explanations of and possible solutions to what many in the field now refer to as an obesity epidemic.

This book has arisen out of an undergraduate special topics course "Psychology of Eating" we first taught about a decade ago. Our impetus was to develop an integrative or capstone course for undergraduates who simply want to learn more about their own eating, who are contemplating a career in one of the for-profit industries mentioned earlier, or in a related government or nonprofit activity. With more than 50% of the adult population and up to 25% of children now classified as overweight or obese, this field will provide considerable employment opportunities for the foreseeable future! Our book might also serve as background material from which to launch discussions at a graduate level. Most of our chapters include citations to primary or additional resources.

Most human behaviors, and misbehaviors, have biological and sociocultural determinants. Eating is an excellent example of this, and in addition uses commodities (foods) that themselves have defined physical and chemical properties. So you cannot understand eating without knowing something about nutrition, energy, genes, chemical sensing, and brain structures. This book contains information about all of these, and it would have been easy to write an entire book on these topics. Instead, we have tried to present these topics in a relatively simple form within the context of the science background typical of many psychology majors. That is, you don't have to be an expert in all or any of these areas to be able to read and hopefully understand the book. We believe that even if your primary interest is in the sociocultural topics, taking the time to read about biological foundations will enrich your understanding. Conversely, we do not believe that exclusive focus on the basic science aspects enables you to appreciate the complexity of human thought and behavior that dominates most people's decisions about what, when, and how much they eat. The book is not organized in a rigidly linear or progressive manner: Each chapter stands alone and can be sequenced in more or less any order, but this order works for us! In the last chapter of the book, which you probably should leave for last, we discuss treatments or strategies to reverse this trend toward an obese world—a trend that is economically unsustainable. It's convenient to point the finger of blame at the food industry, and some entities have done just that by implementing controversial taxes or other restrictions.

But we regard the real problem as the love affair that people have with food and its manifestations such as marketing. What strategies have the best chance to cool off this affair and implement sustainable lifelong relationships with food?

The "obesity problem" is not fundamentally different from other contemporary issues, for example, climate change. In both cases, technologies have over time enabled humans to develop unsustainable behaviors: We have to find technological and psychological approaches to change those behaviors.

We want to thank the editors and staff at Pearson for encouragement and help throughout this project. We also thank the reviewers of earlier drafts of these chapters for their insightful comments that have improved every aspect of the book: Charlotte Markey, Rutgers University; Jennifer Harriger, Pepperdine University; Deb Briihl, Valdosta State University; Sarah Savoy; Alison Ventura, Drexel University; Doris Davis; Thomas Alley, Clemson University; Steven St. John, Rollins College; Lori Forzano, The College at Brockport, State University of New York; Bryan Raudenbush, Wheeling Jesuit University; Kevin Myers, Bucknell University and Carla Bluhm, College of Coastal Georgia, and especially all of our students who are our enduring inspiration.

Psychology of Eating: The Nexus of Nutrition, Brain, and Behavior

After reading this chapter, you will be able to

- Understand the relevance of many scientific disciplines to the psychology of eating
- Define the terms *motivation*, *hunger*, and *satiety* as they relate to eating

- Be able to relate the concept of body mass index to health and obesity
- Realize the economic burden that is borne by a society that is increasingly obese

INTRODUCTION

"You are what you eat" is a commonly heard slogan, and coincidentally the title of a 2006 best seller by Gillian McKeith. Although this slogan does contain elements of truth, it begs the central question of why you eat, with the immediate follow-up questions of what, where, when, and how much. This text is all about the science behind eating that tries to answer these questions. If you think about eating as a scientific problem, it very quickly becomes apparent that many branches of science are involved, including psychology, biology, nutrition, and neuroscience. We believe a well-rounded approach to eating behavior must include each of these elements and, further, that psychological science is an integrative discipline that is uniquely well positioned to bridge the streams of scientific thought that are relevant to eating and its problems (Figure 1.1). Whereas we

do not assume or require an in-depth background in these areas, readers who believe they do not have an adequate preparation are invited to read the two short appendices that review a few basic principles of neuroscience and genetics.

Several books or monographs bear the title or subtitle "The Psychology of Eating," including those by Capaldi (1996), Logue (2004), and Ogden (2010), as well as numerous nonacademic offerings in the field. The coverage in our book builds on these foundations, but with a new point of emphasis on obesity. Some texts focus on eating disorders such as anorexia and bulimia nervosa, and these are of particular interest and relevance to college-age readers. About 1% to 3% of the population suffer from these serious disorders (Hudson, Hiripi, Pope, & Kessler, 2007), but the prevalence of overweight (33%) and obesity (36%) in adults is each an order of

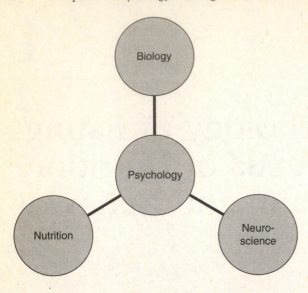

FIGURE 1.1 Psychology occupies an interdisciplinary and integrative role with regard to feeding behavior.

magnitude greater (Flegal, Carroll, Kit, & Ogden, 2012). Obesity is associated with emotional problems and reduced life expectancy (Luppino et al., 2010). Further, overweight and obesity have a devastating economic impact in direct (e.g., health care) and indirect (e.g., lost work days) costs, estimated in 2008 to be $147 billion in the United States (Finkelstein, Trogdon, Cohen, & Dietz, 2009), or about $500 per year for every man, woman, and child. These costs are rising rapidly—as we write this, it is probably nearer $1,000. Can you think of better ways to spend "your" $1,000 (Figure 1.2)?

Then there's the problem of deniability or "it won't happen to me" (Weinstein, 1984). In our own classrooms, we ask students (who are mostly about 20 years old and not overweight) how many of them think their parents are overweight or obese. About half say "yes." Then we ask how many of them believe they will be overweight when they reach their parents' current age. Almost no one believes that. How would you have answered these questions? The fact is that (U.S.) population statistics indicate that middle-aged people have at least a 65% chance of being overweight or obese, so what makes you so sure you will come out on the thin side of this coin toss? In many modern societies, obesity is widely considered to be an undesirable condition, but like

many other undesirable conditions (e.g., poverty, drug addiction, fatal illness), almost no one aspires to it or believes that it will happen to him or her. So, right from the start, we are trying to convince you of something that you may not see as relevant. We hope to persuade you that obesity is a problem that will impact you, if not personally then certainly indirectly, for example, by paying higher health insurance premiums. That's where "your" $1,000 per year disappears: It's like a tax on all of us. Our call to you, the student, is to choose a career or lifestyle to prevent or fix this problem. Let's face it—your authors' generation has been spectacularly unsuccessful in this endeavor!

This book is divided into several sections that we believe encompass the broad range of topics that are relevant to the title of our book. These need not be approached in a strictly sequential manner, although we find some logic in our organization. The first section examines food as an energy source (nutrition), as a stimulant of our senses (chemosensation), and as a commodity that has shaped our past physiology and behavior (evolution). The second section looks at factors that influence an individual's eating such as learning, development, the sociocultural milieu, and emotions. The third section is focused on biology of normal and abnormal eating, including genetics, eating disorders, and treatments for

FIGURE 1.2   The approximate per capita annual cost of obesity, as health care and lost work productivity, in the United States in 2012 dollars.

obesity. Finally, we will try to synthesize all of this diverse information to stimulate your thoughts about future approaches to inappropriate eating and obesity, including roles for business and government.

Before we embark on this journey, it seems appropriate to address two general questions. The first is "what is the goal of eating?" This will be considered in several chapters, but for now we should give you a little background on the theoretical concepts that have been advanced. The second question is "what is the definition of obesity?" Maybe you already asked yourself this question several paragraphs ago, and if you did, then you are already thinking like a scientist! Science requires precision of definition as well as precision in measurement, so, as you read this text, we challenge you to ask yourself "what do you mean by that" and "what's the evidence?"

WHAT IS THE GOAL OF EATING?

Psychologists often talk about "goal-directed behaviors." If you think about it, most behavior has a goal such as waiting for a bus to get you to a destination or developing some commercial material to present to a potential customer. But these examples are really steps along the way: What will you do at the destination and why do you need another customer? To help make this distinction more explicit, scientists have used the terms *distal* (or ultimate) and *proximate* to describe causes of behavior (Alessi, 1992) or, as we will use in the present context, **appetitive behaviors** that bring us from an environment with no food into the immediate vicinity of food and **consummatory behaviors** that deliver the food into our mouth and to our digestive system.

TALKING POINT 1.1

The terms *appetitive* and *consummatory* can be used broadly. Imagine you are shopping at the mall: Which of your behaviors would you consider appetitive and which consummatory?

Compare your lists with those of your classmates. Are there any behaviors that show up on both lists or that you found hard to categorize?

These terms are mostly descriptions of the relationship between an individual and an object in the environment, but they do not specifically address the internal forces or mechanisms that energize or sustain a behavior. In an influential book, Clark Hull (1943) was one of the first psychologists to theorize about such internal mechanisms and used the term *drive* to describe the force(s) that power and direct behavior. Others such as Robert Bolles (1967) used the term *motivation* (from latin *movere*), which can include both thoughts and actions. These terms are now used less frequently as explanatory constructs, in part because it is evident that different behaviors have different internal energizing mechanisms. For example, you might be motivated to find food but not water. The motivational states that underlie these two behaviors are called hunger and thirst, respectively. We will focus on **hunger**. If you see someone eating and ask him or her why, there is a good chance he or she will say "because I'm hungry." This statement might be refined by intensity (a lot or a little) or object specificity (e.g., cookie or celery), but it's hunger nonetheless.

Perhaps the most easily understood occasion for hunger is one that develops following an extended period without eating at all or eating very little. You may have experienced a period of food deprivation or been on a diet. If you're like most people, your thoughts and actions become progressively more dominated by food. If you are hungry right now, you might start drawing food in your notebook or looking up restaurants on your electronic device! Also, you are more likely to engage in behaviors that bring you in contact with food—visiting the vending machine or cafeteria or calling for food to be delivered to you. And maybe you become less picky about what

you will eat—perhaps potato will do just fine instead of parfait. Without much if any conscious effort, all of these thoughts and behaviors lead us to food.

The concept of *hunger* has solved the problem of mechanism, right? No—and if it had, then this would be an extremely short text! Instead, it has reframed the question to "what is it that makes us hungry?" And there's a second question: "If food is available all the time, do we eat only when we are hungry, or are there times we eat when we are not hungry?" This is an important question because if the answer is that there are times we eat when we are not hungry, or even that we start eating on different occasions at different levels of hunger (i.e., there is a different threshold), then there will not be a one-to-one or quantitative correspondence between hunger and behavior. Think again about the time when you were without food for an extended period of time. Did your sensation of hunger get more and more intense as time went by, or did it come and go in waves? In general, people rate their hunger as increasing with time since food and decreasing after eating (Barkeling, King, Naslund, & Blundell, 2007). Many theories of feeding now talk about **satiety** or **fullness** rather than hunger. *Satiety* is often defined as the absence of hunger.

Aside from regulating sensations of hunger or satiety, is there any other goal to eating? To answer this, it is useful to step outside of ourselves for a moment and realize that all animals eat. We cannot be sure that all (or any) other animals experience hunger or satiety in the way that we do, or indeed that your subjective experience is the same for your parents, classmates, or anyone else. We do know that many aspects of animals' feeding

FIGURE 1.3 Monkey eating a banana in its natural habitat.

behaviors are similar to our own (Figure 1.3). So why do animals eat? Chances are that you might answer this "in order to survive"; after all, that's the message you've all seen on wildlife TV shows.

This brings up another important point: Because all animals eat, the study of feeding behavior of animals can give us important insights into human behavior. Further, for animals that have similar feeding habits to our own (i.e., mammalian omnivores), there is every reason to believe that the physiological and brain mechanisms underlying feeding are similar to our own. Although many aspects of feeding and the brain can be directly studied in humans, and many examples will be given in this book, there are some scientific procedures and measures that we cannot do in humans but instead turn to suitable animal models to address the questions. Most such research uses rats or mice, and we will occasionally refer to some of these studies. All animal research is highly regulated and reviewed by both institutional and national entities with regard to rigorously humane treatment and scientific necessity.

The relatively new specialty area of evolutionary psychology considers how psychological traits (thoughts and behaviors) may have been molded by evolutionary forces in play at the time of the emergence of modern humans. Fossil records appear to show that the earliest hominids emerged about 4.5 million years ago; they were **hunter-gatherers**—food acquisition was central to their survival (Figure 1.4). In the next 4.3 million years of hominids' existence, prior to

FIGURE 1.4 The earliest hominids were hunter-gatherers and developed simple tools that allowed them to improve their hunting success.

the emergence about 200,000 years ago of modern humans (*Homo sapiens*), various species of *Australopithecus* and *Homo* evolved only to suffer extinction. A common theme of hominid evolution is the progressive alteration of body shape or size, including erect stature and the development of bigger brains. One major function of these brains must have been improved ability to garner and manage food resources. It follows that most of our psychological functions may be linked to food in one way or another!

In 200,000 years, *Homo sapiens* have developed complex societies (White, 1959). Culture and technology distinguish us from our distant ancestors and from other species of animals. Archaeological data suggest that from the earliest times, humans asked questions concerning the origin of life and the concept of *mortality*, but until recently they had only a religious or cultural context within which to consider these questions. Over the past few hundred years, the scientific method has emerged to provide a universal observation-based framework to advance knowledge, often with spectacular results. One consequence of scientific progress is the accelerated rate at which we can and do alter our environment, including food-relevant categories such as large-scale agriculture and transportation. In some ways, we have a stone-age body (and brain) living in an unforeseen world in which reality is now often virtual.

WHAT IS THE DEFINITION OF OBESITY?

In 1943, the Metropolitan Life Insurance Company published actuarial standard weight-for-height tables, giving ideal or healthiest weights for various heights and at three body-frame sizes (small, medium, and large, determined by bone size measured as breadth at the elbow—although most people self-categorize!) and for men and women separately. Select entries from its tables are shown in the top panel of Figure 1.5. In more recent years, **body mass index (BMI)** has been used. BMI = mass in kilograms divided by the square of height in meters (thus, the units for BMI are $kg.m^{-2}$). You can find your own BMI easily using any one of the many online BMI calculators or from Table 1.1.

It is evident that for a given frame size, BMI tends to be greater in men than women of the same height, and lower in tall compared with short people. BMI values that we derived from the Metropolitan Life ideals are shown in the lower panel of Figure 1.5. All values fall between 19.6 and 26.0 $kg.m^{-2}$, which are in or close to the range of BMI now classified as normal or healthy:

- BMI less than 18.5 = underweight
- BMI 18.5–24.9 = normal or healthy
- BMI 25–29.9 = overweight (also known as pre-obese)
- BMI 30 or more = obese (class I = 30–34.9, class II = 35–39.9, etc.)

Another way of viewing the data in Figure 1.5 is that the Metropolitan Life ideals recommend a lower BMI for tall people and women compared with short people or men. For this and other reasons, the Metropolitan Life standard has been abandoned in favor of BMI—but is BMI a perfect index? One assumption underlying the interpretation of BMI is that all weight change in adulthood reflects changes in body fat, and that too much fat is bad. This may often be the case, but there are certainly

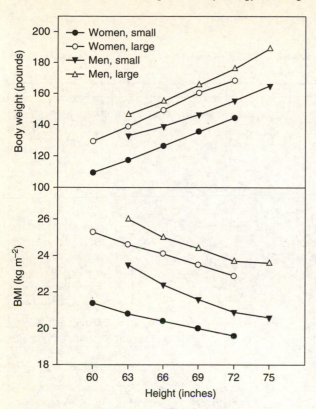

FIGURE 1.5 Weight for height standards.
The top panel shows the mean ideal weight for various heights of men and women and for small or large frame (medium frame data are intermediate but not shown for clarity). Numbers are derived from Metropolitan Life Insurance Company tables (1943) for adults ages 25–59 wearing 1-inch heels and indoor clothing. The bottom panel shows the BMI values derived from these mean data. Weight in kg is ~0.45 × weight in pounds; height in meters is ~0.025 × height in inches.

exceptions. For example, strength athletes have high muscle mass, hence high BMI, but this does not reflect excessive fat. Likewise, from a health perspective, not all fat is created equal. In particular, excess fat in the abdominal region (more common in males) imparts increased risk of cardiovascular disease, whereas the same extra fat in the hips (more common in females) does not carry the same risk (see Arsenault, Beaumont, Despres, & Larose, 2012, for review). Measures that specifically gauge abdominal fat are waist circumference and the ratio of waist to hip circumferences. Bear in mind that when most health professionals use the term *obesity*, they have a precise BMI criterion in mind. BMI is a useful snapshot of population trends (as will be discussed next) or an individual's changes across time. Thus, in an adult whose height does not appreciably change, deviations in his or her body weight will result in strictly proportional changes in BMI (see the following "do the math" exercise).

DO THE MATH

Imagine a 5'2" female starting college at a weight of 120 pounds. Over the next year, she gains the mythical "freshman 15 (pounds)." Use an online calculator to compute BMI at the start and end of that year. The next year, she gains an additional "sophomore 15." What are the new numbers, and how do they map onto the recommended BMI categories? Her friend is a 6'2" male weighing 160 pounds at the start of his freshman year, and he has the same weight gains of 15 pounds per year. What are his BMI numbers and categories? *(Answers are at the end of this chapter.)*

TABLE 1.1 Body Mass Index Table

Obese (>30)   Overweight (25–30)   Normal (18.5–25)   Underweight (<18.5)

HEIGHT in feet/inches and centimeters

WEIGHT lbs (kg)	4'8" 142cm	4'9"	4'10" 147	4'11" 150	5'0" 152	5'1" 155	5'2" 157	5'3" 160	5'4" 163	5'5" 165	5'6" 168	5'7" 170	5'8" 173	5'9" 175	5'10" 178	5'11" 180	6'0" 183	6'1" 185	6'2" 188	6'3" 191	6'4" 193	6'5" 196
260 (117.9)	58	56	54	53	51	49	48	46	45	43	42	41	40	38	37	36	35	34	33	32	32	31
255 (115.7)	57	55	53	51	50	48	47	45	44	42	41	40	39	38	37	36	35	34	33	32	31	30
250 (113.4)	56	54	52	50	49	47	46	44	43	42	40	39	38	37	36	35	34	33	32	31	30	30
245 (111.1)	55	53	51	49	48	46	45	43	42	41	40	38	37	36	35	34	33	32	31	31	30	29
240 (108.9)	54	52	50	48	47	45	44	43	41	40	39	38	36	35	34	33	33	32	31	30	29	28
235 (106.6)	53	51	49	47	46	44	43	42	40	39	38	37	36	35	34	33	32	31	30	29	29	28
230 (104.3)	52	50	48	46	45	43	42	41	39	38	37	36	35	34	33	32	31	30	30	29	28	27
225 (102.1)	50	49	47	45	44	43	41	40	39	37	36	35	34	33	32	31	31	30	29	28	27	27
220 (99.8)	49	48	46	44	43	42	40	39	38	37	36	34	33	32	32	31	30	29	28	27	27	26
215 (97.5)	48	47	45	43	42	41	39	38	37	36	35	33	33	32	31	30	29	28	28	27	26	25
210 (95.3)	47	45	44	42	41	40	38	37	36	35	34	33	32	31	30	29	28	28	27	26	26	25
205 (93.0)	46	44	43	41	40	39	37	36	35	34	33	32	31	30	29	29	28	27	26	26	25	24
200 (90.7)	45	43	42	40	39	38	37	35	34	33	32	31	30	30	29	28	27	26	26	25	24	24
195 (88.5)	44	42	41	39	38	37	36	34	33	32	31	31	30	29	28	27	26	26	25	24	24	23
190 (86.2)	43	41	40	38	37	36	35	34	33	32	31	30	29	28	27	26	26	25	24	24	23	23
185 (83.9)	41	40	39	37	36	35	34	33	32	31	30	29	28	27	27	26	25	24	24	23	23	22
180 (81.6)	40	39	38	36	35	34	33	32	31	30	29	28	27	27	26	25	24	24	23	22	22	21
175 (79.4)	39	38	37	35	34	33	32	31	30	29	28	27	27	26	25	24	24	23	22	22	21	21
170 (77.1)	38	37	36	34	33	32	31	30	29	28	27	27	26	25	24	24	23	22	22	21	21	20
165 (74.8)	37	36	34	33	32	31	30	29	28	27	27	26	25	24	24	23	22	22	21	21	20	20
160 (72.6)	36	35	33	32	31	30	29	28	27	27	26	25	24	24	23	22	22	21	21	20	19	19
155 (70.3)	35	34	32	31	30	29	28	27	27	26	25	24	24	23	22	22	21	20	20	19	19	18
150 (68.0)	34	32	31	30	29	28	27	27	26	25	24	23	23	22	22	21	20	20	19	19	18	18
145 (65.8)	33	31	30	29	28	27	27	26	25	24	23	23	22	21	21	20	20	19	19	18	18	17
140 (63.5)	31	30	29	28	27	26	26	25	24	23	23	22	21	21	20	20	19	18	18	17	17	17
135 (61.2)	30	29	28	27	26	26	25	24	23	22	22	21	21	20	19	19	18	18	17	17	16	16
130 (59.0)	29	28	27	26	25	25	24	23	22	22	21	20	20	19	19	18	18	17	17	16	16	15
125 (56.7)	28	27	26	25	24	24	23	22	21	21	20	20	19	18	18	17	17	16	16	16	15	15
120 (54.4)	27	26	25	24	23	23	22	21	21	20	19	19	18	18	17	17	16	16	15	15	15	14
115 (52.2)	26	25	24	23	22	22	21	20	20	19	19	18	17	17	16	16	15	15	14	14	14	14
110 (49.9)	25	24	23	22	21	21	20	19	19	18	18	17	17	16	16	15	15	14	14	13	13	13
105 (47.6)	24	23	22	21	20	20	19	19	18	17	17	16	16	15	15	14	14	13	13	12	12	12
100 (45.4)	22	22	21	20	20	19	18	18	17	17	16	16	15	15	14	14	13	13	12	12	12	11
95 (43.1)	21	21	20	19	19	18	17	17	16	16	15	15	14	14	13	13	12	12	12	11	11	11
90 (40.8)	20	19	19	18	18	17	16	16	15	15	15	14	13	13	13	12	12	12	11	11	10	10
85 (38.6)	19	18	18	17	17	16	16	15	15	14	14	13	13	13	12	12	12	11	11	11	10	10
80 (36.3)	18	17	17	16	16	15	15	14	14	13	13	13	12	12	11	11	11	11	10	10	10	9

Source: body-mass-index-chart.gif

Note: BMI values rounded to the nearest whole number. BMI categories based on CDC (Centers for Disease Control and Prevention) criteria. www.vertex42.com BMI = Weight[kg]/(Height[m] × Height[m]) = 703 × Weight[lb]/(Height[in] × Height[in]) ©2009 Vertex42 LLC

TABLE 1.2   **Obesity Trends in the United States in Terms of Number of States**

Percentage of adult population with BMI >30 kg.m^{-2}	1994[a]	2005[b]	2011
Less than 20%	50	3	0
20%–30%	0	44	38
More than 30%	0	3	12

[a]The first year that data are available for all 50 states.
[b]The first year that any state had >30% prevalence of obesity.

The U.S. Centers for Disease Control and Prevention (CDC) publishes annual data showing the percentage of the adult population in each of the 50 states that falls within BMI classes (as well as related data, such as incidence of diabetes and stroke). These color-coded maps are easily found online and Table 1.2 is a summary. In 1994, *all* of the reporting states had less than 20% of their adult population with BMIs in the obese range (≥30), and the national mean was about 14%. Eleven years later, in 2005, most states were in the 20% to 30% prevalence category; for the first time, some states had more than 30%; and the national mean was 20%. The data from 2011 show a progressive increase in the fraction higher than 30% as well as in the national mean (27%). These data support the concept of an *obesity epidemic*, showing an additional ~1% of the population entering the obese category every year (see additional statistics in Flegal et al., 2012).

Obesity often has a negative connotation: Most of us would not like to have the word applied to us. Yet, by the CDC statistics, within 20 years, more of us will be obese (BMI >30) than not. Can we define obesity as abnormal if it is found in more than half the population? Can't we just raise the criterion as the population gets heavier? Is obesity bad for you? And, if obesity is caused by eating too much, how do we know what is too much and why doesn't our biology stop us? Many of these questions don't have simple or clear answers and are the topics that we will discuss and challenge you to think about in the pages of this book. The fact remains that obesity causes distress for many individuals and detracts from physical health. Statistically, obesity is associated with increased risks of the so-called noncommunicable diseases: high blood pressure, stroke, diabetes, metabolic syndrome, and cancer (e.g., Wagner & Brath, 2012). Their treatment takes an enormous fraction of the health care budget, regardless of whether the funds are public or private. Uncontrolled growth of expenditure in health care is not a sustainable trajectory, and so prevention of poor health by minimizing risk factors such as obesity is a concern for all of us.

BIOMEDICAL OR ENVIRONMENTAL OR BOTH?

Given that overeating and obesity are significant 21st-century problems for individuals and society, as are other eating disorders such as anorexia and bulimia, how do we solve these problems that are in essence problems of interactions between individuals and their food environment?

The biomedical approach advocates that these problems are best solved by direct manipulation or treatment of an individual, either because something internal is broken or malfunctioning or because the treatment will change the way in which the individual interacts with food. One example of this is the popular concept of taking drugs to suppress appetite: The mode of action of such drugs is to change some aspect of the physiology or brain so that food is more filling and/or less attractive. They are designed to change the body's internal signals related to food; evaluating this approach requires a background in the physiology and brain mechanisms of feeding.

As we will review, many claims about diet drugs are unsubstantiated, so it is important that you are able to evaluate such claims critically.

A completely different approach is to consider that in most cases of obesity, nothing is fundamentally broken within individuals, but rather it is the environment—broadly defined—that is causing the problems. Indeed, the obesity epidemic has been fueled by increases in the energy content and amount of food available and decreases in physical activity—a so-called obesifying or **obesogenic** environment. But even if we could find completely safe and effective biomedical interventions to counteract this obesogenic environment, is it more ethical and/or cost effective to treat the environment? Do you think that businesses are eager to reduce the attractiveness of their food products (e.g., serve smaller portions, lower the taste quality by reducing fat and sugar content) to enhance the health of their customers? If not, should government take on this task? The mayor of New York, Michael Bloomberg, tested this issue by promoting legislation prohibiting the restaurant sale of very large (>16 ounces) portions

of sugar-sweetened beverages, based on a body of scientific evidence supporting a link between consumption of sugary beverages and obesity-related health problems (Brownell et al., 2009; Vartanian, Schwartz, & Brownell, 2007). Some New Yorkers and other Americans supported Bloomberg's initiative; others believed that people should be free to make their own food or beverage choices (even if they were bad choices). Some health advocates support increased taxes on sugary beverages and unhealthful snacks such as candy. What do you think about these issues? If you believe that individual liberties should not be limited, would you support the government restricting the access that children have to sugar-sweetened drinks and "junk" food, for example, in school? How about regulating the marketing of these types of foods to children? How else could we make our environment less obesogenic and, thus, reduce our risk of disordered eating? We hope that you consider these questions as you read this book and become more knowledgeable about the biological, psychological, and sociocultural aspects of eating. We will return to these issues in the final chapter.

Do the math BMI calculation

A 120 lb female has a BMI of about 22 (normal). One and two years later, her BMIs are 25 and 28, respectively: she has become substantially overweight.

A 170 lb male has a BMI of about 21 (normal). One and two years later, his BMIs are 22.5

and 24, respectively: he is still in the normal range.

Note that despite the same initial BMI and the same weight gain of 30 pounds, the individual (female in this example) with the lower initial weight ends up as overweight.

Glossary

Appetitive behaviors   Actions that bring us from an environment without or remote from food (or other desired goal) into the immediate proximity of a desired food source, for example, hunting and foraging.

Body mass index (BMI)   Body weight (in kg) divided by height (in m) squared: thus, the unit is $kg.m^{-2}$. This is the most commonly used clinical

measure to define underweight (<18.5), normal body weight (18.5–24.9), overweight (25–29.9), obese class I (30–34.9), obese class II (35–39.9), obese class III (>40).

Consummatory behaviors   Actions that deliver food from a nearby source into our mouths: for example, eating from a plate or shelling nuts to eat them.

Fullness A subjective sensation relating one's current state to the (comfortable) fullest that one could imagine after eating a large meal.

Hunger Internal (unpleasant) sensation that diverts our thoughts and actions to acquiring and eating food; one cause of hunger is a prolonged period since last eating.

Hunter-gatherer Term given by anthropologists to describe the dominant lifestyle of early hominids.

Obesogenic Term used for an environment (or specific food) that promotes the development of obesity.

Satiety The absence of hunger. It is closely related to the sensation of fullness.

References

Alessi G. (1992). Models of proximate and ultimate causation in psychology. *American Psychologist, 47,* 1359–1370.

Arsenault, B. J., Beaumont, E. P., Despres, J. P., & Larose, E. (2012). Mapping body fat distribution: A key step toward the identification of the vulnerable patient? *Annals of Medicine, 44,* 758–772.

Barkeling, B., King, N. A., Naslund, E., & Blundell, J. E. (2007). Characterization of obese individuals who claim no relationship between their eating pattern and sensations of hunger or fullness. *International Journal of Obesity,* 31, 435–439.

Bolles, R. C. (1967). *Theory of motivation.* New York: Harper & Row.

Brownell, K. D., Farley, T., Willett, W. C., Popkin, B. M., Chaloupka, F. J., Thompson, J. W., & Ludwig, D. S. (2009). The public health and economic benefits of taxing sugar-sweetened beverages. *New England Journal of Medicine,* 361(16), 1599–1605.

Capaldi, E. D. (1996). *Why we eat what we eat: the psychology of eating.* Washington, DC: American Psychological Association.

Finkelstein, E. A., Trogdon, J. G., Cohen, J. W., & Dietz, W. (2009). Annual medical spending attributable to obesity: Payer- and service-specific estimates. *Health Affairs,* 28, w822–w831.

Flegal, K. M., Carroll, M. D., Kit, B. K., & Ogden, C. L. (2012). Prevalence of obesity and trends in the distribution of body mass index among US adults, 1999–2010. *Journal of the American Medical Association,* 307(5), 491–497.

Hull, C. L. (1943). *Principles of behavior: An introduction to behavior theory.* New York: Appleton-Century.

Hudson, J. I., Hiripi, E., Pope, H. G., & Kessler, R. C. (2007). The prevalence and correlates of eating disorders in the National Comorbidity Survey Replication. *Biological Psychiatry,* 61(3), 348–358.

Logue, A. W. (2004). *The psychology of eating and drinking,* 3rd ed. New York: Brunner-Routledge.

Luppino, F. S., de Wit, L. M., Bouvy, P. F., Stijnen, T., Cuijpers, P., Penninx, B. W., & Zitman, F. G. (2010). Overweight, obesity, and depression: A systematic review and meta-analysis of longitudinal studies. *Archives of General Psychiatry,* 67(3), 220–229.

Ogden, J. (2010). *The psychology of eating: From healthy to disordered behavior,* 2nd ed. Malden, MA: Wiley-Blackwell.

Vartanian, L. R., Schwartz, M. B., & Brownell, K. D. (2007). Effects of soft drink consumption on nutrition and health: A systematic review and meta-analysis. *Journal Information,* 97(4), 667–675.

Wagner K.-H., & Brath, H. (2012). A global view on the development of noncommunicable diseases. *Preventative Medicine, 54*(suppl.), S38–S41.

Weinstein, N. D. (1984). Why it won't happen to me: Perceptions of risk factors and susceptibility. *Health Psychology, 3,* 431–457.

White, L. A. (1959). *The evolution of culture: The development of civilization to the fall of Rome.* New York: McGraw-Hill.

2

Macronutrients and the Food We Eat

After reading this chapter, you will be able to

- Understand the basic concepts of *metabolism*, *energy input,* and *expenditure*

- Know the three basic macronutrients: carbohydrates, proteins, and fats

- Know the roles for minerals and vitamins, and the unique case of sodium appetite

MACRONUTRIENT CLASSES

You can't go into many restaurants or shops these days without finding food items or meals that carry slogans such as "heart healthy" or "low carb."

The idea behind this is that by changing the type of food you eat, you will be healthier and lose weight. The fact that obesity rates continue to rise is all the evidence you need to see that these dietary slogans are completely ineffective at the population level. Even individuals who adopt a diet and lose weight often regain that weight, and more. Have you been on such a diet, or do you know someone who has? Chances are you answered "yes" to these questions. We will discuss the effectiveness of diets later in this book, but behind such diets is the basic science of nutrients, energy, and energy balance that will be the focus of this chapter.

Natural foods contain, in varying proportions, three energy-yielding **macronutrients**: carbohydrates, fats, and proteins. Each of the macronutrient classes is chemically different, and each can be subdivided, for example, into simple and complex carbohydrates or unsaturated and saturated fats. Their intrinsic chemical energy is extracted by cells in a series of basic biological reactions known collectively as **metabolism**. The collective speed of those reactions is called the **metabolic rate**.

The yield of that metabolism is expressed in energy units; one common unit is the kilocalorie (kcal): 1 kcal = 1000 calories. One (small "c") calorie is the amount of energy needed to heat 1 gram of water by 1°C. Food energy can also be expressed in joules or kilojoules (kJ). You can convert calories to joules by the multiplier 4.2 (1 kJ = 0.239 kcal). For example, if you wanted

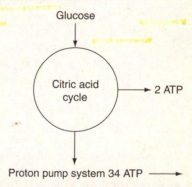

FIGURE 2.1 Structure of ATP.

to heat a cup of water (~250 grams) from room temperature to boiling (a rise of about 80°C), you would need 80 × 250 calories = 20,000 calories = 20 kcal or 84 kJ. This is approximately the amount of energy derived from one level teaspoon (5 grams) of sugar. Biological metabolic cycles are not perfectly efficient, so the energy actually derived from a food is sometimes known as its **metabolizable energy**.

Almost all of the energy produced by animals comes from a process called **aerobic metabolism**, meaning that air and specifically oxygen are required. All of the cells in our body consume energy, and some cells such as those in the brain or heart do so at a much higher sustained rate than others. How does this energy get formed and used? Well, you could take a whole course on that! Instead, we will simplify this into a few sentences (and those of you so inclined can hit the biochemistry books for more!). The universal chemical currency of work inside cells is **adenosine triphosphate (ATP)**, a molecule that is in a high-energy state and acts as an energy donor. As its name implies, a molecule of ATP has three phosphate (-PO_3) groups (Figure 2.1).

These can be removed one at a time to yield a lower energy form, thereby donating energy to cellular processes. The low-energy forms are then regenerated to ATP by an enzyme, ATP synthase, that itself is powered by a proton gradient

or pump (called the **chemiosmotic potential**) set up as a result of reactions in the **citric acid cycle**. This is a cycle of chemical transformations that is "turned" by burning the basic nutrient-derived fuels (carbohydrates, proteins, fatty acids) with oxygen into carbon dioxide (Figure 2.2). "Burning" is used in a figurative sense because no actual flames occur although oxygen (carried from our lungs into the bloodstream) is consumed in the cycle. These reactions occur in **mitochondria**, which are specialized organelles inside each cell. Cells that are metabolically most active often have more mitochondria than cells that are less active.

Energy-yielding molecules in food that fuel the citric acid cycle and generate ATP are called

Glucose

↓

(Citric acid cycle) → 2 ATP

↓

Proton pump system 34 ATP →

FIGURE 2.2 Simplified example of aerobic metabolism showing a common fuel (glucose) entering the citric acid cycle (several chemical steps are involved that are not shown), and subsequent generation of ATP. The theoretical maximum yield is 36 molecules of ATP from one of glucose, although the system is not completely efficient and the actual yield is often ~30.

macronutrients. As mentioned before, there are three classes of macronutrients:

- Carbohydrates (net yield: ~4 kcal or ~17 kJ per gram)
- Proteins (net yield: ~4 kcal or ~17 kJ per gram)
- Fats (net yield ~9 kcal or ~38 kJ per gram)

It is quite rare to consume a pure macronutrient. Most natural foods are mixtures of all three, and, in addition, most contain non-energy-yielding substances including water, nondigestible fiber, vitamins, and minerals. Most processed foods have nutrition labels that disclose the amount of each macronutrient (and other information) per serving. The **energy density** (or caloric density, meaning the energy yield per unit weight of food) of a food thus depends on the relative amounts of the three macronutrients and of the non-energy-yielding molecules. As a rule, foods with highest energy densities are high in fat. Conversely, foods with the lowest energy densities (e.g., vegetables) usually contain a lot of water, which has no usable energy.

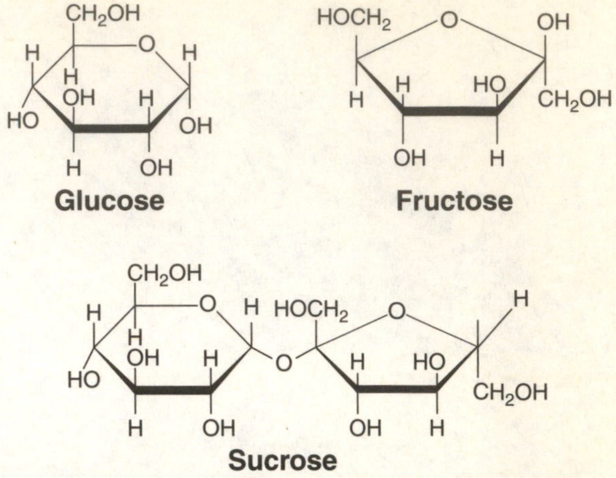

Carbohydrates

In terms of chemical structure (Figure 2.3), the simplest natural carbohydrates are **monosaccharides** such as glucose (also known as dextrose), fructose (in fruits), and galactose (in milk). If we eat a food containing one of these monosaccharides, which are also sugars because they taste sweet, the molecules are absorbed quickly from the upper part of the digestive system and lead to a rapid rise in the concentration of this sugar in our blood (a "sugar rush"). These sugars are then used in

FIGURE 2.3 Structures of monosaccharides glucose and fructose, and the disaccharide sucrose that is formed from these two components.

the metabolic processes mentioned earlier. The size (actually a combination of the height and its duration) of the spike in blood sugar after eating a particular food is called the **glycemic index**. Relative to pure glucose, which is assigned a glycemic index of 100, high-carbohydrate foods such as rice or potatoes have glycemic indices higher than 70, whereas most beans and fruits have indices of 55 or lower (Foster-Powell, Holt, & Brand-Miller, 2002). (Note these relative numbers are meaningful only if the actual weights or amounts consumed are the same for each substance.) Food with a high glycemic index exacerbates the metabolic disease diabetes, so diets of low glycemic index are recommended to help treat this disease.

The next class of sugars is **disaccharides**. It includes sucrose—the common sugar you buy in the grocery store that is extracted from sugar cane

TALKING POINT 2.1

Collect some nutrition labels from foods in your kitchen and discuss these with your classmates. Did you ever look at these labels closely before, and do you think they are useful? Were there any macronutrient contents or energy densities that you found surprising? How many of these foods contained more than 50% energy from fat? Conversely, were any labeled "low fat" and, if so, how low does it have to be to get this label?

or beets, maltose, and lactose—the main carbohydrate in milk. Disaccharides are two monosaccharide molecules joined together:

- Sucrose = glucose + fructose
- Maltose = glucose + glucose
- Lactose = glucose + galactose

When these disaccharides are eaten, they first have to be broken apart by enzymes in your gut into the component monosaccharides, which are then absorbed into the bloodstream. You may have heard the term *lactose intolerance,* which occurs in many individuals after infancy; the enzyme that breaks lactose apart is no longer produced.

Many carbohydrates are called **starches** or **complex carbohydrates**. The main form in

O-O-O-O-O-O   O-O-O-O-O-O-O

Amylose   O-O-O-O-O-O-O Glycogen

FIGURE 2.5 Polysaccharides: Amylose (linear) and glycogen (branched). Each circle represents a molecule of glucose and the dashes represent chemical linkages between them.

which glucose is stored in animals and plants is as polymers (chains) composed of many glucose molecules. Plants store carbohydrates as either amylose (a head-to-tail or chain polymer) or amylopectin (a chain with branching), whereas in animals this is called glycogen (Figure 2.5). After being eaten, these molecules first have to be broken down to the single glucose building blocks and then absorbed; this process is slower when compared to eating pure glucose. Thus, the glycemic index of starches is often lower than for simple sugars, particularly the branched forms.

Cellulose is a structural component of many plants and is glucose polymer much like amylose except that the chemical joining is in a slightly different location on the glucose molecule. As a result of this difference, most animals including humans have an extremely limited ability to break it down to glucose, and for the most part it serves as **dietary fiber** that yields no energy. Such fiber absorbs water and produces bulk in the gastrointestinal tract, and this tends to keep us feeling full and our bowels moving nicely! Some animals are able to digest cellulose because they have microorganisms that live symbiotically in their gut and can break cellulose into glucose. These animals (herbivores) typically eat large amounts of plant material. Termites are also able to digest cellulose, which is why wood is one of their favorite foods and why those of us living in warmer climates have to treat our homes regularly to prevent structural damage.

Proteins

Proteins are made up of building blocks called **amino acids**, joined head to tail to form long chains (Figure 2.6). Short chains of amino acids (usually less that 100) are called peptides.

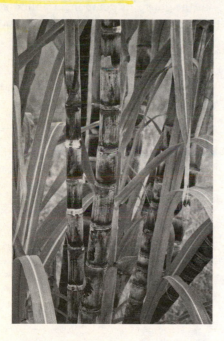

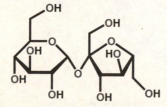

FIGURE 2.4 Sugar cane is one of the major commercial sources of sucrose, the structure of includes the glucose (left) and fructose (right) rings.

TALKING POINT 2.2

Using a table of glycemic indices (available with a simple web search), estimate the average or composite glycemic index of all the food you eat in a typical day. What is the range of these glycemic index estimates for your classmates? How would you have to change your diet to decrease your index by, say, 10%? Do you know anyone (e.g., grandparent) who has received medical advice to lower the glycemic index of his or her diet? Look for commercial diets that advertise a low glycemic index and, if so, which ailment(s) are these designed to improve?

Twenty l-amino acids occur naturally; each of these amino acids has a different shape, size, and chemical properties. The "l-" refers to the fact that these molecules come in two nonidentical but mirror image forms—like your left and right hands. Only the l-forms are used in constructing proteins, like a handshake grasps the same hand of the other person. (Glucose also has d- and l-forms and only the d-form is usable.) Each amino acid is distinct, and the function or role of the specific protein depends entirely on the sequence.

When protein is eaten, it has to be broken down in the gut to its component amino acids and then absorbed. Once absorbed, these amino

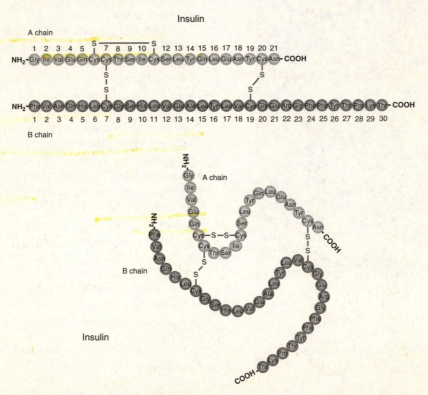

FIGURE 2.6 Schematic of how amino acids (each shown as a ball with a three-letter abbreviation) join head to tail, in this case to form the peptide insulin. It is composed of two short chains joined by a disulfide bridge between two cysteine molecules.

acids are used to build proteins inside the body (structural proteins), as well as to form enzymes, receptors, signal molecules and to provide energy. Some amino acids can also be made in the body; those that cannot are called **essential amino acids** (leucine, isoleucine, valine, phenylalanine, tryptophan, threonine, methionine, arginine, lysine, histidine) not because the others are non-essential, but because we must eat enough protein containing these particular amino acids to meet our body's needs or demands. An **imbalanced protein** is one that is relatively deficient in one or more essential amino acids, and so eating that protein exclusively will not satisfy our body requirements. Most proteins from animal sources are balanced, whereas plant proteins may not be: Vegetarians and vegans must carefully mix and match their protein sources to achieve an overall balance.

Fats

Fats are esters, a chemical combination of one molecule of glycerol and three molecules of **fatty acids** (Figure 2.7). Chemically, fatty acids are relatively long carbon-based chains.

The links between adjacent carbon atoms in these chains can be single chemical bonds (saturated) or double bonds (unsaturated). **Saturated fats** have fatty acid chains that contain

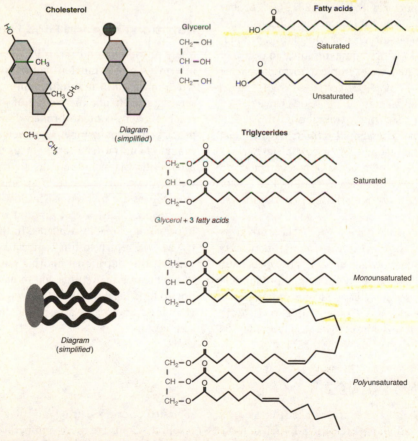

FIGURE 2.7 The structure of fatty acids formed from three ester bonds between glycerol and fatty acids. The different classes of fatty acids discussed are shown. Also shown is cholesterol, which, although not a fatty acid, is a health risk.

all single bonds and tend to give the molecule a "long" profile and are solid at room temperature (e.g., lard). **Unsaturated fats** have all three of the fatty acid chains and contain some double bonds that tend to give the molecule a "round" profile and are liquid at room temperature (e.g., olive oil). There are graded degrees of unsaturation depending on the number of double bonds: monounsaturated fats (MUFA) have one double bond per chain, whereas polyunsaturated fats (PUFA) have two or more. It has been claimed that eating saturated fats (these tend to be animal-derived products such as lard) may be detrimental to cardiovascular health, whereas unsaturated fats may be more "heart healthy." However, the differences in health outcome are generally small and are quite controversial (e.g., Siri-Tarino, Sun, Hu, & Krauss, 2010). It's probably better advice to eat less fat regardless of type! Partial hydrogenation is a chemical food production process in which some unsaturated bonds of oils are saturated, for example to form margarine from oil.

Some fatty acids can be made or rearranged by chemical reactions in our body; those that cannot are called essential fatty acids and must be derived from our diet. Essential fatty acids include PUFAs known as n-3 or omega-3 and n-6 or omega-6. Oily fish such as salmon, herring, or sardines have a particularly high content of n-3 fatty acids.

Triglycerides have to be broken down by gut enzymes (lipases) into the component fatty acids and glycerol, which are then absorbed. Fatty acids can be used directly for energy production, but a lot of the fat we eat or make endogenously is stored in **adipose tissue**. Adipose tissue in humans contains about 87% triglycerides by

weight, and because fat molecules repel water, fat tissue contains very little water. This is why adipose tissue, at ~9 kcal per gram, is the densest form of energy storage.

Nutrition Facts and Food Labels

Many of today's foods are sold in packages that inform us of the nutrient content of that food. Often included in that information is portion or serving size (hence the weight of food) and the macronutrient content, broken down by principal class of carbohydrate (sugar versus starch, for example) and fat (saturated versus unsaturated). Micronutrients including salts are often listed, as well as the calories per serving. Sometimes, specific entries are marked as "healthy" along some dimension. Thus, a vast amount of nutritional information is readily available. In the final chapter, we will return to this topic and in particular whether this nutritional information is well used. In the meantime, we urge you to pay more attention to food labels and whether you might change your food choices as a result of this additional scrutiny.

TALKING POINT 2.3

Make a list of the sources of fat that you eat in a typical day—including in fried food, meat, baked products, and so on. Break those down as best as you can into unsaturated and saturated categories, using food labels or a web resource. Compare these numbers with those of classmates. If you have a high saturated fat intake, what steps could you take to reduce it?

DO THE MATH

Suppose your body uses 2,700 kcal per day—just a bit higher than the average person expends. If this energy were derived entirely from stored fat, how many grams of fat (assume 9 kcal/g) would need to be used per day? If an individual weighs 200 pounds and has 30% body fat (depending on height, this person would probably be in the overweight but not obese category), how many grams or kilograms of fat does he or she carry (use the approximation that 2 pounds = 1 kilogram).

If that person stopped eating completely and his or her energy use remained constant, how long would it take for the fat stores to become completely depleted? Suppose instead the person goes on a strict diet and eats only half as much (1,350 kcal/day). How long would the stored fat last? If he or she set a more reasonable goal of losing half his or her stored fat (to 15%), how long would it take to achieve this on the same strict diet? (*Answers are at end of the chapter.*)

Nutrition Facts

Serving Size	1 Cup (53g/1.9 oz.)
Servings Per Container	About 9

Amount Per Serving

Calories 188	Calories from Fat 25

	% Daily Value*
Total Fat 3g	5%
Saturated Fat 0g	0%
Trans Fat 0g	
Cholesterol 0mg	0%
Sodium 80mg	3%
Potassium 300mg	9%
Total Carbohydrate 37g	12%
Dietary Fiber 8g	32%
Soluble Fiber	
Insoluble Fiber	4%
Sugars 13g	
Protein 9g	14%
Vitamin A 0%	C 0%
Calcium 4%	10%
Phosphorus 10%	0%

* Percent Daily Values are based o
  Your daily values may be higher o

MICRONUTRIENTS

In addition to energy-giving macronutrients, we require a relatively large number of dietary components that do not yield energy but act as essential constituents for the structure and function of our bodies. The most common of these, which we will consider here, are salts and vitamins. We should note in passing that water is a noncaloric necessity for which we have an entire separate regulatory system, including the sensation of thirst. Further, some level of dietary fiber, mentioned previously, is certainly desirable.

Salts

Chemically, salts are molecules that contain positively charged cations, usually of a metal element such as sodium, and negatively charged anions such as chloride. Salts are sometimes also called minerals. Most foods contain tiny or trace amounts of specific salts; if we eat a balanced diet, we will usually consume adequate amounts of all the essential elements. We will note here that people who are not eating adequate amounts, such as in those with anorexia, or who are not absorbing food normally, such as after bowel surgery, are at particular risk for mineral deficiencies. The most abundant mineral in our body is calcium (~1,000 grams) followed by phosphate (750 grams). Bone mass is mainly calcium phosphate, but calcium is also of critical importance for many cellular processes including release of neurotransmitters. Deficiency of calcium leads to loss of bone mass, and possibly osteoporosis. Dairy products are particularly rich sources of dietary calcium, which is why milk-related products are recommended. Other ions that are abundant in our bodies include sodium, potassium, and chloride, which are the principal constituents of the fluid inside and surrounding most cells in our body. Other diet-derived minerals stored in much smaller amounts in the body include chromium, cobalt, copper, fluoride, iodide, magnesium, manganese, molybdenum, selenium, sulfide, and zinc.

If your diet did not contain enough of a trace element, or you had an abnormal need for it, the most common symptom would be tiredness—a general sensation that you're not quite right. (Some people call tiredness a lack of energy, but here we are using the term *energy* in a specific scientific sense. So we will stick with tiredness because energy as in ATP is usually not compromised!) One of the most common mineral deficiencies is that of **iron**. Because iron is a key component of hemoglobin (the oxygen-carrying protein in blood), women who have particularly heavy menstrual periods lose relatively large amounts of iron and risk anemia and the associated tiredness.

Sodium and Sodium Appetite

Sodium is an abundant cation in our body and is the principal ion in extracellular fluid, which is the fluid that surrounds all of our cells including those in the bloodstream. The concentration of sodium in the extracellular fluid, together with the principal negatively charged anion **chloride**, is approximately 150 millimolar (a millimolar is a common physiological unit of concentration; this concentration of sodium is also called **isotonic**). Sodium chloride—common or table salt—is contained in many natural foods and is added as a preservative and flavoring agent in many other foods and cuisines. We continuously lose some sodium, chloride, and water from our bodies in the form of sweat and urine. Such loss produces two types of dehydration: intracellular (primarily water) and extracellular (primarily isotonic fluid). Both quickly lead to impaired function—unlike energy, the body has

no reserves of fluid upon which to call—and must be addressed by drinking water or water plus sodium chloride, respectively. The body has osmoreceptors that detect intracellular dehydration (normally, an increase from ~150 millimolar), and baroreceptors that detect extracellular dehydration (indirectly by a decrease in blood volume). Deviations of only ~2% in these values are sufficient to cause thirst and lead to drinking. There is good evidence that there is a **specific appetite for sodium** associated with loss of blood volume (Denton, 1982).

Sodium is the only mineral for which a specific appetite for salty solutions or foods has been characterized, although a case has also been made for calcium (Tordoff et al., 2008). Sodium appetite will be mentioned at other places in this

FIGURE 2.8   Cattle exhibiting sodium appetite by licking a commercial salt block.
Grass and other vegetation can have low sodium content (depending on the sodium content of the soil), so herbivores have a high risk of sodium deficiency. In winter, wild herbivores such as deer can be a driving hazard because they seek salt that has been spread on roads.

TALKING POINT 2.4

You have heard that high levels of dietary salt are generally considered bad, especially for people with cardiovascular problems such as high blood pressure. The daily amount of salt that is recommended for a healthy individual is about 2 grams. Examine food labels for the amounts of salt in the foods that you eat routinely. How much salt do you consume per day? (Remember that most prepared foods, such as pizza, contain lots of salt!)

book, but we emphasize that this is unique or nearly so among the minerals.

Vitamins

Vitamins are chemicals that are normally found in trace amounts in many natural foods and are essential to a variety of metabolic reactions in your body. Like minerals, a normal balanced diet should provide all of the necessary vitamins, but select vitamin deficiencies are associated with a variety of generally diffuse symptoms that include tiredness (of course!). Vitamins come in two main classes: water-soluble vitamins that cannot be stored in the body and are a continuous dietary need, and fat-soluble vitamins that require dietary fat to be absorbed (Table 2.1).

Vitamin C (abundant in fresh fruits) deficiency was experienced as scurvy by the pioneering sailors who had no fresh produce on prolonged voyages. Of all the vitamins listed in Table 2.1, most have daily requirements of milligrams (mg) per day or less, except for niacin (~20 mg) and vitamin C (~40 mg). Many people take vitamin supplements, for example, as multivitamin pills that contain many times the estimated daily need (recommended daily allowance, RDA) for each of the constituents. However, the body has limited ability to store excess vitamins, so why do you think that the vitamin pill industry is so lucrative?

ENERGY BALANCE

Energy balance is the difference, over a given time frame (e.g., 24 hours), in the energy input and the energy expenditure. How do we measure these inputs and outputs?

Energy Input

Measuring energy input is a matter of knowing the metabolizable energy of each food you eat and exactly how much (by weight) of each food you eat. Many publicly available food tables summarize the average yield for common types of food, as well as individual food labels. The amounts we eat are hard to track retrospectively—can you say, even approximately, how many grams of each food you ate for lunch yesterday? Some investigators use electronic food diaries to help individuals keep track because people generally underreport. The most accurate intake data for humans come from single meals in a laboratory setting rather than from the real world. This is one of the reasons that many studies of food intake use laboratory animals for which we can know precisely how much they eat and when.

TABLE 2.1	Vitamin Classes
Fat-soluble vitamins (*These are families; only one in each is named.*)	A (retinol), D (cholecalciferol), E (α-tocopherol), K (phylloquinone)
Water-soluble vitamins	B_1 (thiamin), B_2 (riboflavin), B_3 (niacin), B_5 (pantothenic acid), B_6 (pyridoxine), B_9 (folate), B_{12} (cobalamin), C (ascorbic acid), H (biotin)

Energy Output

The same is not true of energy output or expenditure. Part of the problem has to do with measurement: Whereas eating occurs in discrete episodes and portions (meals or snacks), energy output is continuous and changes from moment to moment as our activity level changes. Another part of the problem is that energy expenditure has three main categories: resting or **basal metabolic rate (BMR)**, metabolic cost of **activity** or exercise, and **thermogenic** effect of food. Estimates are that for people with a normal level of daily activity, BMR accounts for 60% to 70% of daily energy expenditure, activity for 20% to 30%, and thermogenesis only a few percentage points. Any activity, from walking across the room to competing in an athletic event, is a relatively discrete episode. Accurate measurement of total metabolic rate over time must include basal and activity components. These are often difficult to measure at the same time. Energy expenditure can be measured either by determining whole-body heat generation over a suitable time period (done using an instrument called a calorimeter) or by measuring oxygen consumption and/or respiratory quotient (RQ: the ratio of carbon dioxide exhaled divided by oxygen consumed).

Whole-body calorimetry is a method to measure total heat production over a period of time by having the individual live in a special chamber—often a small cubicle with a bed and table—for a period of hours or even days. Although accurate, this is highly specialized equipment that is not widely available, and the chamber size severely limits activity. A recent invention called the "Bod Pod" is a small sealed cubicle in which subjects sit still for a few minutes while their respiratory exchanges are measured by ultra-sensitive detectors. Again, this is limited to BMR because there is no space to engage in physical activity. Metabolism during activity can be measured as oxygen consumption and carbon dioxide production; this uses simpler but not easily portable equipment and often incorporates stationary activities such as a treadmill or gym bike. However, subjects have to wear a tightly fitting mask, and people are willing to tolerate this for only a relatively short time, so that whole-day or multi-day measures are not feasible. In summary, none of these methods for measuring basal or activity metabolic rate is completely satisfactory.

The combination of basal and activity metabolism can be measured over days in free-living humans going about their normal lives using the **doubly labeled water** method. The catch here is that it's expensive and involves injecting people with radioactive isotopes, which, although quite common in modern nuclear medicine, is not acceptable to everyone. In this procedure, a known amount of water that has been radioactively labeled with tiny amounts of the isotopes ^2H and ^{18}O (present in negligible amounts relative to the normal and nonradioactive isotopes ^1H and ^{16}O) is administered intravenously. After a short time when the labeled water has mixed and equilibrated with normal water in the body, a sample (blood or saliva) is taken, and the amount of each radioactive isotope measured using a suitably sensitive radioactivity counter. Identical samples are then taken at later intervals (e.g., several days) and counted. What has happened in the time between the two measures is that hydrogen in water, including the ^2H, has been lost from the body by secretion or excretion in sweat, urine, and so on, and the decline in the radioactive counts of ^2H from the first sample to subsequent samples is a measure of that rate of loss. In contrast, oxygen in water, including the ^{18}O, has been lost from the body not only by the same secretion/excretion, but in addition as exhaled carbon dioxide. Thus, the rate of decline of ^{18}O counts is faster than the decline in ^2H (Figure 2.9). The greater an individual's metabolic rate, the more carbon dioxide expired and the faster the relative drop in ^{18}O counts. What is derived uniquely by this method is the sum of basal and metabolic rates over the period of study. Now that we've talked about problems of measurement, let's look at factors that contribute to BMR.

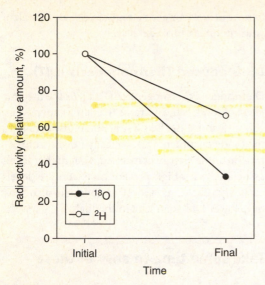

FIGURE 2.9 Hypothetical result from a doubly labeled water experiment.
Soon after injection, the concentrations of ^2H and ^{18}O are high. After several days, the concentrations of both have fallen, but the ^{18}O declines faster. The difference between the two lines reflects the integrated metabolic rate between the two measurements.

Basal Metabolic Rate (BMR)

BMR is the amount of energy expended over a given interval when you are physically resting (including during sleep). Several factors affect BMR:

- Body weight: The more you weigh, the more cells to feed, so the higher the BMR.
- Age: BMR is higher in the young than the old, partly a result of changes in body composition.

- Height: Tall, thin people have higher BMR than shorter people of the same weight.
- Growth: Children and pregnant women have higher BMR to support new tissue growth.
- Body composition: High lean body mass supports high BMR; high body fat, low BMR.
- Stress: Stress hormones can raise BMR.
- Environmental temperature: Both very cold and very hot temperatures raise BMR.
- Fasting/starvation: Hormones released during fasting lower BMR.

Measurement of BMR in a large cross-section of people has led to population-based or average mathematical expressions that allow individuals to estimate their BMR from simple measures:

1. **The quick and dirty:** BMR (in kcal per day) = your body weight in pounds × 10. The equivalent in metric units is BMR (in kJ per day) = body weight in kg × 92. This is a one-size-fits-all calculation, notwithstanding the bulleted list presented earlier!
2. **Harris-Benedict equations:** These compute BMR with sex, weight, and height adjustments and will give a more accurate result. Most online calculators (point your web browser to Harris-Benedict) adjust BMR by a factor related to your self-assessed level of activity; some include stress level as well.

Activity: Metabolic Cost of Exercise

Exercise-related energy expenditure, like BMR, is a function of body weight. Several online resources can be used to estimate the cost of

TALKING POINT 2.5

Calculate your BMR using both the quick-and-dirty method and a Harris-Benedict calculator. How close are the two values? If they differ, why in your case do you think this is? Compare your results with those of others in your class.

exercise for a typical person. This ranges from ~200 kcal/hour for domestic activities or walking to almost 1000 kcal/hour for fast cycling. People who live sedentary lives may expend as little as 15% of their daily energy budget on activity. Elite endurance athletes may spend 80% of their energy on activity. For most people, extreme levels of activity such as biking at 40 km/h (25 mph) for an extended period of time is beyond their reasonable reach, but increasing the duration of activity is a simple lifestyle change that almost everyone can do—for example, walk up a flight of stairs rather than take the elevator, stand up from time to time at work or get a stand-at desk, or lose all of your remote control devices.

Diet-Induced Thermogenesis (DIT)

Diet-induced thermogenesis (DIT), or the thermic effect of food, is the increase in energy expenditure above (fasting) BMR as a function of the energy in the food consumed. DIT typically ranges from 5% to 15% of the energy consumed, with higher levels associated with high protein diets and low levels with high fat diets. Obese individuals also may have lower DIT than lean individuals.

Let's review and apply your knowledge. Take some time to answer these chapter questions

1. What are the subdivisions of carbohydrates? What are some sources of these?
2. Describe the subdivisions of fats and what makes them different. Which are the most healthful and which can be detrimental to health?
3. What is essential about essential amino acids and fatty acids? How could you most easily ensure that your diet contains adequate amounts of these?
4. What are the three main ways that energy expenditure occurs? Can these be influenced by factors under our control? Explain. What accounts for the majority of energy output?
5. Name three ways in which you can measure energy expenditure, and the most important limitation of each method. How could you estimate BMR without doing an experiment?

Do the math energy calculation

Three hundred grams of fat per day yield $300 \times 9 = 2{,}700$ kcal. The individual carries $200 \times .30 = 60$ lb $= 30$ kg fat. At 300 grams used per day, this would last 100 days. On a 50% diet, it would last twice as long (200 days). To lose half the overweight (to 15% fat) would take half the time (100 days).

Note that a reasonable weight loss even on a strict diet takes months to achieve. Commercial claims of massive weight or fat loss on proprietary diets are scientifically impossible to achieve.

Glossary

Activity Physical movement that involves energy expenditure above metabolism at perfect rest.

Adenosine triphosphate (ATP) The universal molecular "currency" of work within cells. ATP is made in organelles inside cells called mitochondria.

Adipose tissue   Tissue clumps or depots that are made of cells that store large amounts of triglycerides.

Aerobic metabolism   Biochemical cycles that use oxygen in transformation of food-derived fuels into cellular energy.

Amino acids   Series of 20 naturally occurring molecules containing an organic acid ($^-$COOH) and an amine ($^-$NH$_2$) group.

Basal metabolic rate   The rate at which energy is expended when a person is at physical rest.

Cellulose   A fiber made up of glucose molecules, but joined in such a way that they cannot be broken down and used for energy by humans and many other animals. It is one of the most common dietary fibers.

Chemiosmotic potential   A chain of reactions inside cells that involves transferring protons (H$^+$) between molecules (or electrons in the other direction) that eventually generate most of the ATP in cells.

Chloride   (Cl$^-$) is the negatively charged ion (anion) of chlorine. It is the cation in common salt (sodium chloride).

Citric acid cycle   A cyclic chain of chemical reactions that transforms metabolic fuels into energy.

Complex carbohydrate   Also known as starch. A metabolizable molecule composed of many glucose molecules joined in either linear (amylose) or branched (amylopectin) chains. To be nutritionally useful, these chains have to be broken down to glucose by enzymes in the digestive tract.

Dietary fiber   Refers to large molecules derived from plants that are not broken down by human and some other animal digestive systems so no energy can be derived. These molecules pass essentially unchanged through our digestive tract and constitute bulk or "roughage."

Disaccharide   A carbohydrate formed by chemical union of two monosaccharide rings. Examples include sucrose (glucose + fructose) and lactose (glucose + galactose).

Doubly labeled water   Doubly radioactive form of water (^{2}H$_2$^{18}O) that can be used to determine metabolic rate in free-living individuals.

Energy balance   The difference, over a suitable time frame, between energy input as food and energy expenditure as metabolic rate.

Energy density   The metabolizable energy of a food. A given foodstuff is usually a mixture of the three macronutrients, plus non-nutritive materials such as water. Foods with high water or fiber content have low energy density. Foods with high fat content have high energy density.

Essential amino acid   Any one of 10 (of the 20) naturally occurring amino acids that cannot be made in the body. These have to be obtained by eating food containing adequate amounts.

Fatty acid   A carbon-based chain ending with an organic acid ($^-$COOH) group that is a component of dietary fat. It is usually esterified with glycerol to form triacylglycerol molecules.

Glycemic index   The increase above basal in blood glucose level, integrated across time until it returns to baseline, following consumption of a unit weight of a food. By convention, pure glucose has an index of 100, and other foods are compared to this standard.

Imbalanced protein   A protein that is deficient in one or more essential amino acid.

Iron   An element (Fe) that is essential to several biological reactions in our body. For example, iron is part of the hemoglobin complex that carries oxygen in our bloodstream.

Isotonic   Literally means exerting the same (iso) osmotic pressure (tonic) as the fluids inside and outside the cells in our body. As sodium chloride is the main extracellular osmotic force, isotonic is close to the concentration of sodium chloride in blood or plasma.

Macronutrient   An energy-yielding food component of carbohydrate, protein, or fat classes.

Metabolic rate   The rate at which energy is expended over a suitable period of time. It includes basal metabolic rate, energy cost of physical activity, and that used to generate excess heat (thermogenesis).

Metabolism   Complex series of chemical reactions inside the body that transform nutrients into the heat and energy necessary to sustain life.

Metabolizable energy   The actual energy yield derived from unit mass (most usually 1 gram) of a macronutrient. The metabolizable energies of carbohydrates, proteins, and fats are approximately 4, 4, and 9 kilocalories per gram (kcal/g) or 17, 17, and 38 kilojoules per gram (kJ/g).

Mitochondria   Energy-generating organelles inside cells.

Monosaccharide   Also known as simple sugar; a carbohydrate in which each molecule consists of a single basic ring of four to five carbon and one oxygen atoms. Examples include glucose, fructose, and galactose.

Protein   A protein is typically a chain of several hundred amino acids joined chemically. The order in which the amino acids are joined is specified by our genes, and different sequences give rise to different proteins that have various functions in our bodies such as structural proteins or enzymes that catalyze specific chemical reactions.

Saturated fats   Triglyceride molecules in which the three fatty acid chains contain only saturated (single) bonds in the carbon backbone.

Specific appetite for sodium   Taste-guided behavior seeking sodium salts in the environment.

Starches   Generic name for glucose polymers, most usually in plants, that can be broken down for usable energy.

Thermogenic   Chemical or physiological reaction or series of reactions that generate heat.

Triglyceride   An ester of glycerol and fatty acids. Fatty acids can be saturated or unsaturated, and the latter occur either as monounsaturates (MUFA) or polyunsaturates (PUFA, notably, some fish oils).

Unsaturated fats   Triglyceride molecules in which one or more of the three fatty acid chains contain unsaturated (double) bonds in the carbon backbone.

Vitamins   Compounds that occur in trace amounts in various foods and are essential for optimal metabolic and other life processes.

References

Denton, D. A. (1982). *The hunger for salt*. New York: Springer-Verlag.

Foster-Powell, K., Holt, S. H. A., & Brand-Miller, J. C. (2002). International table of glycemic index and glycemic load values: 2002. *American Journal of Clinical Nutrition, 76*, 5–56.

Siri-Tarino, P. W., Sun, Q., Hu, F. B., & Krauss, R. M. (2010). Meta-analysis of prospective cohort studies evaluating the association of saturated fat with cardiovascular disease. *American Journal of Clinical Nutrition, 91*, 535–546.

Tordoff, M. G., Shao, H., Alarcon, L. K., Margolskee, R. F., Mosinger, B., Bachmanov, A. A., Reed, D. R., & McCaughey, S. (2008). Involvement of T1R3 in calcium-magnesium taste. *Physiological Genomics, 34*, 338–348.

3

The Chemical Senses

After reading this chapter, you will be able to

- Describe the basic mechanisms of smell and taste
- Understand their integration to form a sense of flavor
- Appreciate the gut as a major chemosensory and endocrine system
- Understand the brain stem and other structures relevant to these senses
- Describe specific examples of eating behaviors guided by these senses

"L'appétit vient en mangeant" ("appetite comes as you eat") is an old French proverb dating from well before 1534 when it was cited in *Gargantua* by François Rabelais. Using the rate of eating as a measure of appetite in both animals and humans, some studies have found empirical support of this proverb, which leads to the question of which feature(s) of the early stages of an eating bout might lead to acceleration of eating (Sclafani & Ackroff 2012). The consciously perceived features are those derived by our senses of smell and taste. Imagine yourself walking down a street in town and smelling a food aroma—say, freshly baked bread. Does that make you think about eating the bread? Do you start salivating? What are the chances you find the bakery and buy the bread? The odor that you have learned is associated with attractive food now produces physiological (salivation) and behavioral changes to bring you into contact with the food. (There are food-repulsive odors too; which odors might stop you from enjoying your bread?)

In this chapter, we first review the two traditional chemical senses of smell and taste, and then we talk about their integration in the brain to form the perception of flavor. Then, we will describe how parts of the digestive tract (stomach, intestine) "taste" in essentially the same way as the mouth. Although the signals generated by the gut are generally not part of our conscious experience of food, they do affect behavior. Lastly, we will examine the input zone in the brain for taste and gut sensing that will serve as an introduction to a broader treatment of the brain and feeding later in this book.

OLFACTION: THE SENSE OF SMELL

What is the function of olfaction? Most animals, and presumably our human ancestors, have an acute sense of smell and use this to locate food or other odors at a distance, sometimes miles away. To do so requires high sensitivity of the receptors and the ability to exhibit *chemotaxis*—moving toward the source of the odor (or away if it is dangerous). As one gets closer to an odor source, the concentration of the odor molecules gets larger; chemotaxis thus requires the ability to judge changes in intensity across time. Modern humans are not called on to use this ability often for survival purposes, although you may perceive the smell from and be attracted to a bakery that is around the corner! Another function of olfaction is the sensation of flavor and its actions to make nearby food more attractive: The smell of dinner in the kitchen may cause you to feel hungry, for example.

Odorants and Receptors

Odorants are molecules emitted from a source, dispersed in a carrier medium, and detected by receptors in sensory organ(s). For terrestrial animals, air is the carrier medium and the nose is the sensory organ. Although normal breathing is sufficient to bring odorants to the sensory surface inside the nose, we often sniff to draw more outside air across the sensory surface.

Odorants are volatile (airborne) molecules that have specific chemical shapes and sizes. Some chemical structures and what they smell like are shown in Figure 3.1. These chemicals can be

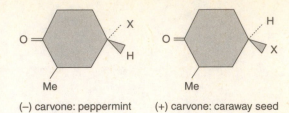

(−) carvone: peppermint   (+) carvone: caraway seed

Isoamyl acetate: banana

FIGURE 3.1   Chemical structures of (+) and (−) carvone (mirror image compounds such as a left and right hand) that are perceived to have extremely different odors. Esters such as isoamyl acetate often have fruity flavors, in this example, very banana!

presented as pure odorants in a laboratory: They may smell similar to but not exactly the same as natural objects (e.g., a banana) because natural objects almost always emit several odorants. Thus, to identify "banana" means analyzing a mixture of odors in a characteristic combination of constituents and relative concentrations. How does our olfactory system reliably achieve this sophisticated chemical analysis?

The chemical analysis is performed by chemical detectors called **olfactory receptors** that are clustered on the dendrites of **olfactory receptor neurons** that are supported in the **epithelium** lining the roof of the nasal cavity (Figure 3.2).

TALKING POINT 3.1

How many different odors can you name? If you detected them in the future, would you be able to identify the source by smell alone? Make a list of about five odors that you find pleasant and five that you find unpleasant, and compare it with the lists of others in your class. How many of these items are specific (e.g., "my roommate's cologne") and how many generic (e.g., "new car smell")? What do you think is the difference in olfactory sense between average people and "professional noses" for whom odor discrimination is their job (e.g., perfumiers or food testers)?

Olfactory

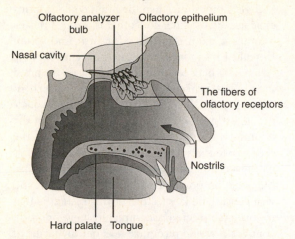

Olfactory analyzer bulb

Olfactory epithelium

Nasal cavity

The fibers of olfactory receptors

Nostrils

Hard palate   Tongue

FIGURE 3.2   The mammalian olfactory system, showing receptors in the nasal epithelium and convergence of connections from a given class of receptors.

These receptors all belong to a superfamily called **G-protein coupled receptors (GPCRs)** that are found in most tissues of the body. GPCRs are typically protein chains of at least 300 amino acids that thread through the cell membrane seven times. Thus, they have three domains or loops outside the cell that form a specific shape or pocket for binding chemicals called *ligands* (see also Appendix 1). Different GCPRs have different amino acid sequences in these loops that cause the pocket to vary and in turn attract a different ligand shape (Mombaerts, 1999).

The human genome encodes about 1,000 GPCRs, although more than half of these are called *pseudogenes* because they are not functional (Rouquier & Giorgi, 2007). More than half of all the GPCRs are expressed only in this tiny part of our body, the **nasal epithelium**. Each of the 300–400 or so human olfaction-specific GPCRs straddle the dendritic membrane of olfactory receptor neurons in the nasal epithelium, and each olfactory neuron expresses only one type of receptor. Like all GPCRs, they have structural regions outside of the cell that impart a particular shape and chemical characteristic that in turn allows a particular GPCR to bind

or interact with only a narrow range of possible odorant molecules. Thus, by virtue of its shape and size, a given odorant will interact or bind well with one or a small number of olfactory receptors, less well with another subset, and not at all with the rest. A second but chemically different odorant will bind to a different subset of receptors. Thus, each pure odorant will give rise to a unique pattern of stimulation of the entire olfactory receptor population.

Let's try to illustrate this point with a situation in which you may have found yourself. There are 500 people, all with different first names, in a noisy waiting area. Think of each person as a unique receptor for the sound of his or her name. One name is called over a loudspeaker, let's say Brenda. Brenda will most likely come forward, but because of background noise and/or poor speaker quality, so might Brandon, Wanda, and people with names that share phonetic features with Brenda, but not Veronica or Albert or most of the other 500 present. If a different name, say Henry, is called, a different subset of people would come forward. Each stimulus (name) will engage a unique group of people, and that is more or less how odorants engage receptors.

Although only about 500 receptor types are expressed in the nose, there are many more than 500 receptor cells (actually, about 40 million); thus, each type of GPCR occurs in thousands of olfactory receptor neurons. These same-GPCR cells are distributed across the area of the olfactory epithelium but a remarkable feature is that *all* of the distributed receptors containing a particular GPCR are connected, in humans, to only about 1,000 **glomeruli**. Olfactory receptor neurons send axons called the *olfactory nerve* through what is basically a bone with small holes (the cribriform plate) above the epithelium and to the glomeruli, which are in the **olfactory bulb**. Thus, given 300–400 unique receptors, on average, there are only a small number of glomeruli per receptor. Glomeruli are relay stations: They collect incoming signals from thousands of olfactory nerves and transmit them to the dendrites of mitral cells that are located in the main olfactory bulb). The axons of mitral cells then send digital electrical pulses called **action potentials** to the brain via the olfactory tracts.

So far, we have talked about smell from a source outside the organism—sometimes called *nasal* or *orthonasal* olfaction because the odor enters the nose from the front or "normal" direction. But there is a second source of odorants, via **retronasal olfaction** (Figure 3.3). When we bite and chew food, small molecules inside the food item may be released into the mouth. These odorants are often different from or additional to those detected by orthonasal stimulation and travel up the retronasal passage, a conduit running from the back/roof of the mouth into the nasal cavity, where they are detected by the olfactory receptor neurons (Gautam & Verhagen, 2012).

Projections to the Brain

The brain areas that receive the digital signals along thousands of afferent axons from the mitral cells have to decode these signals. If the axons from a single mitral cell were influenced only by a single glomerulus, then the brain could in principle use a cross fiber code; that is, axon *A* means odorant *a*, axon *B* means odorant *b*, and so on. In reality, it's more complicated because there is "cross talk" between mitral cells; instead, the brain uses a **pattern code**—each unique pattern of incoming signals codes a particular odorant quality, as distinct from another. The *intensity* of the odorant is coded mainly by the *frequency* of the action potentials (i.e., number of action potentials in a given time) as is true in all sensory systems: Many action potentials mean a strong odor, and vice versa. One key feature of this system is that if you encountered a completely new odorant, your brain would recognize it as new by virtue of a novel pattern of incoming digital signals.

Axons of the mitral cells form the olfactory tracts that run caudally and enter the front of the brain, including parts of the telencephalon such as cortex and amygdala. The amygdala is involved in emotional processing, and so olfaction may in

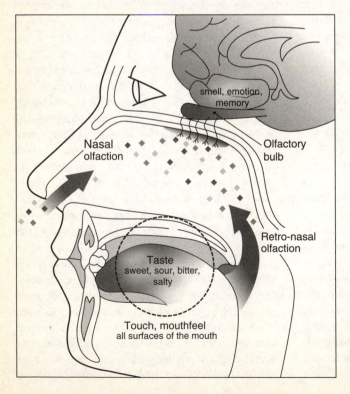

smell, emotion, memory

Nasal olfaction

Olfactory bulb

Retro-nasal olfaction

Taste
sweet, sour, bitter, salty

Touch, mouthfeel
all surfaces of the mouth

FIGURE 3.3 Nasal and retronasal olfaction, and relation to taste. *Source*: From "The Senses and the Psychology of Quality, Part 1" http://www.enologyinternational.com/articles/senses.html, Printed by permission of Jordan Ross.

BOX 3.1   Do You Smell What I Smell—or Your Dog Smells?

Scientists often make a distinction between macrosmatic species such as dogs that have a well-developed sense of smell that is central to their existence and microsmatic species such as humans for whom olfaction is not generally as important as other senses such as vision. Humans often use dogs to "sniff out" very low concentrations of odorants, such as hunting dogs that can detect the scent of prey or a buried object such as a truffle, and police and rescue dogs that can find concealed people, drugs, or bombs.

What is the basis of this difference in sensitivity or acuity? There are probably several contributing factors. First, although the size of

the olfactory bulb and number of olfactory receptor neurons is not always greatly different, the relative size may be; thus, a dog's olfactory bulb is a larger fraction of its total brain size than it is in humans (Quignon, Rimbault, Robin, & Galibert, 2012). Second, the number of different GCPRs encoded in the genome is typically a little higher in macrosmatic compared with microsmatic species, but the difference in the fraction of those genes that encode functional receptors is greater (e.g., 80% in dogs versus 30% in humans), the balance being nonfunctional or pseudogenes (Rouquier & Giorgi, 2007). Third, the patterns of sniffing, the structure of the nasal cavity, and the flow patterns of air through it differ greatly between dogs and humans (Craven, Paterson, & Settles, 2009). In addition, macrosmatic species have a well-developed vomeronasal organ, which functions a lot like a second and parallel olfactory system but is specialized for species-specific recognition molecules called *pheromones* (as in dogs sniffing other dogs).

---

a direct way be able to influence mood or affect. Indeed, some odors can elicit feelings of either extreme pleasure or disgust. Various parts of the **frontal cortex,** including the insular, orbitofrontal, and prepiriform regions, are where odor memory, complex odor discrimination, and flavor are computed. Different odorants produce activation of different sets of neurons in these regions (Gottfried, 2007; Howard, Plailly, Grueschow, Haynes, & Gottfried, 2009). The response of neurons in the orbitofrontal cortex is sensitive to context and learning; for example, the odorant-evoked response of single neurons in the orbitofrontal cortex of macaque monkeys was greater when they were hungry than after feeding/satiation (Pritchard et al., 2008). Odor memory is typically very good: You may not smell an odor for years; then, when re-exposed, you will recall the object or occasion of the prior exposure. Can you recall smells from your early childhood, such as

your grandmother's kitchen? It should be noted, however, that newborn infants who have minimal prior olfactory experience and an undeveloped frontal cortex make a complex odor discriminations, such as distinguishing their mother from other women (Cernoch & Porter 1985).

Anosmia

Anosmia refers to a complete loss of the sense of smell; *hyposmia* is a partial loss of smell or ability to discriminate one odor from another. Most of our sensory systems deteriorate with age, and olfaction is no exception. By age 80, most humans are hyposmic or anosmic. This decline is accelerated in Alzheimer's disease (Mesholam, Moberg, Mahr, & Doty, 1998). Concussions from frontal head trauma—many related to sports—may be associated with either temporary or permanent anosmia (Van Toller, 1999; Varney, Pinkston, &

TALKING POINT 3.2

Have you ever experienced loss of smell, or do you know someone who is anosmic? Were there symptoms other than loss of smell, such as those listed earlier? Can you be sure that the anosmia is causing these other symptoms, or instead that anosmia is one of several independent results from the trauma? What happens to your sense of smell when you have a cold? What difficulties with everyday life might anosmic people encounter?

Wu, 2001), as well as other symptoms. In the case of permanent anosmia, axons of the olfactory receptor neurons are cut where they pass through the cribriform plate, caused by movement of the brain relative to the skull during the traumatic event. Anosmic individuals often report that food tastes bland, and they have a range of other persistent psychological symptoms including personal isolation and emotional blunting (Van Toller 1999).

GUSTATION: THE SENSE OF TASTE

Taste and smell are closely interrelated (see Figure 3.3); when we talk about different tastes (lemon, strawberry, etc.), we often mean odors or in particular retronasal olfaction in combination with taste. This combination is called *flavor* and will be discussed later. Taste (without flavor) is vitally important for detection and recognition of the many food components that have little or no odor (e.g., salt), as well as contributing to the sensation of flavor. Unlike olfaction, for which there are hundreds of receptors, the number of receptor types involved in taste is far fewer and are organized into discrete classes of sensation. Only some of the taste receptors belong to the GPCR superfamily; others are ion channels (also called *ionotropic* receptors). The five primary taste classes are sweet, salty, sour, bitter, and umami (Chaudhari & Roper, 2010). **Umami** means "savory taste" and is a relatively recent addition to this list. It arises from receptors for the amino acid L-glutamate; monosodium glutamate (MSG)—a common food additive—is a prototypical example.

Taste receptors are located in groups of ~50 cells within onion-shaped structures called **taste buds** (Figure 3.4). Taste buds form the sides of nipple-like structures called *papillae*, which appear as bumps on the surface of the tongue and other parts of the oral cavity including the palate (roof of mouth) and throat. The main types of gustatory papillae found on the tongue are fungiform (anterior), foliate (side), and circumvallate (back).

As in olfaction, different **tastants** (chemicals) impart a particular taste sensation by activating specific receptors. To gain access to taste receptors, the molecules of a tastant have to permeate the papillae and buds, most usually by being soluble in water or saliva. Each taste bud contains several taste receptor cells; although each taste cell expresses a limited range of receptors, different cells in the bud may express different receptors. That said, the relative expression of various taste-related genes does differ between fungiform and circumvallate papillae in primates (Hevezi et al., 2009), suggesting that the taste buds in these regions are more or less "tuned" to a specific taste. The popular myth of a "tongue map"—that certain tastes are detected only by certain parts of the tongue—is not supported by scientific evidence: All parts of the tongue have some sensitivity to all tastes, although not equally (Collings, 1974). Different populations of buds are connected to different sensory nerves. In particular, anterior regions are served by the facial nerve (also known as the seventh cranial nerve or CN7), whereas posterior regions are served by the glossopharyngeal nerve (CN9). Also, a branch of the **vagus nerve (CN10)** innervates the throat regions. Other mouth sensations including information about texture, temperature, and so on (see Figure 3.4) are additionally relayed via the

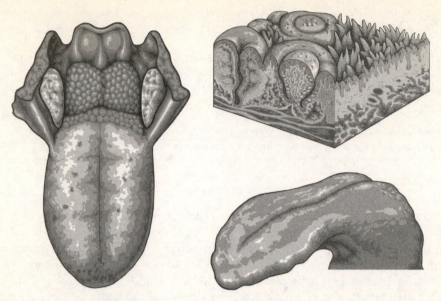

FIGURE 3.4 **Representation of the human tongue and inset detail of organization of a typical taste bud.** The tongue can be regarded as a muscle for moving food through the mouth that additionally has a sensory function.

trigeminal nerve (CN5). Completely unlike the olfactory tracts that enter the front of the brain, these taste-relaying nerves enter the brain stem (rear of the brain) and synapse in the **nucleus of the solitary tract (NST)** (Figure 3.5).

GPCR Taste Receptors: Sweet, Umami, and Bitter

The GPCRs involved in sweet and umami taste are part of the TAS1R family, which has three members: TAS1R1, TAS1R2, and TAS1R3. Each

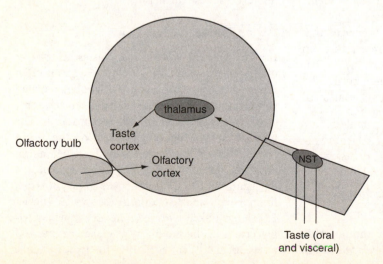

FIGURE 3.5 **Sketch of the human brain showing the different trajectories for olfactory and taste signals.**

Taste inputs synapse in the nucleus of the solitary tract (NST), then project to the thalamus and frontal cortex.

BOX 3.2 Taste Bud Turnover

Some sensory cells, such as photoreceptors in your eyes and hair cells in your ears, are with you for life. That is, they have little or no capacity to be renewed if they are fatally damaged. Taste cells are almost the other end of this spectrum—they typically have a life of only a few weeks after which they are replaced. The lower part of a taste bud is enriched in genes associated with cell cycle and stem cells (Hevezi et al., 2009), suggesting that new taste cells are made there, then migrate toward the tip of the bud, but eventually die. However, the part of the taste neurons (dendrites) that contacts the taste bud is not renewed. Thus, taste nerves are continually being paired with new cells; nonetheless, our sense of taste does not suddenly change.

of these receptor proteins has a long chemical-recognition domain outside the cell and is encoded by *Tas1R1, Tas1R2,* and *Tas1R3* genes, respectively (genes are denoted in italics and the protein products of those genes in uppercase font; see Appendix 2 for a refresher on genes and proteins). Slight modifications or differences in these genes between individuals and across animal species underlie differences in taste perception. Tastants are recognized as a result of nonidentical pairs (called *heterodimers*) of these GPCRs coupling together to form a receptor complex that engages a particular class of tastant: for example, TAS1R1 + TAS1R3 for umami and TAS1R2 + TAS1R3 for sweet (Sbarbati & Osculati, 2005; Treesukosol, Smith, & Spector, 2011).

Bitter taste is encoded by the T2R family which have relatively short domains outside the cell and of which there are more than 30 members. These receptor variants respond best to different bitter-tasting molecules. It appears that several, if not all, of these genes are expressed in each bitter taste receptive cell, which means that each bitter responsive cell will be activated by most or all bitter substances. Thus, because the brain cannot tell which precise bitter tastant gave rise to an action potential in an afferent nerve, our ability to discriminate among different bitter taste qualities is limited.

Ionotropic Taste Receptors: Salty and Sour

The prototypical salty taste is common table or sea salt, sodium chloride (NaCl). Salts are chemically defined as a combination of positively charged cations, in this case sodium (Na^+), and negatively charged anions, in this case chloride (Cl^-). Cations are the more important for taste: Sodium salts (chloride, sulfate, etc.) all taste more or less the same. Far more is known about sodium than other cations (e.g., potassium, calcium). Salty taste is transduced mainly through the transport of sodium ions through the epithelial amiloride-sensitive sodium channels (ENaCs) found in some taste buds. *Amiloride* is a chemical that blocks or obstructs access of sodium to this channel; pretreating the tongue with amiloride largely abolishes the sensation of saltiness.

Sour taste is related to acidity, in particular hydrogen ions (H^+). There are several candidate channels, but functional analysis of these lags far behind that for other taste modalities, so we will not discuss these further.

Other Tastes

In addition to these five primary tastes, at least two others deserve mention. First, pure water is often reported to have a taste, which might be mediated by water channel proteins called *aquaporins*, some of which are expressed in taste receptor cells. The taste of water is highly dependent on the recent taste history of the tongue, including the natural adapting stimulus of saliva. Second, evidence is emerging that in addition to its greasy texture, fat may have a taste (Running, Mattes, & Tucker, 2013), most likely a result of the breakdown of triglycerides in the mouth by a lipase enzyme and access of the liberated fatty acids to taste buds.

TALKING POINT 3.3

You have learned that the receptors that transduce taste come from several very different genes and families. That is, the old psychological distinction between sweet and bitter rests on distinct molecular mechanisms.

From an evolutionary perspective, how do you think that this diverse set of mechanisms became lumped together in the tongue, and indeed from a cluster of sensations that we call taste?

A fatty acid transporter protein expressed in taste receptor cells could be a candidate sensor.

Taste Coding in Higher Brain Regions

We noted earlier that taste and other mouth-related information is conveyed via four nerves to the NST in the brain stem. Most of the afferent taste fibers, as well as cells in the NST, are "broadly tuned," meaning that they are activated by more than one prototypical tastant. Many cells in the NST respond to temperature or touch rather than or in addition to taste, and at least in rats, the timing of firing in the NST is modified by ongoing licking behavior (Roussin, D'Agostino, Fooden, Victor, & DiLorenzo, 2012). Cells within the NST that respond to taste stimulation of the tongue appear to be broadly tuned—that is, they do not respond to only one class of tastant. Thus, recognition of particular tastes seems to involve recognition of patterns of responding across a large population of NST cells.

One other feature of taste input, as in many sensory systems including olfaction, is rapid adaptation to a sustained stimulus. If a tastant is applied continuously to the tongue (e.g., bathing with a continuous stream of the tastant), the stimulated taste buds and afferent nerves first show a large initial or phasic response of many action potentials and then adapt to a later or sustained response of fewer action potentials. Thus, at the level of the NST and higher levels, the nervous system responds best to a *change* of stimulus (taste).

Taste information then flows via the *thalamus* to two regions of the frontal cortex, the *anterior insular cortex* and the *frontal operculum*. These neuroanatomical descriptions suggest that the gustatory system is organized hierarchically, but, as for all sensory systems, the brain does not simply transfer the same information from regions A to B to C. Instead, it actively analyzes, prioritizes, and extracts relevant information along the way. An important question is the functional role of taste-responsive cells at the highest level (cortex) compared with those at a lower level such as the NST. Data in this regard are quite sparse because available methods to look at the human brain such as **functional magnetic resonance imaging (fMRI)** do not allow for analysis at the level of individual neurons. On the other hand, the most popular lab mammals for taste research (rats and mice) do not have a taste cortex that is as well developed as that in humans. The relatively few studies of single cells in the gustatory cortex of nonhuman primates have indicated that some cells have much more specific taste profiles than at other brain levels and also integrate across time and with other senses (Thorpe, Rolls, & Maddison, 1983).

Flavor

As we noted before, the stimulation of taste cells is almost always accompanied by olfactory (ortho and/or retronasal) and oral trigeminal stimulation. Certainly this is true for most of the foods that we eat that require active oral manipulation such as chewing. Food or drink tasters have long known that keeping the commodity in the mouth for a long period enhances the flavor and indeed is necessary to appreciate the nuances of a complex edible item. Surprisingly little is known about the integration of these sensory streams to form the concept of **flavor**.

BOX 3.3 So You Think You Can Taste?

Here's a fun exercise to demonstrate that "taste" is often more a function of smell. First, select a classmate or friend as a partner for this experiment. You'll then need a good supply of jelly beans or other candies with distinct flavors (e.g., blueberry, cotton candy, popcorn, pear). Now, close your eyes, hold your nose closed with your fingers, and have your partner give you a flavored jelly bean. Hold your nose closed the entire time you chew the candy; then try to name the taste. Repeat several times with your partner feeding you different colors (flavors), and then switch places with your partner. Most people cannot reliably distinguish the different tastes because the distinction depends on seeing the color and/or retronasal olfaction (which is stopped when you hold your nose). A similar experiment can be done with raw potato and apple slices; these have similar textures. This explains why food "tastes" so bland when we have a cold: Odorants cannot bind to receptors in the nasal epithelium very well.

In humans, neuroimaging studies have been performed relevant to flavor. Small et al. (2004) used fMRI to examine activation of brain regions to a taste alone, an odor alone, and to their combination. Either stimulus presented alone activated the frontal operculum, the ventral insula, and the cingulate cortex. Their combination produced a supra-additive response that was greater than the sum of the components. Although not all fMRI studies have found supra-additivity, all have implicated these same regions. In a behavioral study using intensity ratings, Frank and Byram (1988) showed a taste-odor interaction for only certain pairs. For example, strawberry odor enhanced the sweetness rating of a sucrose solution, but the odor of peanut butter did not. Further, perceived saltiness of a salt solution was not enhanced by strawberry odor. It is possible that experience plays a role in this specificity of pairing: Strawberries are often eaten with sugar, but typically not with peanut butter or salt, and adults obviously come to these tests having extensive prior exposure to complex foods. You might want to keep this in mind during the discussion of associative learning in later chapters; would Would learning a novel taste-odor association cause synaptic reorganization so that a supra-additive response might now occur in one or more of the cortical areas we have discussed? Changes in synaptic organization and strength are known to underlie many types of learning and memory, so there is every reason to think this will also be true for taste-related learning. In rats,

damage to the insular cortex prevents taste-odor associative learning (Sakai & Imada, 2003).

TASTE-OR FLAVOR-GUIDED BEHAVIORS

We now focus on the behaviors (or changes in behavior) that are associated with chemical senses. In studying this in the laboratory, several features are important to consider.

Stimulus Presentation

Because of sensory adaptation, brief or intermittent tests are best. For example, in rodents, some methods to test either discrimination or preference for a tastant involve only a few seconds of licking (Treesukosul, Smith, & Spector, 2011). The analog in humans is a "sip and spit" test. For solutions with post-ingestive benefit (e.g., sugars), tests for purely taste properties should not be long enough that gut sensory factors (see later discussion) influence the results. In studies that involve prolonged exposure to the food (e.g., daily food choice), preferences or aversions observed probably reflect post-ingestive in addition to taste or flavor characteristics.

Innate or Learned

Long before the discovery of taste receptors, it was recognized that newborn infants accept and suck on an artificial, sweet-coated nipple, but they will spit out a bitter-coated nipple. Thus,

TALKING POINT 3.4

To what extent do you think alliesthesia, sensory specific satiety, and receptor adaptation are related? Traditionally, meals are served as a succession of courses that progress from savory to sweet. Do you think this is purely by chance or that it has a physiological basis?

the basic accept/reject functions of sweet and bitter are innate. The term *innate* implies never before experienced, but in the case of taste, how innate is innate? In a later chapter, we will tell you that certain tastants ingested by a pregnant woman may be transmitted into amniotic fluid and affect an infant's postnatal diet preferences, presumably because the fetus can detect these chemicals. Preterm infants are known to swallow substantial volumes of amniotic fluid; so, provided that the taste (or gut) receptors are functional at the particular age of gestation, there is certainly the potential for prenatal tasting. The taste of sodium (salt) may also be innate; recall that there are specific ENaCs and, from an earlier chapter, the discussion of the special nature of sodium appetite.

Palatability

Palatability refers to the acceptability of an item on the basis of its taste, that is whether a substance would be moved from the tip of the tongue to the palate and then swallowed. The infant's reflexive behaviors toward sweet and bitter are good examples of this definition. However, the use of the term in research literature is sometimes confounded with the quantity consumed (palatable substances are often consumed in greater amounts than unpalatable substances). This is not a trivial issue. For example, you are hungry and start eating a food item. By the definition of acceptance, the food is palatable. After some time eating, you stop. By definition of rejection, the food is no longer palatable. The same food has decreased in palatability. How can that be?

The term **alliesthesia** describes this decline in acceptance for a food as it is consumed. When humans are asked to rate the pleasantness of a tastant (or a range of tastants) at various times during a meal, a downward shift in pleasantness occurs as the meal proceeds. In a more general sense, the acceptance of a tastant is dependent on the internal state of the organism. The term *sensory specific satiety* describes a related phenomenon, namely that satiety for one particular food does not mean satiety for all foods. In general, a variety of foods stimulates appetite and intake (Rolls, 1985).

Finally, we should mention that palatability is dependent not only on the tastant but also its concentration. For example, maybe you habitually add one spoonful of sugar to your coffee or tea. If you add less than that, it is not so tasty (which is why trying to cut out sugar is hard!). Conversely, if you add much more than that, it is "unpleasantly sweet." Thus, most pure tastants show a preference-aversion function (Figure 3.6) in which a midrange concentration is most preferred. When we talk about palatability, we are in fact also

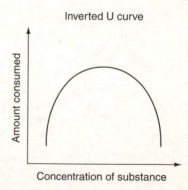

Inverted U curve

FIGURE 3.6 Idealized preference-aversion function for a tastant in which the amount consumed (or its palatability) varies according to an inverted U with concentration. High preference occurs in the midrange.

considering sensitivity to a specific concentration of tastant. To return to sodium appetite, animals that are sodium depleted show increased acceptance or palatability to both low and high concentrations of NaCl—that is, the preference-aversion function is broadened.

CHEMICAL SENSING AND THE ENTERIC NERVOUS SYSTEM

Once you swallow something, does it become part of your body? Is your skin the largest sensory surface in your body? You may be surprised to learn that the answer to both of these questions is "no." It is not until nutrients are absorbed through the walls of the intestine into the bloodstream that they become an integral part of the organism. For this reason, we consider the **gastrointestinal (GI) tract** to be a food tube with the mouth its top end (Figure 3.7).

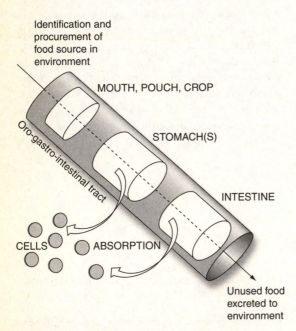

Identification and procurement of food source in environment

Oro-gastro-intestinal tract

MOUTH, POUCH, CROP

STOMACH(S)

INTESTINE

CELLS   ABSORPTION

Unused food excreted to environment

FIGURE 3.7 The food tube.
Food passes from the mouth to the stomach to the intestines. Food is digested or broken down into component nutrients and then absorbed across the walls; undigested food and indigestible material are excreted.

The role of the food tube is to process the foods that we eat into energy-yielding molecules that can be absorbed across the walls of the tube, to propel food along the tube during this digestive process (or to eject it by vomiting), and to discard the unwanted material as feces. The food tube in an adult human is folded and about 6 meters (20 feet) long. Further, the walls of the food tube are highly convoluted (i.e., containing ridges and furrows), so that the total surface area is about 100 times that of your skin! More than 200 million neurons are associated with the food tube, forming the **enteric nervous system**. So, quite literally, the mouth and its taste receptors are merely the top end of the food tube. Just as we need to know about stimuli impinging on the outside of our body (including smell and taste), it is important for the body to be informed about what is in the food tube. Many of the sensory mechanisms that accomplish this are similar or identical to how taste works, except that we are not consciously aware of enteric sensing (Mayer, 2011).

The walls of the food tube are made of many types of cells, and for our present purposes, we will focus only on a subset called **enteroendocrine cells** (*entero*—of the intestine; *endocrine*—secreting hormones internally) that are dispersed along the length of the food tube (Sternini, Anselmi, & Rozengurt, 2008). These cells express chemosensory receptors that send sensory information both locally within the enteric nervous system or the gut and to the brain. The signals to the brain are of two main types: action potentials in sensory afferents of the vagus nerve and specific hormones that are released into the bloodstream (thence to the brain) as a result of specific enteroendocrine cell stimulation. Different classes of these cells (identified by a letter, e.g., G-cell) secrete different hormones. For completeness, we should add that there are also receptors in the food tube for stimuli such as toxins and physical stretching, and this information goes to the brain via spinal afferent neurons.

Primary vagal afferents first synapse in the brain in the nucleus of the solitary tract (NST) in the brain stem (see Figure 3.5), the same region as taste afferents, but whereas taste information

TALKING POINT 3.5

Because it is so large, the enteric nervous system is sometimes known as the gut brain or second brain. However, we are generally unaware of its function—for example, the sweet receptors in your tongue give rise to a conscious perception whereas those in your gut do not. What sensations from your gut are consciously available? What do you think is the origin of the term *gut feeling*?

goes mainly to the rostral or front part of the NST, the gut (vagus) input is to the caudal or back part. This linear organization reinforces the idea that the sensory surface of the gut is best viewed as a continuation of the mouth.

Hormones are carried in the blood and access the brain mostly in two tiny regions that have a weak blood-brain barrier (see Appendix 1)—the **area postrema** and the **arcuate nucleus**. The area postrema is situated between the left and right sides of the NST, and together with a motor output region, they make up what is known as the *dorsal vagal complex*. Because of the diversity of enteroendocrine cell types and receptors, the dorsal vagal complex receives diverse information about the food we eat and controls some output to the gut (Young, 2012). Next, we

identify some key chemical signals in this system; all are peptide hormones and, collectively, are often called *gut hormones*. They are important in the context of this text because they directly affect feeding behavior.

GUT HORMONES THAT AFFECT FOOD INTAKE

Cholecystokinin (CCK) is the most-studied of these. It is released from a specific class of cells (I-cells) found mainly in the first segment of the intestine (the duodenum). CCK release starts very soon after a meal begins and, in addition to digestive actions, locally stimulates afferent vagal activity to the NST and is carried in the bloodstream to the AP. CCK was found to have a specific

BOX 3.4 What's the Evidence That CCK Is an Anorectic Agent?

First, injection of laboratory-made CCK causes rats (and humans) to stop an eating episode sooner than they otherwise would. Second, this satiety effect occurs even in "sham feeding" rats in which an ingested liquid diet does not pass to the intestine but rather drains out of the stomach through a surgically implanted port. Third, antagonist drugs that prevent the action of endogenous CCK at its receptors increase the size of a meal. Fourth, damage to vagal sensory fibers in rodents after injection of a high dose of capsaicin (active ingredient of chili pepper) attenuates CCK-induced satiety as well as that by nutrients. So you like spicy food? Don't worry—capsaicin is absorbed slowly and it is partly

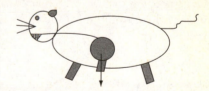

Sham feeding rat.
Licked fluid can drain out of stomach when fistula open.

degraded before entering the general circulation; it would be exceedingly difficult to consume enough to achieve neurotoxic levels. The sweating you may experience when eating spicy food is due to a benign action of capsaicin in the mouth (salivary glands) that triggers facial sweating. Do rats eat less simply because CCK makes them feel ill? The **behavioral satiety sequence** (briefly, grooming followed by resting) seen after natural meals or CCK suggests this is not the case; this sequence is not seen in sickness. Do humans have a comparable behavioral satiety sequence?

appetite-suppressing action (Moran, 2000; Wren & Bloom, 2007).

Other, more recently characterized satiety hormones include glucagon-like peptide-1 (GLP-1) and peptide YY (PYY) that are released from L-class cells throughout the intestine, especially the lower part (ileum); thus, as food takes a while to move through the intestine, their release relative to a meal is considerably later than release of CCK.

Ghrelin is the only gut peptide discovered thus far that increases food intake. Ghrelin is released from cells in the stomach, not in response to food but rather to the absence of food in the stomach and hence a state of hunger. Consistent with this idea, injection of ghrelin to rats and humans stimulates food intake (Wren & Bloom, 2007) by reducing the latency to meal onset.

Insulin

The pancreas, an organ near the stomach and upper intestine, has long been recognized as an endocrine organ with major implications for energy regulation. The pancreas secretes two main hormones, the anabolic (tissue-building) peptide **insulin** from β-cells and the catabolic (tissue-breaking) peptide **glucagon** from α-cells. Some enteroendocrine cells also secrete these hormones. Physiologically, these hormones have somewhat opposite effects, so we'll focus only on insulin, which appears to have a major role in communication to the brain about metabolism.

The primary stimulus to insulin release is a rise in blood glucose as a carbohydrate-containing meal starts to be absorbed, typically within 5 minutes of the start of a meal. This occurs because walls of the β-cells contain glucose sensors (actually glucose transporters that move glucose across the cell membrane). Other chemical triggers for insulin release include CCK and GLP-1 released from enteroendocrine cells. There is also a so-called cephalic phase: It takes several minutes after the beginning of a meal for food to start being absorbed; yet, insulin secretion starts almost immediately or even in anticipation of food, the result of sensations of taste and smell triggering a neural signal to the pancreas (whence the term *cephalic*—involving the brain). A functional role of such cephalic reflexes may be to prepare the body for the arrival of food. Insulin increases transport of glucose into cells, primarily muscle and adipose tissue, leading to nutrient storage. The rapid time-course of insulin release would be consistent with a role in meal termination, and consistent with this, administration of small amounts of insulin into rats' brains decreases food intake via receptors in the brain.

Amylin is a peptide that is co-secreted from the pancreas along with insulin, although in much smaller amounts. Amylin administration into the brain of rats suppresses food intake, but via a separate mechanism from insulin. There seems to be a synergy between amylin and insulin in brain: Together, their anorectic action is greater than the sum of their independent effects. Indeed, all of the hormones described in this section are known to interact in various ways.

BOX 3.5 Diabetes

A symptom of untreated diabetes is high blood sugar (hyperglycemia). If untreated, chronic hyperglycemia leads to a number of serious consequences such as neuropathy (damage to neurons) and vascular collapse causing degeneration of many systems including the retina, causing blindness. Clearly, this is not a disease to leave untreated! There are two types of diabetes. Type 1 diabetes manifests quite early in life and is caused by a lack of insulin synthesis by the pancreas. It can be treated by replacing the body's insulin with insulin from an external source. Type 2 diabetes is far more common than type 1 and is caused, paradoxically, by too much insulin. In this type of diabetes, insulin receptors become insensitive (insulin resistance); giving more insulin is of limited use as a treatment. Type 2 diabetes is caused by obesity and weight loss is the best treatment.

Let's review and apply your knowledge. Take time to answer these chapter questions

1. How do we "smell" different odors in our environment? Why is smell important?
2. What are the five primary tastes? How are these encoded (different receptors, etc.)?
3. Summarize the neuroanatomy of taste. Make a sketch of the pathway for taste information from receptors in the tongue to areas within the cortex.
4. What is meant by the term *flavor*? What have fMRI studies indicated about brain activity associated with processing of flavor information? What are the main functions of the enteroendocrine system?
5. Name three peptides released from this system that inhibit food intake.

Glossary

Action potential   The brief digital (all-or-none) electrical signal (about 100 millivolts in amplitude and 1 millisecond in duration) used by axons to transmit information rapidly from the cell body to the terminal (see also Appendix 1). The number of action potentials in unit time is called the *firing rate*.

Alliesthesia   The change in perception of a stimulus (in this context, smell or taste) as the internal state changes (e.g., from hunger to satiation).

Anosmia   Inability to smell. This often occurs in the elderly, as well as after concussive brain trauma.

Arcuate nucleus   The most ventral part of the hypothalamus; has a weak blood-brain barrier allowing penetration of blood-borne hormones. This region is involved with eating behaviors.

Area postrema   Small midline nucleus in the brainstem, located on the floor of the 4th cerebral ventricle. Has a "weak" blood brain barrier so circulating small molecules such as peptides can gain access to this nucleus and activate (or inhibit) the neurons.

Behavioral satiety sequence   A sequence of behaviors that normally occurs immediately after the end of a natural meal; in rodents, this normally starts with grooming and ends with sleeping or resting.

Cholecystokinin (CCK)   A hormone released from cells in the upper part of the digestive tract in response to stimulation by food. Some of this released CCK contacts receptors on sensory nerve endings in the gut and these generate neural signals to the brain (NST).

Enteric nervous system   A comprehensive network of neurons that are involved in the various sensory and motor functions of the gastrointestinal tract. It is also popularly known as the "gut brain," although for the most part, we are not consciously aware of its functions.

Enteroendocrine cells   Specialized cells in the wall of the gastrointestinal tract that secrete hormones in response to stimulation by specific nutrients.

Epithelium   Epithelium is one of four basic types of tissues found in animals. Epithelial tissues are composed of densely packed cells and line most structures in the body. Many substances are actively transported across epithelia. Some epithelial cells aggregate into clusters forming glands that secrete hormones.

Flavor   A property ascribed to a food resulting from the combination of its taste and smell qualities.

Frontal cortex   The front lobe of the brain, particularly large in humans, that is involved in many high-level behaviors such as decision making and receiving distinct olfactory and gustatory inputs to several subdivisions. Flavor most likely is integrated at this level of the brain.

Functional magnetic resonance imaging (fMRI)   A popular method by which to "map" regions of high metabolic activity within the living human brain. Typically, data (which are derived from signals related to blood oxygen level) are presented as differences between a stimulus condition such as odor presentation and a baseline condition with no stimulus of interest (e.g., odor in this chapter) present.

Gastrointestinal (GI) tract   Also called the food tube; it is the tube that connects the mouth to the anus. If straightened out, it would be about 20 feet long. Because the walls are highly ridged or convoluted, the actual surface area is up to 100 times that of your external skin! The role of the GI tract is to detect and selectively absorb desired nutrients to fuel cells of the body.

Glomerulus (plural glomeruli)   A spherical structure located in the olfactory bulb of the brain where synapses form between the terminals of olfactory receptor neurons and the dendrites of mitral (and other) cells that project to the brain. Each glomerulus is "odor coded": It receives input from many receptor neurons but all of these express the same specific receptor type.

Glucagon   A peptide hormone secreted by alpha cells of the pancreas, usually during fasting, that functions to raise blood glucose levels by breaking down stored glycogen into glucose.

G-protein coupled receptor (GPCR)   A superfamily of receptors, including ~1,000 olfaction-specific instances in the human genome that on binding a ligand (e.g., odorant for olfaction) at the outer surface of a cell, initiate a cascade of G-protein–mediated events inside the cell.

Insulin   A peptide hormone secreted by beta cells of the pancreas, usually during and after eating, that serves to promote storage of absorbed nutrients as glycogen and triglycerides.

Nasal epithelium   Specialized surface or skin, about 1 square centimeter in area in humans, in the nasal cavity and supporting the olfactory receptors.

Nucleus of the solitary tract (NST)   A long, skinny nucleus of cells (one on each side of the brain) found in the brainstem. It is the first region in the brain contacted by incoming neural signals from the gut and from the tongue.

Odorant   Molecules emitted from a source, dispersed in a carrier medium, and detected by receptors.

Olfactory bulb   Front or rostral part of the brain that contains glomeruli and mitral cells whose output axons form the olfactory tracts and project rearward or caudally to various brain regions.

Olfactory receptors   Protein molecules on olfactory receptor neurons whose three-dimensional shape forms a binding site or pocket for odorant molecules that have a corresponding shape. As a result of this binding, the receptor initiates a cascade of chemical events inside the receptor neuron.

Olfactory receptor neuron   Specialized neuron (bipolar) class whose dendrites express the olfactory receptors and whose axon projects to and synapses in a glomerulus in the olfactory bulb. Each neuron expresses only one type of olfactory receptor and projects to only one glomerulus.

Pattern code   The "rule" that allows the brain to decode or use incoming information; in the case of olfaction, this input is from the mitral cells. A pattern code extracts which fibers were active (the pattern) and the relative frequency (which codes intensity) of action potentials.

Retronasal olfaction   Occurs when volatile molecules are released in our mouth as we chew food, and these enter the nasal cavity via a channel from the roof of the mouth.

Tastant   A molecule that by virtue of its shape and other characteristics stimulates taste receptor(s) on the tongue and gives rise to a sensation of taste.

Taste buds   Onion-shaped structures composed of many cells, including taste receptor cells, that are embedded in the tongue and shaped to allow access of tastant molecules to the taste receptors.

Umami From Japanese "pleasant savory taste"; it is the fifth and most recently characterized basic taste category. It is received or transduced by a specific class of taste receptors. The prototypical tastant is the common food additive monosodium glutamate (MSG).

Vagus nerve (CN10) A mixed nerve (both sensory afferents to the brain and efferent motor fibers from the brain) that innervates a large number of organs in the chest and abdomen.

References

Cernoch, J. M., & Porter, R. H. (1985). Recognition of maternal axillary odors by infants. *Child Development, 56,* 1593–1598.

Chaudhari, N., & Roper, S. D. (2010). The cell biology of taste. *Journal of Cell Biology, 190,* 285–296.

Collings, V. B. (1974). Human taste response as a function of locus of stimulation of the tongue and soft palate. *Perception & Psychophysics, 16,* 169–174.

Craven, B. A., Paterson, E. G., & Settles, G. S. (2010). The fluid dynamics of canine olfaction: Unique nasal airflow patterns as an explanation of macrosomia. *Journal of the Royal Society Interface, 7,* 933–943.

Frank, R. A., & Byram, J. (1998). Taste-smell interactions are tastant and odorant dependent. *Chemical Senses, 13,* 445–455.

Gautam, S. H., & Varhagen, J. V. (2012). Retronasal odor representations in the dorsal olfactory bulb of rats. *Journal of Neuroscience, 32,* 7949–7959.

Gottfried, J. A. (2007). What can an orbitofrontal cortex-endowed animal do with smells? *Annals of the New York Academy of Sciences, 1121,* 102–120.

Hevezi, P., Moyer, B. D., Lu, M., Gaeo, N., White, E., Echeverri, F., ... Zlotnik, A. (2009). Genome-wide analysis of gene expression in primate taste buds reveals links to diverse processes. *PLoS ONE, 4,* e6395.

Howard, J. P., Plailly, J., Grueschow, M., Haynes, J.-D., & Gottfried, J. A. (2009). Odor quality coding and categorization in human posterior piriform cortex. *Nature Neuroscience, 12,* 932–938.

Mayer, E. A. (2011). Gut feelings: The emerging biology of gut-brain communication. *Nature Reviews Neuroscience, 12,* 453–466.

Mesholam, R. I., Moberg, P. J., Mahr, R. N., & Doty, R. L. (1998). Olfaction in neurodegenerative disease: A meta-analysis of olfactory functioning in Alzheimer's and Parkinson's diseases. *Archives of Neurology, 55,* 84–90.

Mombaerts, P. (1999). Molecular biology of odorant receptors in vertebrates. *Annual Review of Neuroscience, 22,* 487–509.

Moran, T. H. (2000). Cholecystokinin and satiety: Current perspectives. *Nutrition, 16,* 858–865.

Pritchard, T. C., Nedderman, E. N., Edwards, E. M., Petticoffer, A. C., Schwartz, G. J., & Scott, T. R. (2008). Satiety-responsive neurons in medial orbitofrontal cortex of the macaque. *Behavioral Neuroscience, 122,* 174–182.

Quignon, P., Rimbault, M., Robin, S., & Galibert, F. (2012). Genetics of canine olfaction and receptor diversity. *Mammalian Genome, 23,* 132–143.

Rolls, B. J. (1985). Experimental analyses of the effects of variety in a meal on human feeding. *American Journal of Clinical Nutrition, 42,* 932–939.

Rouquier, S., & Giorgi, D. (2007). Olfactory receptor gene repertoires in mammals. *Mutation Research, 616,* 95–102.

Roussin, A. T., D'Agostino, A. E., Fooden, A. M., Victor, J. D., & DiLorenzo, P. M. (2012). Taste coding in the nucleus of the solitary tract of the awake, freely licking rat. *Journal of Neuroscience, 32,* 10494–10506.

Running, C. A., Mattes, R. D., & Tucker, R. M. (2013). Fat taste in humans: Sources of within- and between-subject variability. *Progress in Lipid Research, 52,* 438–445.

Sakai, N., & Imada, S. (2003). Bilateral lesions of the insular cortex of the prefrontal cortex block the association between taste and odor in the rat. *Neurobiology of Learning and Memory, 80,* 24–31.

Sbarbati, A., & Osculati, F. (2005). The taste cell–related diffuse chemosensory system. *Progress in Neurobiology, 75,* 295–307.

Sclafani, A., & Ackroff, K. (2012) Role of gut nutrient sensing in stimulating appetite and conditioning food preferences. *American Journal of Physiology Regulatory Integrative and Comparative Physiology 302*, R1119-33.

Small, D. M., Voss, J., Mak, Y. E., Simmons, K. B., Parrish, T., & Gitelman, D. (2004). Experience-dependent neural integration of taste and smell in the human brain. *Journal of Neurophysiology, 92*, 1892–1903.

Sternini, C., Anselmi, L., & Rozengurt, E. (2008). Enteroendocrine cells: A site of "taste" in gastrointestinal chemosensing. *Current Opinion Endocrinology, Diabetes and Obesity, 15*, 73–78.

Thorpe, S. J., Rolls, E. T., & Maddison, S. (1983). The orbitofrontal cortex: Neuronal activity in the behaving monkey. *Experimental Brain Research, 49*, 93–115.

Treesukosul, Y., Smith, K. R., & Spector, A. C. (2011). The functional role of the T1R family of receptors in sweet taste and feeding. *Physiology and Behavior, 105*, 14–26.

Van Toller, S. (1999). Assessing the impact of anosmia: Review of a questionnaire's findings. *Chemical Senses, 24*, 705–712.

Varney, N. R., Pinkston, J. B. & Wu, J. C. (2001). Quantitative PET findings in patients with post-traumatic anosmia. *Journal of Head Trauma Rehabilitation, 16*, 253–259.

Wren, A. M. & Bloom, S. R. (2007). Gut hormones and appetite control. *Gastroenterology, 132*, 2116–2130.

Young, A. A. (2012). Brainstem sensing of meal-related signals in energy homeostasis. *Neuropharmacology, 63*, 31–45.

4

You Are What You Eat: Evolution, Energy, and Foraging

After reading this chapter, you will be able to

- Understand the process of natural selection as it applies to feeding behavior
- Understand the concept of energy and its flow through organisms

- Apply the concept of optimal foraging to the economics of energy acquisition
- Interpret the relation of portion size in the modern world to the previously mentioned concepts

Two of the fundamental scientific foundations for understanding eating and obesity are the theory of **evolution** and the physicochemical concept of **energy**. We have already introduced some aspects of these concepts in previous chapters. We hope you will acquire a working idea of these concepts, although we certainly don't require you to be a theoretical expert in either!

ANCESTORS AND EVOLUTION

The first comprehensive evolutionary theory is attributed to Charles Darwin, who proposed in the mid-1800s that species evolve by a very slow process called **natural selection**. To simplify greatly, this means that a species will change over a long time span and eventually may become a new species if that change allows the individuals to exploit or compete for resources better than

their ancestors or competitors. These individuals are said to have higher biological "fitness" because they live to produce more offspring to whom they pass on the fitness traits that are encoded in their genes, or heritable. Most scientists, including psychologists, are swayed by overwhelming evidence that humans and all creatures living are products of natural selection. The fundamental mechanism for this heritability of fitness change lies at the level of cells in the **genes**. At the behavioral level, choices and decision making are crucial to survival and fitness in a particular environment. Slow environmental changes, for example, ice ages, occurred on a time scale that was compatible with genetic adaptations. In contrast, rapid environmental changes will overwhelm the slow pace of genetic adaptation, and failure to adapt behavior fast enough may lead to extinction of a species. Humans as a species are doing well when viewed from these fitness criteria of reproduction and survival: The global population recently passed 7 billion, double the number just 40 years ago (United Nations, 2010). That population explosion has been driven by technological innovation (sanitation, medicine, agriculture, etc.) and not by any biological process of natural selection.

It is important to appreciate our own evolutionary heritage in order to understand ourselves in the context of these rapid changes in the late 20th and early 21st centuries of the Common Era. In the constantly changing web of life, today's human species **Homo sapiens** is a relatively recently evolved member of the hominid family. From fossil records, the earliest true hominids appeared about 4.5 million years ago; they were hunter-gatherers—food acquisition was central to their survival (Figure 4.1).

In the 4.3 million years of hominids' existence prior to the emergence of *Homo sapiens*, various species of *Australopithecus* and *Homo* evolved only to become extinct. A common theme of hominid evolution is the progressive alteration

of morphology—body shape or size, including erect stature—and in particular the development of bigger brains. The Smithsonian Institution is an excellent reference resource (http://humanorigins.si.edu/evidence/human-fossils/species).

Homo sapiens have roamed this planet for about 200,000 years. During that time, we have developed complex societies, cultures, and technologies. The latter two in particular are what distinguish *Homo sapiens* from their evolutionary ancestors and from other species. Archaeological data suggest that early humans asked questions concerning the origin of life and the concept of mortality. These and many other questions were historically considered within a prevailing local religious or cultural context. Over the past few hundred years, scientific methods have been developed to provide a universal observation-based framework to catalog or advance knowledge, and with spectacular results. One consequence of scientific progress is that the rate at which we have altered our own environment, including in areas such as agriculture,

FIGURE 4.1   Artist's impression of the size and posture changes during hominid evolution.

TALKING POINT 4.1

How would you classify the rate of environmental change for humans over the past 100 years in relation to food and health? Is that affecting the "classical" process of natural selection, and if so, how? Is that sustainable on an evolutionary time scale? Why or why not?

urbanization, education, health technology, and telecommunications, has greatly exceeded the rate at which our bodies and brains have been able to undergo any sort of meaningful structural evolution. (You could argue we make up for this by packing extra "brains on board" in our laptops and smart phones.)

All living organisms are composed of building blocks called cells. Most cells are too small to be seen with the naked eye and were not discovered until the invention of the microscope (Figure 4.2; the term *microscope* was applied in 1625 to a multi-lens device made by Galileo—the same genius who deduced planetary motion with a far-seeing optical device called the *telescope*). Imagine the excitement of the first anatomists who found that organisms were collections of cells rather than, say, elaborate blobs of jelly. The simplest organisms are single cells, but most organisms are collections of many cells—in the case of a human being, billions of them. These cells require energy to fuel the fire of life.

We have bigger brains and correspondingly more brain cells than our hominid ancestors. Big brains come at a significant cost because brain cells are energy gluttons. Table 4.1 illustrates this fact.

Comparing ourselves with nonhuman primates of similar body size (chimpanzees), we find that brain size is twofold to threefold higher in humans. At birth, the human brain weighs about 500 grams, or 15% of typical newborn body mass, and that brain accounts for up to 85% of the total energy budget or metabolic rate. By age 2, the brain has grown to near the adult size, whereas the body is still only about 20% of adult size. This large and disproportionate early development of the brain in humans poses uniquely large demands on energy intake by human infants, first in the form of uterine growth, then as milk, and

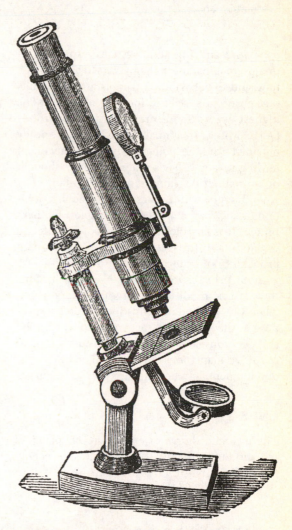

FIGURE 4.2   An early microscope.

later as nutritious or energy-yielding foods. In the absence of adequate nutrition, the body and brain will fail to develop normally.

To support the evolutionary growth of the brain, natural selection must also have favored

TABLE 4.1	Relative Sizes and Costs of Chimpanzee, Human Newborn, and Adult Brains		
	Average brain weight (grams)	Brain weight as percentage of body weight (approx.)	Metabolic cost of brain (percentage all energy)
Adult chimpanzee	500	1	10
Human newborn	500	15	85
Adult human	1400	2	20

behaviors and digestive systems, especially in infants, that maximize their access to high-energy food and to behaviors in parents or other adults that ensure a supply of food for offspring. The highest energy foods are **animal source foods (ASF)**: Milk is an animal source food, historically obtained from the biological mother. Many infant feeding-related behaviors are sometimes thought of as instinctive—for example, an infant cries when hungry with the result of attracting attention or sucks on objects that resemble a mother's nipple. It is instinctive for adults to comfort a crying infant. Instinctive behaviors have a high probability of occurrence in a specific situation without prior exposure. But, like all behaviors, they can be modified as a result of experience. Allen (2012) has taken this idea further to propose a "theory of food" according to which food and decisions about eating are considered neurocognitive adaptations that are acted on by cultural development, in much the same way as language.

ENERGY

The ultimate source of energy on our planet is radiation from the sun. Plants harness the energy from the sun directly and transform it into chemical energy in the form of molecules that can store and later release energy to drive cellular reactions and interactions. Some of these are discussed in other chapters. Although we and other animals may use the sun's rays to warm us, the proximate source of energy for animals including ourselves is in the form of chemical energy that we know more commonly as food, derived from eating plants or animal source foods. That's the intent behind the title of this chapter, "You Are What You Eat": We eat chemical energy and transform, store, and use that chemical energy to fuel our own cells.

To understand eating, you have to understand energy flow through an organism. Although this might sound complicated, it isn't. Think about a bank account. There is one source of input—deposits—that are analogous to food we eat. Some deposits may be bigger than others, and they may occur at irregular intervals, but they have a common currency in which they can be expressed (e.g., dollars). Food also has a common currency, energy, most often expressed in kilocalories (kcal) in the United States or kilojoules (kJ) almost everywhere else! A bank account also has outputs—withdrawals—some of which might occur on a regular basis (e.g., a phone bill)

TALKING POINT 4.2

Insufficient energy content or availability leads to death and before that to loss of reproductive capacity, meaning loss of biological fitness. An example of this occurs in young women in "appearance" activities that encourage extreme thinness (e.g., modeling, gymnastics); they often experience amenorrhea (their menstrual cycles stop). Do you think that the converse condition, excessive energy, has or will have consequences for biological fitness? If so, what are they?

and some of which are occasional (e.g., buying a birthday present). These outputs are expressed in the same currency as the inputs. If, over time, inputs exceed outputs, the balance in the account increases (energy is stored by the organism). On the other hand, if outputs exceed inputs, the balance in the account falls (stored energy is used or mobilized). When the account is depleted below a critical level, it cannot function (the organism will die of energy starvation). Here's the point: In order to live and do the things for which our bodies have evolved to do, we need to have an adequate source of food and the physiological means to store and mobilize the energy in that food.

OPTIMAL FORAGING

We previously introduced the idea of the gastrointestinal tract as a "food tube." However, this function is dependent on finding or identifying suitable energy sources or food to "load" the food tube from time to time. The food environment has potent control over what and when we eat. Our hunter-gatherer ancestors had no long-term way to preserve food: Because hoards or caches of food were insecure in the sense that they might spoil or be stolen, early hominid existence was substantially hand to mouth. Animals likewise have only limited ways to store food. For them, and our ancestors, the only truly secure store was inside the body, and this occurs mostly as fat or adipose tissue. Food availability is of course essential for eating to occur at all, and this availability is dependent on factors including the weather, season of the year, and presence of potentially dangerous competitors for the same food sources. Gathering commodities such as nuts, fruits, grasses, and grains is particularly subject to these variables. Further, as one commodity is harvested, a new place or patch has to be exploited until the resource is renewed, and this might not occur until the next growing season. Thus, gatherers must move across a large territory to harvest the food of the day or season. On the other hand, by exploiting known habitats of animals, hunters can wait for prey to come to them. Furthermore, the payoff is a nutrient-rich animal source food. But catching and killing prey, especially large prey, with primitive tools is dangerous and has a low success rate. The combination of the distinct foraging strategies of hunting and gathering has been very successful for *Homo sapiens*. Indeed, hunter-gatherers have been characterized more by their diversity and adaptability than by any specific pattern of behavior (Rowley-Conwy, 2001).

All animals have to forage for food, and each species has specialized behaviors. **Optimal foraging theory** posits that individuals of a given species will adopt the best possible set of behaviors in a given environment. The meaning of *optimal* in this context is founded on the two now-familiar concepts of evolution and energy. It is also linked to the concept of *inclusive fitness*, which considers not how well any one individual survives but how well the offspring of that individual survive. Reproduction entails additional energy costs—for example, we discussed earlier how the newborn human brain is energetically costly—a cost most often borne by the parents. Although energy balance is at the core of foraging theory and will be the focus of our discussion, another consideration is that foraging is not risk free, and injury or loss of life during foraging is an energy-gathering "cost" that affects the inclusive fitness of a population or species.

From the perspective of energy balance, most foraging behavior is associated with increased physical activity and so will increase metabolic rate. Thus, some fraction of the energy yield of food has to be "written off" as the cost of obtaining that food, as in this equation:

Net energy yield of food = metabolizable energy minus energy used in foraging

There's another factor that we haven't yet considered: body mass or weight. (Strictly, when we put something on a scale, we are measuring weight; mass refers to the actual amount of matter present in the body. The two are related by the force of gravity *g*, but because for most of us *g* never changes, weight and mass are often used interchangeably, as in BMI). Both basal metabolic rate—what it costs just to keep the body at

DO THE MATH

Suppose it costs 120 kcal per hour for a foraging activity in addition to a basal metabolic rate of 80 kcal per hour. Suppose too that food occurs in metabolizable energy units of exactly 1000 kcal (that's approximately the energy value of a large cheeseburger and fries). After what duration of foraging does the net yield of one food unit become negative?

Next, you invent the wheel and your foraging costs drop to 20 kcal per hour. What is the new critical duration per food unit? Then, climate change causes the food unit to become "mega-sized" to 2000 kcal. What is the new critical duration? *(Answers are at the end of this chapter.)*

rest—and the cost of exertion are roughly proportional to body mass. It follows that a lean or light individual will get more return from a particular quantity of food relative to his or her body mass than a heavier individual. Weight (strictly, mass!) loss is an effective way of reducing obligatory energy expenditure by increasing the energy yield (or gross energy gain, which is the energy in food minus the energy required to obtain it) from foraging (Figure 4.3).

Like big automobiles, big bodies use a lot of fuel to move them, so when food is scarce or expensive and foraging costs high, being big is a disadvantage. Conversely, if foraging costs are low, optimal theory will predict a high net yield of food, and most of the excess yield will be eaten (i.e., hand to mouth) and stored in the body as fat. Accumulation of fat, in the limit to the level of obesity, is a completely predictable result of

plentiful and inexpensive food. From this theoretical perspective, obesity is not caused by a defective physiology but is the inevitable result of a modern evolutionarily improbable environment that some have termed **obesogenic** (promoting obesity).

The shortcoming of optimal foraging theory is that it does not consider the psychology of the individuals or subjects. It regards the individual as ready to take optimal advantage of a food resource when it appears. We will use the term **opportunistic eater** to describe this type of person. In an environment in which food is scarce, being highly opportunistic is essential to survival. However, in an environment where food is plentiful and easily available, being an opportunistic eater leads to overconsumption. To take this a step further, we could ask whether, in the 21st-century world of humans, opportunism may have become

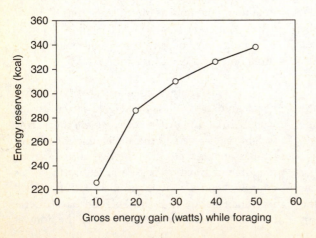

FIGURE 4.3 Change in energy reserves (i.e., mainly body fat) as energy yield during foraging changes.

Note that higher effort and lower yields are to the left, whereas low effort and high yields are to the right. As the cost of acquiring energy increases, the organism would move toward the left and so maintain lower body fat reserves. *Source:* Data from Houston A.I. and McNamara, J.M. (1989). The value of food: effects of open and closed economies. Animal Behaviour 37:546–62.

TALKING POINT 4.3

You are most likely well nourished, with no immediate risk of starvation. And you know that food is close at hand—in your refrigerator, at the store, in the vending machine. How much time do you spend each day thinking or talking about food? Do you spend as much time on average thinking about other essentials—your computer, your car, or even a loved one? If you have a thought about food, how often do you move that thought (obsession) to an action (compulsion)? Why do you think that TV food shows or competitions are so popular?

obsession. *Obsessions* are defined as frequent and irrational or nonfunctional thoughts. Many individuals, obese people in particular, show characteristics of obsession with food (Kessler, 2009).

ECONOMICS OF FOOD

Optimal foraging theory places a measurable cost, in units of energy, on the acquisition of food. However, for most of the urbanized and industrialized world, very little physical effort is expended in obtaining food; instead, the effort takes the form of a token—money—that is exchanged for the asking price of the commodity. Elapsed time may also be a relevant cost for food insofar as it impinges on other behaviors including earning tokens (Figure 4.4).

One branch of economics is the study of consumer demand for a commodity as its cost or **unit price** changes. The relationship is called a **demand function** (Figure 4.5).

The curvature of this function is called **elasticity:** The more steeply that demand declines as unit price increases, the greater the elasticity (or flexibility) of the demand. Demand is inelastic if it does not change at all regardless of price.

FIGURE 4.4 In a modern or token economy, time and money are interrelated "costs" for food.

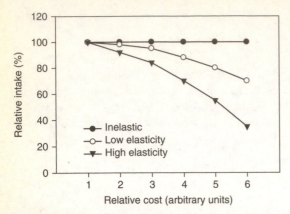

FIGURE 4.5 Idealized demand functions of intake (demand) as unit cost varies.
The more curved the line, the greater the elasticity.

Unit Price and Access Cost

This type of analysis can be applied to energy and feeding behavior. As we noted earlier, the demand imposed by energy expenditure is continuous and increases above basal with increasing physical activity. Thus, averaged across a suitably long time frame (e.g., days or weeks), energy consumption is relatively continuous and predictable. Energy supply to meet this demand comes from two sources: food consumed in the present, and excess food consumed in the past that has been stored as adipose tissue. This stored energy acts like a buffer that allows food intake to be episodic or to fluctuate. The amount and timing of food intake is under a considerable degree of economic control.

Foraging behavior can be divided into at least two components. The first is a search phase: The animal is looking for food but has not yet located or reached it. This type of search may be quite energy and time consuming, particularly if long distances have to be traveled and food is scarce. We will call the effort associated with this **access cost**. This search may have a relatively low probability of success—hunters may come home empty-handed some days. The second phase occurs when food has been located or secured and is nearby. This includes activities such as

gathering fruit from a tree, food preparation, and direct costs of eating (hulling seeds, chewing, etc.). We call this **consumatory cost** and it is essentially the same as the unit price, introduced previously. The only way that consumatory cost of a particular food can be minimized is to eat less of it!

Access and consumatory costs may be in different units (e.g., energy or time) and/or hard to separate, but under controlled laboratory conditions, it is possible to isolate them. To emulate access cost, Collier, Hirsch, and Hamlin (1972) had rats perform a certain number of lever press responses in order to open a gate and thereby gain access to a large bowl of food. Once the animals left the food bowl for more than 10 minutes (detected by photocells), the gate closed and another access cost would be needed to get at the food. The researchers found that as access cost increased, the overall food intake did not change much but the pattern of eating changed (Figure 4.6).

Specifically, the number of feeding opportunities initiated (meals, see later discussion) declined as access cost increased, and the size of the meals taken increased in a compensatory manner. Another way of expressing this result is that low access costs promote many small meals, or snacking. Note that at a cost of 100 responses, animals initiated a mean of five meals per day, or half that at the lowest cost; that translates to a total access cost of 500 responses per day which, for a typical rat, takes a cumulative time of less than 10 minutes or less than 1% of the 24-hour day—hardly an enormous time investment! A similar study, but with the cost in time rather than effort, was performed with macaque monkeys trained to respond on a lever followed by a 30-minute waiting period before food was presented (Foltin, 2006). Monkeys ate three or four meals per day. In contrast, when food was available all the time at no cost, in addition to about four large meals, rhesus monkeys took several small meals or snacks, although considerable individual variation was seen (Hansen, Jen, & Kalnasy, 1981). When the response requirement was consumatory—animals had to respond a determined number of

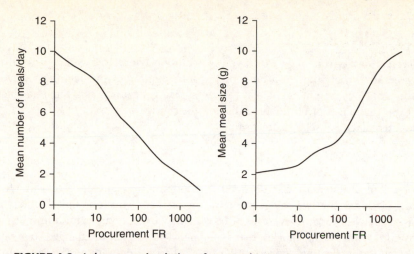

FIGURE 4.6 **Laboratory simulation of approach costs in rats.**
As the cost of gaining access to food increases, the mean number of meals
initiated per day drops (left panel), whereas the size of each meal increases (right
panel).   *Source:* Data from Collier G, Hirsch E, Hamlin P (1972). The ecological
determinants of reinforcement in the rat. Physiology and Behavior 8:705–16.

times for each small pellet of food within a meal,
a unit cost—three major differences emerged.
First, meal pattern did not change substantially
as unit cost increased; second, food intake or
demand declined some as unit cost increased
(see Figure 4.5); and third, intake did not start
to show elasticity (or decline significantly) until
some 10,000 responses per day (some 3 hours
cumulative responding) were emitted (Atalayer &
Rowland, 2011; Collier et al., 1972).

Meal-Defining Criteria

In the previous section, we started talking about a
term we will meet in several places in this text, the
meal. You all probably have your own idea about

what constitutes a meal: Perhaps it has to do with
how much food is consumed, the time of day, or
the social milieu within which the eating occurs.
Eating episodes that do not qualify as meals are
usually called snacks. Thus, a scientist has to
define precisely what is meant by a meal, especially when dealing with animal studies, including the minimum amount that will qualify to be
called a meal as well as the minimum duration of
time between eating episodes that will separate
one meal from the next.

There is no "correct" or universally agreed-
upon meal criterion, but, like the monkeys studied at low or no consumatory cost by Hansen
et al. (1981), humans typically engage in a small
number (two to three) of large feeding episodes

TALKING POINT 4.4

The results of the animal studies indicate that
high costs need to be applied at the consumatory stage to affect total intake, whereas a com-
paratively small cost at the access stage greatly
affects the prevalence of snacking. What
implications do these results have for dietary

moderation in humans if "barriers" such as
restriction or taxation were to be considered?
These animal experiments all used a single
food, but humans live in a much more varied
food world. What do you think would be the
effect if only certain foods were so taxed?

TALKING POINT 4.5

During a typical day at school or work, you probably consume morning or afternoon snacks and lunch. Now, for a moment, play the role of an experimental subject: Imagine that an invisible intergalactic observer is recording your behavior. How would "The Observer" be able to analyze your feeding behavior to recognize your lunch as a separate episode from the snacks?

per day that we call meals interspersed with small or brief feeding episodes that we categorize as snacks. Insofar as many of today's beverages also contain a substantial number of calories, drinks should be included in these eating categories. We know from the studies described earlier that the incidence of snacking is dependent on access cost, but once someone has made a decision to eat (and for now not distinguishing between meals and snacks), what determines how much—the size of the portion—he or she will eat?

PORTION SIZE

Thus far, we have considered the effect of effort and cost for a more or less uniformly sized food unit. But what would happen if the size of the food unit were altered? According to optimal foraging theory, if a food unit doubles in size *and* the energy expended per food unit also doubles, the net yield will not be changed so organisms should eat half as many units (i.e., the same quantity). However, as we will see, this is not what actually happens.

Before reviewing some laboratory studies, it is informative to consider the magnitude of this problem in a typical Western-style food environment. Table 4.2 shows the energy associated with a typical serving or portion size today and 20 years ago. In most cases, the portion size has doubled. For coffee, for example, this occurred because more high-fat additives such as cream are typically included. All of the foods show an increase in physical portion size. For example, a muffin

TABLE 4.2	Increase in Average Retail Portion Size Between 1990 and 2010	
kcal in 1990	Food item	kcal in 2010
500	Pizza 2 slices	850
337	Cheeseburger	590
500	Spaghetti and noodles plate	1025
435	Chicken stir fry (take out)	865
320	Turkey sandwich	820
390	Caesar salad	790
210	French fries	610
140	Bagel	350
260	Cheesecake	640
210	Muffin	500
55	Chocolate chip cookie	275
270	Movie popcorn	630
97	Soda	242
45	Coffee	330

Source: Data from National Heart, Lung and Blood Institute (http://hp2010/nhlbihin.net).

today is made of more or less the same ingredients as 20 years ago—but it's more than twice the energy because it's more than twice the mass. Further, the typical diameter of dinner plates has increased during this time from 10 inches to 12 inches, a 44% increase in the area of the plate.

In almost every example, the dispensed portion size is not under the control of the consumer—it is determined by the food industry. The food industry is of course responding to actual or perceived consumer demand, including how to maintain that demand or market in the future. The cost of manufacturing or producing food today is typically only a small fraction of its retail price; much of the retail cost is fixed and not related to food mass (e.g., personnel costs involved in serving or selling to the customer), so it costs little more to serve a large portion than to serve a small portion. Thus, increasing portion size is an inexpensive way for a business to attract customers. Industry advocates often consider that a large dispensed portion sizes give customers a choice—that is, they may choose to eat only part of the portion. In practice, however, people are very poor at exerting this choice: They tend to eat everything they are served, so an increase in portion size results in increased consumption.

To test the extent to which intake is influenced by portion size, Brian Wansink and colleagues performed several experiments in which they showed that internal control over portion size is surprisingly small. Instead, intake is determined mainly by the dispensed portion size or the presentation, and the perception of how much has been consumed. In one study performed at an ice cream social (Wansink, van Ittersum, & Painter, 2006), subjects were given either a small or a large bowl and self-served ice cream using either a small or a large scoop. Subjects given a larger scoop took more (14.5%) ice cream than those given the smaller scoop, but an even bigger effect was found with bowl size: Subjects given a large bowl took (and consumed) 31% more than those given a small bowl. By the way, the subjects at that ice cream social were nutritional scientists!

In a study at a movie theater, subjects were dispensed portions of free popcorn (Wansink & Kim, 2005). Different groups of subjects received either a medium or a large container (120 g versus 240 g popcorn).

Half of each size group received fresh popcorn, whereas the other half received stale popcorn (14 days old: presumably this was less palatable!). The amount eaten was determined by measuring the amount remaining in each

container after the movie. As in the ice cream study, container size made a large difference, with subjects eating 45.3% more from the large compared with the small container when the popcorn was fresh and 33.6% more when it was stale. Even when the popcorn was stale, container size had a large effect on consumption.

Not all studies have found this effect when varying container or serving size. Rolls, Roe, Halverson, and Meengs (2007) served subjects with the same lunch menu on three occasions, each one with a different plate size (17, 22, or 26 cm diameter—the largest is a standard dinner plate size). The subjects, tested in individual cubicles, were given a large serving bowl containing 800 g (at least twice as much as anyone actually ate) of macaroni and cheese. Subjects could replenish their plate from the serving bowl as often as they chose. There was no significant effect of plate size on consumption. A second study eliminated the replenishment aspect by serving subjects 700 g of macaroni and cheese on either 22 or 26 cm diameter plates. Again, the amount eaten did not differ with plate size. They also found that when a multi-item buffet was given instead of just macaroni and cheese, the lack of effect of plate size on caloric intake was still evident, even though subjects with the small plate made more trips to the buffet than those with the larger plates. Rolls et al. (2007) suggested that the individual eating condition in their studies might be the critical difference from the social eating situations used by ansink and colleagues.

Economics and humans

We noted that increased effort implies increased time and often decreases food demand. However, simply slowing the rate of eating by chewing each mouthful for longer is sufficient to reduce intake: This is known as **fletcherism,** named after Dr. Horace Fletcher who in the 19th century advocated that food should be chewed exactly 32 times (!) before being swallowed. In a recent empirical test of the effectiveness of this strategy in young women, Andrade, Greene, and Melanson (2008) presented a test lunch with directions to eat either quickly or slowly. Subjects were tested under both conditions, on different days and in random order. The lunch was a large (600 g) portion of seasoned dilatini pasta (small unit size) and water, and subjects could eat as much as they liked. In the fast-eating condition, subjects were given a large spoon and told to consume their meal as fast as possible with no pauses between bites. In the slow-eating condition, subjects were given a small spoon and were told to take small bites and chew each mouthful 20 to 30 times. Subjects ate 11% more in the fast than in the slow condition, and their meal took an average of only 8.6 min compared with 29.2 min.

An apparently opposite result was found by Yeomans, Gray, Mitchell, and True (1997), also using a pasta lunch protocol; they showed that imposing pauses of up to 60 seconds after every 50 g were consumed produced an increase in intake relative to the no pause condition. Together, these studies suggest that Dr. Fletcher was right: Chewing, rather than simply slowing the rate at which food reaches the stomach, seems to be critical. One evolutionary trend in hominids has been a decrease in the size of molar teeth, indicating to anthropologists a shift in diet from raw plant material that required extensive chewing to animal source and/or cooked food that requires less chewing.

TALKING POINT 4.6

Compared with when you eat alone, do you think you eat less, the same, or more than when you are eating with friends? Do you think that the group composition (e.g., friends versus acquaintances, same versus mixed sex, some versus all overweight) would make a difference? Why or why not?

TALKING POINT 4.7

Do you ever make a conscious effort to eat slowly? Many modern or pre-prepared foods require little or no chewing, and most of our food comes in bite (mouthful) sizes or is easily made into a convenient bite size using a knife and fork—rather than with our molars! Which food that you eat routinely do you chew the most, and which the least? How does that correlate with portion size and/or calories per serving?

What about price? Several laboratory studies have shown that changes in relative price can affect consumption. For example, in a simulation of shopping for food, Epstein, Dearing, Paluch, Roemmich, and Cho (2007) gave mothers a low or high spending allowance and asked them to select cards depicting low- and high-energy density items. The cards were price coded either at a standard price or 25% above or below that price, and one food category was held at the standard price, whereas the other varied in price. Subjects selected foods from both low- and high-energy categories, but as the price of the variable item increased, the number of items selected declined by almost 50% between the low- and high-price limits, whereas the number of the fixed price items was unchanged. One purpose of this type of purchasing study is to see whether eating is affected by selective pricing (including taxation). The result shows that within a limited budget situation, the number of items and as a result the mass of an item purchased can be influenced more or less directly by unit price and the choice available. But it should be borne in mind that what is purchased, especially in this virtual study, does not tell us about the portion size in the home (a carton of food often contains more than a single serving) and/or the amount actually eaten.

CONCLUDING REMARKS

In the first part of this book, we have focused on the physical and chemical properties of food, and how food is acquired from the environment. It should now be evident that food choice and food intake are the result of a complex interaction between individuals and the food environment. In the following section of the book, we adjust the focus to emphasize the factors that operate at the level of an individual's eating behavior, including development, learning, and social factors.

Let's review and apply your knowledge. Take some time to answer these chapter questions

1. Explain the optimal foraging theory. What factors influence energy expenditure during foraging?
2. Describe food economics using the terms *unit price* and *access cost*.
3. Discuss the impacts of increased portions and serving containers over the past 20 years on energy intake.
4. Summarize the main points and implications of the Collier et al. (1972) study.
5. What is fletcherism? What is its involvement in food economics?

Answers to Do the Math

1. Metabolic rate while foraging = basal + cost of activity = 120 + 80 = 200 kcal/hour. Thus, a 1000 kcal payoff is worth a maximum of 1000/200 = 5 hours of effort. Once more than 5 hours of foraging are involved, energy expenditure exceeds 1000 kcal.
2. In this condition, metabolic rate while foraging is the same 80 plus only 20 as the cost of activity = 100 kcal/hour. Thus, 10 hours of foraging will now cost 1000 kcal.
3. The expenditure is the same as (2)—100 kcal/hour. But the food unit is now 2000 kcal, and so it would take 20 hours of foraging before the payoff would not be worth the effort. Note that increases in size of the food item have a strictly proportional effect on duration.

Glossary

Access cost   Sometimes also called procurement or foraging cost: the cost, in relevant currency, of gaining access to a commodity (e.g., time spent traveling to a restaurant).

Animal source foods (ASF)   Foods that are directly derived from animals, such as meat, milk, or eggs.

Consumatory cost   The cost (in suitable units of measurement) of eating a unit such as a mouthful of food once the food is nearby. Example: price at a food vending machine.

Demand function   The relationship between consumption or demand for a commodity and its price, most usually unit price.

Elasticity   A mathematical description of the curvature of the demand curve. If demand does not change with price, the demand is inelastic. If one commodity is more vital (say, for survival) than another, you would expect a higher elasticity for the less essential commodity.

Energy   In physics, energy is a force or entity that is necessary for performing mechanical work. In biology, the same concept of energy is embodied in specific molecules that drive biological reactions (including mechanical movement such as walking) essential for life.

Evolution   The change in inherited (genetic) traits or characteristics across generations in a species. When, over a long period, such changes have become large, a new species is definable.

Fletcherism   Extensive chewing of each mouthful of food, with the goal of slowing eating rate.

Gene   A segment of the genome that encodes a single heritable trait—the smallest functional unit.

Homo sapiens   Our current human species. Appeared in fossil records only about 200,000 years ago, or more than 4 million years after the divergence of our hominid ancestors from apes.

Natural selection   first proposed by Charles Darwin, the heritable mechanism by which new species can evolve by competition or biological fitness, usually meaning more surviving offspring.

Obesogenic environment   An environment in which calorically dense foods are available at low cost, thus promoting excess intake and ultimately obesity.

Opportunistic eater   Term we use to imply that an optimal strategy for feeding in an uncertain food environment is to take advantage of each and every feeding opportunity that comes along.

Optimal foraging theory   A general theory that individuals will adopt the best possible set of food acquisition behaviors in a given environment to maximize net energy gain.

Unit price   The cost (in relevant currency, e.g., energy, money, time) to acquire a unit of a commodity once it has been reached. Most usually applied to situations in which each unit is the same (e.g., a pellet of food or a slice of pizza) but could also be applied to a derived quality such as kcal.

References

Allen, J. S. (2012). "Theory of food" as a neurocognitive adaptation. *American Journal of Human Biology, 24,* 123–129.

Andrade, A. M., Greene, G. W., & Melanson, K. J. (2008) Eating slowly led to decreases in energy intake within meals in healthy women. *Journal of the American Dietetic Association, 108,* 1186–1191.

Atalayer, D., & Rowland, N. E. (2011). Structure of motivation using food demand in mice. *Physiology and Behavior, 104,* 15–19.

Collier, G., Hirsch, E., & Hamlin, P. (1972). The ecological determinants of reinforcement in the rat. *Physiology and Behavior, 8,* 705–716.

Epstein, L. H., Dearing, K. K., Paluch, R. A., Roemmich, J. N., & Cho, D. (2007). Price and maternal obesity influence purchasing of low- and high-energy-dense foods. *American Journal of Clinical Nutrition, 86,* 914–922.

Foltin, R. W. (2006). "Tasting and wasting" behavior in non-human primates: Aberrant behavior or normal behavior in "times of plenty." *Physiology and Behavior, 89,* 587–597.

Hansen, B. C., Jen, K.-L. C., & Kalnasy, L. W. (1981). Control of food intake and meal patterns in monkeys. *Physiology and Behavior, 27,* 803–810.

Houston, A. I., & McNamara, J. M. (1989). The value of food: Effects of open and closed economies. *Animal Behaviour, 37,* 546–562.

Kessler, D. A. (2009). *The end of overeating: Taking control of the insatiable American appetite.* New York: Rodale.

Rolls, B. J., Roe, L. S., Halverson, K. H., & Meengs, J. S. (2007). Using a smaller plate did not reduce energy intake at meals. *Appetite, 49,* 652–660.

Rowley-Conwy, P. (2001). Time, change and the archaeology of hunter-gatherers: How original is the "Original Affluent Society"? In C. Panter-Brick, R. H. Layton, & P. Rowley-Conwy (eds.), *Hunter-gatherers: An interdisciplinary perspective* (pp. 39–72). New York: Cambridge University Press..

United Nations. (2010). World population prospects. Retrieved from http://esa.un.org/wpp/

Wansink, B., & Kim, J. (2005). Bad popcorn in big buckets: Portion size can influence intake as much as taste. *Journal of Nutrition Education and Behavior, 37,* 242–245.

Wansink, B., van Ittersum, K., & Painter, J. E. (2006). Ice cream illusions bowls, spoons, and self-served portion sizes. *American Journal of Preventive Medicine, 31,* 240–243.

Yeomans, M. R., Gray, R. W., Mitchell, C. J., & True, S. (1997). Independent effects of palatability and within-meal pauses on intake and appetite ratings in human volunteers. *Appetite, 29,* 61–76.

5

Basic Learning Processes and Eating Behavior

After reading this chapter, you will be able to

- Understand the role of associative learning on eating behavior and the associated practical implications
- Know how food preferences and aversions are formed

- Appreciate that knowing when to start and stop eating is shaped by learning
- Understand the neurobiology of food learning

Learning can occur in many ways. Several forms of basic associative learning have been identified in eating behavior research as having particular relevance to the development of food likes and dislikes and on the establishment of meal patterns (i.e., amount, timing, and rituals of meals and food selection). The types of learning explored in this chapter are rooted in classical conditioning (or Pavlovian conditioning). This basic form of learning shapes many human and animal behaviors, and the effects can be long lasting. Before we explore this further, take a moment and imagine going to a movie theater for the premiere of a movie you've been looking forward to seeing. What foods are you likely to want? For some people, it is nearly unthinkable to watch a movie in a theater without eating popcorn or candy. Why are these associations so pervasive? Associative learning, as you will see in this chapter, is quite simplistic, yet very influential on our eating behaviors.

OVERVIEW OF CLASSICAL CONDITIONING AND TERMINOLOGY

Classical conditioning is a type of basic associative learning in which a stimulus that is previously neutral (or meaningless) to the animal or person comes to elicit a response that another stimulus naturally elicits. Let's briefly review the research of Ivan Pavlov, the Russian physiologist who won a Nobel Prize in 1904 for his research on digestion in dogs. Dogs naturally salivate when food, or in the case of Pavlov's studies, meat powder, reaches their mouths. This is an innate or reflexive response requiring no learning. Pavlov found that his dogs started salivating before the food was delivered to their mouths. For example, they salivated when someone entered the room or neared the food storage area. This salivation, Pavlov realized, was a result of learning. The dogs *learned*

Nobel Prize–winning physiologist Ivan Pavlov.

that when their handler neared the food storage area that food would soon be delivered.

Pavlov conducted many carefully designed studies to more precisely determine the specifics around this type of learning, now known as classical or Pavlovian conditioning. In one well-known example, Pavlov conditioned the dogs to salivate to the sound of a metronome, a clicking device used by musicians to mark rhythm. Metronomes are not usually associated with food, so salivation to their clicking is certainly not an instinctive behavior. In formal learning terminology, before the conditioning process begins, meat powder is an **unconditioned stimulus (UCS)** because dogs naturally salivate to it, salivation is the **unconditioned response (UCR)**, and the metronome is a **neutral stimulus (NS)** eliciting no salivation (see Figure 5.1). After several pairings of the sound of the metronome with the delivery of meat powder, the dogs salivate to the sound of the metronome. The metronome is now the **conditioned stimulus (CS)** and the salivation is the **conditioned response (CR)**.

Classical conditioning allows animals and people to *predict* the occurrence of future events, and physiologically, behaviorally, and/or psychologically prepare for them. The dogs learned that food was soon to come once they heard the metronome, so they were prepared for it. Physiological changes occurred (hormonal, thermogenic, neurochemical, etc.) so that they were ready to eat and digest the soon-to-arrive food. For many college students, hearing a roommate's rustling potato chip bag triggers a sudden craving for potato chips that can be distracting and irresistible as their bodies, just as those of Pavlov's

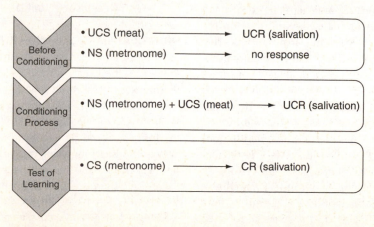

FIGURE 5.1 Schematic diagram illustrating the sequence of events in classical conditioning.

dogs, prepare for the desired snack. This is clearly the result of a learned association between a particular sound and food.

Marketing of food products is largely based on the principles of classical conditioning. What do you think of when you drive past the "Golden Arches"? Many people experience sudden and overwhelming cravings for cheeseburgers; french fries; milkshakes; and, more recently, McCafé lattes and frappés on seeing the golden M sign associated with a McDonald's restaurant. Are you getting hungry now, too? This is classical conditioning; the pairing of the NS (the golden M sign) with the UCS (tasty food) yielding the UCR (eating and liking), and now the M sign serve as the CS triggering a desire for specific foods (CR). The influences of media, society, and marketing are explored in other chapters, but it is important to bear in mind that, despite its simplicity, this type of learning is extremely effective and consequential.

LEARNING OF POST-INGESTIVE CONSEQUENCES: TASTE AVERSIONS AND PREFERENCES

Taste and Food Aversions

Most people have particular aversions to tastes or foods associated with sickness, even when the person knows that the food is actually safe (Schafe & Bernstein, 2004). If one happens to develop symptoms of the flu (nausea, vomiting) on the same evening that eggplant parmesan was tried for the first time, it is likely that eggplant parmesan will never be tried again, or at least not enthusiastically. The likelihood of an aversion is greater if the flavor or food meets one or more of the following conditions: it is *novel*, it is *less preferred*, it is *distinct*, and/or it is *unusual* (something one does not typically consume). Rats are particularly known to develop long-lasting aversions for flavors associated with gastrointestinal illness. Because rats lack the ability to regurgitate food once it has been ingested, it is essential for their survival that they avoid a food or flavor that previously made them ill (assuming they were lucky

enough to survive their first negative experience). So, rats often exhibit **one-trial learning**, learning the negative association between food or flavor and illness with only one such pairing.

In now classic studies of taste aversion, John Garcia and Robert Koelling (1966) showed that rats soon learned to avoid a sweet-tasting liquid (a taste innately liked by rats) when it was followed by an injection of lithium chloride (LiCl) that made them ill. Interestingly, they did not learn to avoid the liquid when they received electric shocks afterward. The rats did, however, learn to avoid the electric shock when it was paired with light and noise (but injection of LiCl paired with light/noise failed to produce such learning). These results indicate that taste is more likely to be associated with visceral illness and audiovisual cues are associated more with pain. Just like these rats, we (humans) are predisposed to develop particular aversions or avoidances associated with biologically relevant stimuli. This insight into conditioned aversions influenced the ways in which behavioral studies have since been conducted.

Brief overview and example of taste aversion:

1. Initial state: UCS (LiCl) → UCR (nausea)
   NS (sweet tasting liquid) → neutral/positive response (drinking)
2. Learning trials: NS + UCS → UCR (nausea)
3. Acquisition of taste aversion:
   CS (sweet tasting liquid) → CR (nausea)

PRACTICAL IMPLICATIONS—ANIMALS Others later applied the newly acquired understanding of learned taste aversions to help ranchers humanely control wolf predation of their livestock (Gustavson, Kelly, & Sweeney, 1976). After eating a sheep carcass contaminated with LiCl, wolves no longer preyed on sheep; in fact, they backed away after smelling their potential victims (LiCl induces nausea and vomiting in wolves). Ranchers have since used this method to prevent predation (from wolves, coyotes, crows, etc.) on other types of livestock (e.g., cows, chickens; Nicolaus, Cassel, Carlson, & Gusysvson, 1983). Conditioned taste aversion is similarly used to prevent agricultural damage caused by black birds and other animals and to protect endangered species (Werner, Kimball, & Provenza, 2008). However, some debate remains around the usefulness of conditioned taste aversion in field conditions (i.e., without experimental controls and manipulation) because the associative learning typically occurs with the use of a carcass rather than live prey.

PRACTICAL IMPLICATIONS—HUMANS When humans or animals eat a particular food before becoming ill because of a virus or before receiving a drug or radiation treatment that induces visceral illness, they avoid that food in future exposures. This is quite problematic for cancer patients undergoing chemotherapy, a treatment that often causes severe nausea. Many patients experience excessive weight loss because of newly developed food aversions, a condition referred to as *cancer anorexia* (Wisse, Frayo, Schwartz, & Cummings, 2001). Unfortunately, many of these patients experience what is known in the learning literature as **stimulus generalization**, developing aversions not only for the foods consumed prior to their nausea-inducing treatment, but also aversions for foods that are similar in taste, appearance, and other qualities.

Efforts have been made to utilize our current understanding of taste aversion learning to prevent or minimize the occurrence of such learning among cancer patients. In a study by Broberg and Bernstein (1987), children who consumed a flavored candy (e.g., coconut or root beer Life Saver®) prior to chemotherapy developed an aversion for that flavor but not for normal menu items. The flavored candy served as a "scapegoat" for the development of food aversions following chemotherapy treatment. The flavor for which the patients developed an aversion was inconsequential in their usual diet (most of us can lead healthy, normal lives without consuming coconut or root beer). Thus, the scapegoat aversion helped prevent the unsafe weight loss that often results from conditioned aversions following cancer treatments. Similar scapegoat food aversions have also been useful among adults undergoing chemotherapy (e.g., Andresen, Birch, & Johnson, 1990).

LEARNING OF FOOD BY EXPERIENCE: INCREASING PREFERENCES

Medicine Effect

Food consumed when we are hungry or deficient in some macro- or micronutrient will be more preferred in subsequent exposures than food consumed when we are sated. And the more severe the deficiency, the greater the food preference we will have. In a classic study by Paul Rozin (1969), rats were fed a thiamine (vitamin B_1)-deficient diet. After some weeks (the deficiency in thiamine takes time to develop), the rats started to reject this diet by eating less and by spilling or spoiling the food. When the deficient rats were given "novel" food that contained the needed thiamine, they sampled it. If more than one novel food was provided, they sampled only one per meal.

The rats quickly came to prefer the food enriched with thiamine. Interestingly, there is no evidence that this preference was guided by the taste of thiamine; instead, other properties of the food (e.g., overall flavor or texture) were what the animal associated with "recovery." This type of learning, known as the **medicine effect**, is an example of a general food learning mechanism. First, deficient animals must become motivated to reject their current food and to overcome **neophobia** (fear of the new) and try a novel food. Then, they must learn the association between feeling better and the sensory properties that will allow them to recognize that food again in the

future. Of course, this is almost the mirror image of the taste or flavor aversion previously discussed, in which animals learn to avoid food that has undesirable post-ingestive consequences. In common with that mechanism, the learning probably can occur in a single trial. That is, the animal need only eat the good food once to learn that it is safe, and there should be an allowable delay (hours) between eating and the consequence. This is why a strategy of discrete (one at a time) sampling of novel foods is adaptive when one is deficient. The biological rule seems to be something like this: Try one new food, wait and see if it is safe; if so, return to it; if not, try another new food. People who are deficient in vitamins or minerals often engage in **pica**—eating objects that are not normally considered food, such as soil, paint, or coins, which contain minerals. Some anthropologists believe that cannibalism may have its roots in dietary deficiency (e.g., de Montellano, 1978).

So, how does this feeling better or medicine effect work? It is believed that learning occurs by a process of reinforcement that is mediated by internal reward system(s). It is likely, then, that recovery from deficiencies in trace elements (and perhaps calories, too) uses the same systems. Research indicates that the pleasurable feeling associated with eating good (safe) food and recovery from a deficiency is mediated by the signaling of the neurotransmitter dopamine and endorphins, among others, acting within the reward pathway of the brain (Berridge, Ho, Richard, & DiFeliceantonio, 2010; Volkow et al., 2003). The neurobiology of food liking and reward is discussed in further detail in other chapters of this book.

Despite our innate liking of the sweet taste, heavily sweetened foods such as candy or sugary beverages are typically not desired when we are truly hungry, at least not to the exclusion of other foods. For example, you would probably not want jelly beans as your only food for dinner. In fact, foods that we normally find appealing, such as a chocolate bar, may seem unappealing or even disgusting when we are energy deficient. Rather, when we are deficient, we tend to seek out and prefer more savory food items. Which types of foods do you prefer after a long day or vigorous

workout? In Western culture, preferred foods include sandwiches, meat or pasta dishes, and burgers (Drewnowski, 1997; Drewnowski, Kurth, Holden-Wiltse, & Saari, 1992). In many Asian cultures, the preferred foods are fish and rice. So, often the food preferences shaped by the medicine effect are foods that are of greater nutritional value than the preferences made through other experiences when we are less deficient. This could indicate that the best way to acquire a liking for Brussels sprouts or other innately less preferred foods is to consume them when you are very hungry. We'll let you try it out!

Mere Exposure

Preferences for particular food items or flavors increase with repeated exposure whether or not the exposure is consciously known (Bornstein & D'Agostino, 1992). This passive type of learning that shapes eating behavior was first termed the **mere exposure effect** in 1968 by Robert Zajonc. Humans and nonhuman animals are somewhat neophobic (wary of novel foods and flavors), yet paradoxically neophilic (liking of the new). Unfamiliar foods and flavors can be either beneficial (providing nutrients and calories) or dangerous (containing toxins). As previously described, humans and animals tend to sample new foods and increase consumption with repeated exposure only if the post-ingestive consequences are positive (or, at least not negative). This process results in increased liking and decreased neophobia: The mere exposure effect and reduction of neophobia necessarily co-occur.

BOX 5.1   Do Food Preferences of Babies Increase with Exposures?

Sullivan and Birch (1994) investigated the liking of novel vegetables in infants who were starting to eat solid foods (age 4–6 months) and found increased acceptance over the course of 10 exposures. Liking of the novel vegetables occurred more quickly in breast-milk-fed infants compared with formula-fed infants, indicating that breast milk "merely exposes" infants to a wider variety of flavors increasing their liking of novel foods. Studies in rats have shown that the pups quickly prefer flavors they experience through mother's milk and show preferences for their mother's diet when they start to consume solid food (Galef & Henderson, 1972; Galef & Sherry, 1973).

As an anecdotal example, most Americans do not consume large portions of sushi (containing raw fish) at their first exposure to that cuisine. Most choose menu options with cooked fish (e.g., the California roll) and gradually increase their liking and consumption of raw sushi over time.

Mere exposure to new tastes and smells actually begins in utero (Beauchamp & Menella, 2009). The fetus is exposed to the flavors of foods consumed by the mother and is seemingly more accepting of these otherwise novel flavors when old enough to eat solid foods during infancy. Menella, Coren, Jagnow, and Beauchamp (2001) found that when women consumed carrot juice for 3 weeks during their third trimester, their infants (6 month later) were more accepting of carrot-flavored cereal compared with non-flavored cereal, demonstrating that the mere exposure effect on the shaping of food preferences begins prior to birth.

The number of exposures needed to increase liking of novel foods or flavors varies. Foods to which children or adults have been previously exposed or that are similar to familiar items (e.g., trying strawberry yogurt when already familiar with strawberries, or trying blueberry yogurt when already familiar with strawberry yogurt) require fewer exposures than entirely novel or innately less appealing foods (e.g., a novel bitter-tasting vegetable). So, some foods may be rated as more appealing after just one exposure, whereas others may require many more exposures. Further, for children, mere exposure seems to be more effective in shaping food acceptance and liking than rewards. Wardle, Herrera, Cooke, and Gibson (2003) found that children who were exposed to samples of sweet red pepper once a day for almost 2 weeks increased their liking and intake regardless of receiving a sticker reward for consuming the vegetable.

Flavor-Flavor Associative Learning

Humans have an innate liking of sweet and salty tastes. The sweet taste is associated with energy and nutrient-dense foods, and the salty taste is associated with foods that help maintain fluid and sodium balance. Humans also have an innate aversion to bitter and sour tastes, which are associated with toxins (Birch, 1999). However, many people regularly enjoy bitter or sour foods and beverages such as coffee, tea, beer, broccoli, sour candies, and so on, which seems to defy our innate predispositions. Why is this?

Pairing a new food or flavor that is not innately preferred with an already liked food or

TALKING POINT 5.1

Have you experienced flavor-flavor learning that increased your preference for a new food? How did you initially experience the food?

Do you prefer the food differently now (e.g., maybe less ketchup on your hamburger than you liked as a child)?

flavor increases the liking of that new food. This is called **flavor-flavor associative learning** (Birch, 1999). Although many adults enjoy coffee, some even preferring it black (without cream or sugar), most are initially exposed to coffee with cream or milk and sweetener. We have an innate liking of cream/milk and the sweet taste. Typically, adults gradually prefer less of the cream/milk and sweetener, but their initial liking of coffee is mediated by flavor-flavor learning. The same applies for tea, often sweetened in first exposures. Similarly, early experience with broccoli often includes cheese or butter sauce (tastes that are innately liked). Despite its bitter taste, the pairing of broccoli with already liked flavors increases its liking.

It is important to note that flavor-flavor associative learning can also result in conditioned aversions. In other words, the learning can work in reverse. In laboratory experiments, rats given a liked flavor mixed with bitter-tasting quinine demonstrated an aversion for the previously liked flavor, avoiding it when it was no longer paired with quinine (Rozin & Zellner, 1985). Theoretically, pairing broccoli with cheese hoping to increase a child's liking of broccoli could actually create a dislike of cheese! This, however, is typically not the case as the liking of cheese is greater than the dislike of broccoli for most humans.

Flavor-Nutrient Associative Learning

Pairing a flavor with calories (or with other needed substances such as vitamins) increases preference. Flavors paired with higher calories will be preferred to those paired with fewer calories (Ackroff & Sclafani, 2006). This **flavor-nutrient associative learning** can result in preference maintained for long durations even without reinforcement. As with taste avoidance learning, flavor-nutrient learning can occur with a delay of hours between conditioned stimulus (flavor) and unconditioned stimulus (benefit). This type of learning is akin to the medicine effect, in which animals and people learn preferences for foods or flavors associated with feeling good and recovering from a deficit in vitamins, minerals, or calories. However, flavor-nutrient associative learning can occur in a non-deficient state.

Although flavor-nutrient associative learning occurs in sated rats, the results are more robust when the rats (or other animals, including humans) are food deprived. It is easy to assume that the actions of nutrients in the gastrointestinal tract are more reinforcing for hungry than for sated animals. The "incentive value" for a food or flavor consumed when in a deficient state will be higher and will result in an increased appetitive approach to and intake of that particular food or flavor (Sclafani, 2004), which is the medicine effect.

BOX 5.2   Can Flavor-Flavor Learning Happen Easily?

In a study conducted by Capaldi and Privitera (2008), college student volunteers were given vegetables (cauliflower and broccoli) on three exposure sessions. One vegetable was sweetened with sugar during the exposures and the other was unsweetened. When subsequently tested with unsweetened vegetables, participants reported a greater liking of the previously sweetened vegetable. So, although the vegetable was no longer sweetened, its taste was preferred because of the association with the sweet taste.

BOX 5.3   Do Animals Learn Associations between Flavors and Nutrients?

Anthony Sclafani has performed many studies to define the limits of flavor-calorie learning. In one experiment, rats had access to two flavors of Kool-Aid (e.g., grape- or cherry-flavored water with no calories). These flavors were presented in water bottles fitted with contact sensors so that when the rat licked, a signal was sent to a computer (Drucker, Acroff, & Sclafani, 1993). The rats otherwise had *ad libitum* (i.e., unrestricted) access to food and water. In the one-bottle training trials, they had one flavor per day. Ingestion of one flavor was accompanied by infusion (programmed via the computer) of a caloric solution into the stomach through a surgically implanted tube. Ingestion of the other flavor was accompanied by infusion of water only. After several days of each flavor consequence, the rats were given a two-bottle preference test without any infusions. They strongly preferred the flavor previously paired with calories. Further, when these preference tests were continued without infusions (this is called *extinction*), the preference for the flavor paired with calories remained for weeks. That is, established preferences can be maintained without continued reinforcement. Sclafani and colleagues have also demonstrated similar flavor-nutrient associative learning by pairing Kool-Aid flavors with intragastric infusions of fat (Lucas & Sclafani, 1989) or protein (Pérez, Ackroff, & Sclafani, 1996).

Flavor-nutrient learning has been demonstrated in humans. Studies show that flavors associated with nutrients (calories, fat, vitamins, or minerals) are preferred. For example, Johnson, McPhee, and Birch (1991) gave preschool children fixed volumes of distinct flavors of pudding (pumpkin and chocolate-orange) that were either high or low in fat and calories (220 or 110 kcal/serving; 14 or < 2 g fat). The low- and high-fat versions were identical in taste, smell, and appearance. After several exposures to the flavor-nutrient pairing, children consumed less food following consumption of the high-fat and high-calorie pudding (compared with the low-fat and low-calorie pudding), even though during the test condition, all puddings were of mid-level caloric and fat content. Further, children reported increased liking for the flavor associated with high energy density, and no change in preference for the flavor associated with low density. These findings suggest that such flavor-nutrient learning shapes food preferences and energy intake. Similar studies (e.g., Booth, 1985) have been conducted in humans of other ages (infants and adults) and in rats, providing evidence that portion size is adjusted based on learned associations with flavors and their energy yield (i.e., flavor-nutrient learning).

It is important to note that flavor-flavor and flavor-nutrient associative learning do not typically occur in exclusion of each other outside of the laboratory setting. In real-life situations, preferred flavors are innately liked because they are associated with nutrients (calories, fat, vitamins, or minerals). For example, increased

liking of peanut butter after pairing it with honey demonstrates both flavor-flavor learning (honey is sweet tasting and innately liked) and flavor-nutrient learning (honey provides added calories). In fact, even increased liking of coffee after repeatedly consuming it with cream and sugar demonstrates both flavor-flavor and flavor-nutrient associative learning.

LEARNING OF APPROPRIATE FOOD QUANTITY: CONDITIONED SATIETY

Experiments conducted in the 1960s and 1970s routinely demonstrated that both humans and nonhuman animals fail to compensate when a previously consumed food is made either more or less energy dense (Stunkard, 1975). For example, after several exposures of a milkshake-like drink, participants in one study drank their "norm" amount even when the drink was diluted, and consequently less energy dense (Jordan, Wieland, Zebley, Stellar, & Stunkard, 1966).

Influential researcher A. J. Stunkard proposed that satiety must be a conditioned reflex, a function of learning rather than of physiological satiety cues. Some of the findings regarding flavor-nutrient learning (discussed earlier in this chapter) are consistent with this theory. For example, Johnson and colleagues (1991) found that children consumed less of the flavored pudding that they had learned to associate with higher calories and fat even when it was no longer high in calories and fat. They liked the flavor but learned to regulate calories and stop eating based on flavor cues supporting the idea that satiety is a conditioned reflex.

How often do you eat three-fourths of a sandwich or cookie? Typically, we finish items of defined quantity and have experience with these

particular quantities. We can assume that in early exposures to a sandwich, for example, consumption of one sandwich was followed by comfortable satiety and an adequate level of energy. We also tend to consume entire portions, often while completely unaware of how energy dense or dilute they

| BOX 5.4 | How Do Rats Know When It's Mealtime? |

In a study conducted by Drazen, Vahl, D'Alessio, Seeley, and Woods (2006), rats either received food *ad libitum* (food available all day) or for 4 hours only per day. The rats in the meal-restricted group soon (within 14 days) learned to anticipate their mealtime and consumed their food much more quickly and robustly. Ghrelin (a hunger-stimulating hormone) levels in the meal-trained rats were significantly higher prior to their anticipated 4-hour access to food in comparison with controls as their dark cycle approached (the time during which rats typically consume the most food). Their findings indicate that rats (and presumably humans) have learned physiological responses in anticipation of mealtimes.

are. For example, many of us consume a "bowlful" of cereal in the morning, regardless of the type of cereal (high or low in calories or other nutrients). Indeed, the popular individual serving bowls of cereals from one commercial source vary between 70 and 120 kcal, and the fat content of the milk you probably add will make even larger differences. We learn in early experiences with particular foods what quantities yield satiety, supporting Stunkard's conditioning theory. However, we can easily be "tricked" especially when eating at restaurants because portion sizes are often larger and more fat and calorie dense than we expect.

LEARNING OF WHEN TO EAT: CONDITIONED HUNGER

If satiety is conditioned, is hunger also conditioned? Consider the frequent long lines at many delis and cafeterias at lunchtime. Why do so many of us eat at similar times of the day, such as lunch around noon in particular? Perhaps we all have similar energy and nutrient needs at the same time of day. Does this seem logical given that many of us wake at different times in the morning, exert varying amounts of energy early in the day, have different metabolic rates, and consume varied calories and nutrients (or none at all) for breakfast? It is more likely that our "hunger" for lunch at noon is a result of learning that this is mealtime. Because of our learned expectation of consumption of food at lunchtime, physiological changes occur (e.g., insulin and ghrelin levels rise; blood glucose drops) that intensify our hunger. (See Box 5.4.)

When rats are placed on a meal schedule (something analogous to breakfast, lunch, and dinner), rather than allowed food *ad libitum*, they consume the most in the meal that precedes the longest between-meal interval. One might expect the opposite, that they eat the most following the longest stretch of deprivation. The fact that this is not the case is quite interesting, and much like with human eating patterns, suggesting that they have learned to anticipate the longest interval without food access and consume more in advance of it. It seems likely that eating behavior (ours and rats') is largely attributed to learning to anticipate and prevent future disruptions to physiological homeostasis (Woods, 2009).

In addition to time-of-day cues, other stimuli associated with food also trigger hunger and eating. As mentioned, we tend to think of and crave particular food items on seeing certain corporate logos. After conditioning, Pavlov's dogs salivated at the sound of a metronome. Animals and people quickly associate food with the stimuli surrounding the experience with the food (physical, visual,

| BOX 5.5 | Do Food Cues Trigger Eating Even in Absence of Hunger? |

In classic experiments conducted in the 1980s by Weingarten (e.g., 1984), food was delivered to rats following a buzzer and light stimulus. After several days of conditioning, rats ate when exposed to the buzzer and light stimulus, despite the fact that they were not food deprived in the test condition.

olfactory, and auditory cues; mood; etc.), and later encounters with these stimuli trigger hunger, even when there is no physiological need for food. Food-associated cues are increasingly ubiquitous in Western society, and their impact on eating (and overeating) is tremendous.

Influence of Learned Contextual Cues

Have you ever noticed feeling hungry when you enter the place in which you typically eat meals or snacks? People and rats tend consume more food when they are in places that they have learned to associate with food. This helps explain the frequent "mindless" behavior of grabbing a soda out of the refrigerator or candy from the kitchen when passing by, even in the absence of thirst, hunger, or a planned intention to snack.

Contextual cues, such as sights, smells, and sounds, are non-food stimuli that we quickly learn to associate with food. This type of learning is simply classical conditioning, which, as mentioned earlier, is basic but effective. Birch, McPhee, Sullivan, and Johnson (1989) examined the impact that a physical setting has on a child's eating. In this study, preschool children were exposed to two playrooms that were similar in appearance and had similar contents (toys, etc.), but in one room they received snacks regularly and in the other room they were never fed. On the test day, both rooms were "baited" with snacks, and half the children were sent to play in one room and half to the other. The group sent to the playroom in which they had experienced snacks before started eating/snacking sooner and ate more than the group sent to the room in which they had not previously experienced snacks. This indicates a powerful influence of social and environmental learning in readiness to eat and/or amount consumed, and this is established early in life.

Rats, too, demonstrate increased eating as a result of learning about physical or contextual cues. Rats eat more quickly and ingest larger amounts when placed in cages previously associated with food, especially if the food to which they were previously exposed was palatable (e.g., cookies;

Boggiano, Dorsey, Thomas, & Murdaugh, 2009). Further, rats and people eat more of palatable and bland food when they are exposed to contextual cues associated with palatable food. It seems that we (rats and humans) feel hungrier when exposed to food-related conditions or places. Learned contextual cues can be more influential on hunger and eating than the actual taste of food (an unconditioned stimulus).

In a study of college students and staff, Ferriday and Brunstrom (2008) found that the sight and smell of pizza were more associated with increased consumption of pizza and other foods than was the taste of pizza. How could this be? Exposure to contextual cues associated with a pleasurable experience such as consumption of palatable food activates the brain's reward pathways and areas associated with wanting and motivation (Berridge et al., 2010). This powerful activation can drive the appetitive behavior toward the desired food. Further, physiological changes (e.g., increase in insulin, decrease in blood glucose) intensify hunger when we are

TALKING POINT 5.3

Are there specific foods that you associate with particular places or other cues? How about the movie theater as discussed in the opening paragraph of this chapter? A local bakery? Grandma's house? A football or baseball game? Write down some of these associations and see how your list compares with your classmates' lists.

exposed to cues associated with particular foods, explaining the difficulty many people have in resisting foods on exposure to those cues.

Conditioned Immune System Activity

Efforts have been made to utilize classical conditioning techniques to boost immune system functioning particularly among clinically ill patients (Exton et al., 2000). Initially, researchers realized that immune system functioning weakens when patients enter the hospital or treatment facility where they receive chemotherapy, a consequence of associative learning. This, however, only puts patients at greater risk for the negative physiological side effects of chemotherapy and the toll it takes on the immune system and overall health (although the benefits of such treatment usually outweigh the risks). In one study, as an example of these experiments, patients consumed particular flavors of sherbet and afterward received an adrenaline injection (which boosts immune system activity and overall physical feeling). After several pairings, the patients' immune systems were more active following consumption of the sherbet even when it was no longer followed by the adrenaline injection (Exton et al., 2000).

Neurobiology of Food Learning

The neurobiology associated with *conditioned* taste aversions and preferences is different from that associated with *innately* disliked and liked tastes. The brain regions associated with *learned* taste dislikes and likes include those associated with memory, emotion, and reward. It seems obvious that emotional memory (e.g., disgust) is important in preventing an organism

from re-exposing itself to a dangerous food or flavor, as the lack of this recall ability could result in fatality. And, pleasant experiences with particular foods, such as warm soup on a chilly night or a substantive pasta dish following an exhausting soccer game, should be remembered so that those positive experiences can be repeated. These types of emotional memories require an intact **hippocampus**. Severe damage to the hippocampus disrupts the ability to form new explicit memories (i.e., memories that can be consciously recalled). Amnesic patients with hippocampal damage will consume a second meal soon after eating a first meal, and often a third meal as well, indicating that physiological satiety signals are not sufficient in regulating their food intake (Rozin, Dow, Moscovitch, & Rajaram, 1998). It seems, rather, that *memory* for food intake (type and amount of food) is more important in making subsequent food choices (Beniot, Davis, & Davidson, 2010).

In addition to the hippocampus, other brain regions associated with emotional memory are important in the establishment of conditioned taste aversions and preferences. Establishing a learned food aversion is unpleasant (often including nausea and vomiting) and can be considered frightening and upsetting. The **amygdala**, a brain region associated with various motivated and emotional behaviors, including fearful and aggressive responses, plays an important role in the formation of learned taste aversions. It seems, though, that different regions within the amygdala function differentially in the *establishment* of a conditioned taste aversion compared to the *avoidance response* in future exposures (Reilly & Bornavalova, 2005; Yamamoto, 2006). Further, regions of the amygdala communicate differently with the **nucleus accumbens** and other brain reward circuitry following exposure to a liked versus disliked taste, which may not be surprising as the neurobiology of conditioned taste preferences and conditioned taste aversions serve different functions. Avoiding harmful foods and flavors is important for the survival of any animal, thus brain stem anatomy and physiology shared among many species including reptiles and mammals likely underlie the basic ability to form conditioned taste aversions. Further, conditioned taste aversions in animals under anesthesia when exposed to the CS-US pairing have been demonstrated (Yamamoto, 2006); this does not occur for conditioned preferences. Conditioned taste preferences (again, these are learned and shaped by experience and are not necessarily innate preferences) are influenced by social and cultural factors (e.g., parents, friends, local cuisine, expectations, accessibility). Although these are extremely important aspects of our eating behaviors, they are not as essential as learning to avoid what may kill us. More recently evolved brain regions (e.g., the forebrain) may be of greater importance in the formation of conditioned taste preferences compared with conditioned aversions. The

involvement of the forebrain, and specifically reward circuitry, in eating behavior is of recent interest as it relates to the concept of excessive and problematic food liking and the possibility of food addiction. The neurobiology of feeding is explored in other chapters; thus, the focus of the remaining discussion in this chapter is on the neurobiology of conditioned taste aversions.

The brain stem **nucleus of the solitary tract (NST)** and the **parabrachial nucleus(PBN)** are the first and second brain relay nuclei, respectively, for taste and gastrointestinal information. Rats with lesions to the PBN do not acquire conditioned taste aversions despite their demonstrated capacity to maintain the ability to process taste and visceral information. And, any previously learned taste aversion is abolished by a lesion to this region. The association between taste and gastrointestinal information occurs in the PBN and not in the NST, an integration that is seemingly necessary for the formation of conditioned taste aversion. Taste and gastrointestinal information from the PBN relay to the medial thalamus, and then to the **gustatory insular cortex** in the frontal cortex. In parallel fashion, the same information projects from the PBN to the amygdala. Severe

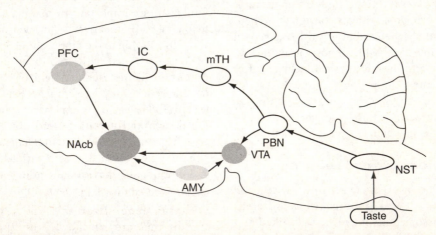

FIGURE 5.2 Brain regions important for the processing of taste information and the development of conditioned taste aversions are shown in this rat brain figure. Yamamoto, T. (2008). Central mechanisms of roles of taste in reward and eating. Acta Physiologica Hungarica, 95, 165–186. Printed with permission from Acta Physiologica Hungarica.

Key: NST—nucleus of the solitary tract; PBN—parabrachial nucleus; VTA—ventral tegmental area; AMY—amygdala; mTH—medial thalamus; IC—insular gustatory cortex; NAcb—nucleus accumbens; PFC—prefrontal cortex.

damage to the gustatory insular cortex (or gustatory cortex), the medial thalamus, or areas within the amygdala (specifically, the basolateral amygdala) can prevent a human or animal from forming a conditioned taste aversion or from retaining the learned association. Although many other regions are likely involved (e.g., hypothalamic nuclei), as the brain circuitry of eating behavior is complex and involves multiple pathways, the PBN, medial thalamus, basolateral amygdala, and gustatory insular cortex are of particular importance for the formation and maintenance of conditioned taste aversions (Yamamoto, 2006; Yamamoto, Shimura, Sako, Yasoshima, & Sakai, 1994).

Let's review and apply your knowledge. Take some time to answer these chapter questions

1. Use classical conditioning terminology (UCR, UCS, etc.) to briefly diagram and describe an example of how classical conditioning has shaped one of your food preferences or aversions.
2. What are the four ways to that food preference can be increased by experience? Give examples of each.
3. Do you think that satiety is conditioned? What is the scientific evidence for this? Describe some evidence in your own eating behavior that supports or refutes this theory.
4. What are some of the learned cues that trigger hunger? Why does this occur?
5. What brain regions are most important for learned food preferences and aversions?

Glossary

Amygdala A forebrain region associated with raw emotion, particularly fear and aggression.

Conditioned response (CR) A learned response to a previously neutral stimulus.

Conditioned stimulus (CS) A previously neutral stimulus that comes to elicit the response of an unconditioned stimulus.

Flavor-flavor associative learning Increased liking of a flavor that is associated with a flavor that is already or innately liked.

Flavor-nutrient associative learning Increased liking of a flavor associated with nutrients, usually calories.

Gustatory insular cortex The primary taste cortex; allows for perception of taste.

Hippocampus A forebrain region involved with the formation of memories.

Medicine effect Increased liking of a food associated with recovery from illness.

Mere exposure effect Increased liking of food resulting from repeated exposures to the food.

Neophobia Fear of the new (for the purposes of this text, fear of new food or flavors).

Neutral stimulus (NS) A stimulus that elicits no response.

Nucleus accumbens A forebrain region associated with pleasure and reinforcement.

Nucleus of the solitary tract (NST) A brain stem region to which taste information from the tongue projects.

Parabrachial nucleus (PBN) A brainstem region that receives taste information from the NST.

Pica The appetite for items that are generally not considered food (e.g., dirt).

Stimulus generalization The response to stimuli that are similar to the conditioned stimulus.

Unconditioned response (UCR) An unlearned response to a stimulus.

Unconditioned stimulus (UCS) A stimulus that triggers an unlearned response.

References

Ackroff, K., & Sclafani, A. (2006). Energy density and macronutrient composition determine flavor preference conditioned by intragastric infusions of mixed diets. *Physiology & Behavior, 89*(2), 250–260.

Andresen, G.V., Birch, L. L., & Johnson, P. A. (1990). The scapegoat effect on food aversions after chemotherapy. *Cancer, 66*, 1649–1653.

Beauchamp, G. K., & Mennella, J. A. (2009). Early flavor learning and its impact on later feeding behavior. *Journal of Pediatric Gastroenterology and Nutrition, 48*, S25–S30.

Benoit, S. C., Davis, J. F., & Davidson, T. L. (2010). Learned and cognitive controls of food intake. *Brain Research, 1350*, 71–76.

Berridge, K. C., Ho, C. Y., Richard, J. M., & DiFeliceantonio, A. G. (2010). The tempted brain eats: Pleasure and desire circuits in obesity and eating disorders. *Brain research, 1350*, 43–64.

Birch, L. L. (1999). Development of food preferences. *Annual Review of Nutrition, 19*(1), 41–62.

Birch, L. L., McPhee, L., Sullivan, S., & Johnson, S. (1989). Conditioned meal initiation in young children. *Appetite, 13*(2), 105–113.

Booth, D. A. (1985). Food-conditioned eating preferences and aversions with interoceptive elements: Conditioned appetites and satieties. *Annals of the New York Academy of Sciences, 443*(1), 22–41.

Boggiano, M. M., Dorsey, J. R., Thomas, J. M., & Murdaugh, D. L. (2009). The Pavlovian power of palatable food: Lessons for weight-loss adherence from a new rodent model of cue-induced overeating. *International Journal of Obesity, 33*(6), 693–701.

Bornstein, R. F., & D'Agostino, P. R. (1992). Stimulus recognition and the mere exposure effect. *Journal of Personality and Social Psychology, 63*(4), 545–552.

Broberg, D. J., & Bernstein, I. L. (1987). Candy as a scapegoat in the prevention of food aversions in children receiving chemotherapy. *Cancer, 60*(9), 2344–2347.

Capaldi, E. D., & Privitera G. J. (2008). Decreasing dislike for sour and bitter in children and adults. *Appetite, 50*(1), 139–145.

de Montellano, B. R. O. (1978). Aztec cannibalism: An ecological necessity? *Science, 200*(4342), 611–617.

Drazen, D. L., Vahl, T. P., D'Alessio, D. A., Seeley, R. J., & Woods, S. C. (2006). Effects of a fixed meal pattern on ghrelin secretion: Evidence for a learned response independent of nutrient status. *Endocrinology, 147*(1), 23–30.

Drewnowski, A. A. (1997). Taste preferences and food intake. *Annual Review of Nutrition, 17*(1), 237.

Drewnowski, A., Kurth, C., Holden-Wiltse, J., & Saari, J. (1992). Food preferences in human obesity: Carbohydrates versus fats. *Appetite, 18*, 207–221.

Drucker, D. B., Ackroff, K., & Sclafani, A. (1993). Flavor preference produced by intragastric polycose infusions in rats using a concurrent conditioning procedure. *Physiology and Behavior, 54*, 351–355.

Exton, M. S., von Auer, A. K., Buske-Kirschbaum, A., Stockhorst, U., Göbel, U., & Schedlowski, M. (2000). Pavlovian conditioning of immune function: Animal investigation and the challenge of human application. *Behavioural Brain Research, 110*(1), 129–141.

Ferriday, D., & Brunstrom, J. M. (2008). How does food-cue exposure lead to larger meal sizes? *British Journal of Nutrition, 100*, 1325–1332.

Galef, B. G., & Henderson, P. W. (1972). Mother's milk: A determinant of the feeding preferences of weaning rat pups. *Journal of Comparative and Physiological Psychology, 78*(2), 213–219.

Galef, B. G., & Sherry, D. F. (1973). Mother's milk: A medium for transmission of cues reflecting the flavor of mother's diet. *Journal of Comparative and Physiological Psychology, 83*(3), 374.

Garcia, J., & Koelling, R. A. (1966). Relation of cue to consequence in avoidance learning. *Psychonomic Science, 4*(3), 123–124.

Gustavson, C. R., Kelly, D. J., & Sweeney, M. (1976). Prey-lithium aversions I: Coyotes and wolves. *Behavioral Biology, 17*, 61–72.

Johnson, S. L., McPhee, L., & Birch, L. L. (1991). Conditioned preferences: Young children prefer flavors associated with high dietary fat. *Physiology & Behavior, 50*(6), 1245–1251.

Jordan, H. A., Wieland, W. F., Zebley, S. P., Stellar, E., & Stunkard, A. J. (1966). Direct measurement of food intake in man: A method for the objective study of eating behavior. *Psychosomatic Medicine, 28*(6), 836–842.

Lucas, F., & Sclafani, A. (1989). Flavor preferences conditioned by intragastric fat infusions in rats. *Physiology & Behavior, 46*(3), 403–412.

Menella, J. A., Johnson, A., & Beauchamp, G. K. (2001). Prenatal and postnatal flavor learning by human infants. *Pediatrics, 107*(6), 88–97.

Nicolaus, L. K., Cassel, J. F., Carlson, R. B., & Gusysvson, C. R. (1983). Taste-aversion conditioning of crows to control predation on eggs. *Science, 220*, 212–214. doi: 10.1126/science.220.4593.212

Pérez, C., Ackroff, K., & Sclafani, A. (1996). Carbohydrate- and protein-conditioned flavor preferences: Effects of nutrient preloads. *Physiology & Behavior, 59*(3), 467–474.

Reilly, S., & Bornaovalova, M. A. (2005). Conditioned taste aversion and amygdala lesions in the rat: A critical review. *Neuroscience and Biobehavioral Reviews, 29*, 1067–1088.

Rozin, P. (1969). Adaptive food sampling patterns in vitamin deficient rats. *Journal of Comparative and Physiological Psychology, 69*(1), 126–132. doi: 10.1037/h0027940

Rozin, P., Dow, S., Moscovitch, M., & Rajaram, S. (1998). What causes humans to begin and end a meal? A role for memory for what has been eaten, as evidenced by a study of multiple meal eating in amnesic patients. *Psychological Science, 9*(5), 392–396.

Rodgers W., & Rozin, P. (1966). Novel food preferences in thiamine-deficient rats. *Journal of Comparative Physiological Psychology, 61*(1), 1–4.

Rozin, P., & Zellner, D. (1985). The role of pavlovian conditioning in the acquisition of food likes and dislikes. *Annals of the New York Academy of Sciences, 443*(1), 189–202.

Schafe, G. E., & Bernstein, I. L. (2004). Taste aversion learning (in Capald, pp. 31–51).

Sclafani, A. (2004). Oral and postoral determinants of food reward. *Physiology & Behavior, 81*(5), 773–779.

Stunkard, A. (1975). Satiety is a conditioned reflex. *Psychosomatic Medicine, 37*(5), 383–387.

Sullivan, S. A., & Birch, L. L. (1990). Pass the sugar, pass the salt: Experience dictates preference. *Developmental Psychology, 26*, 546–551.

Sullivan, S. A., & Birch, L. L. (1994). Infant dietary experience and acceptance of solid foods. *Pediatrics, 93*, 271–277.

Volkow, N. D., Wang, G. J., Maynard, L., Jayne, M., Fowler, J. S., Zhu, W., … Pappas, N. (2003). Brain dopamine is associated with eating behavior in humans. *International Journal of Eating Disorders, 33*, 136–142.

Wardle, J., Herrera, M., Cooke, L., & Gibson, E. (2003). Modifying children's food preferences: The effects of exposure and reward on acceptance of an unfamiliar vegetable. *European Journal of Clinical Nutrition, 57*(2), 341–348.

Weingarten, H. P. (1984). Meal initiation controlled by learned cues: Basic behavioral properties. *Appetite, 5*(2), 147–158.

Werner, S. J., Kimball, B. A., & Provenza, F. D. (2008). Food color, flavor, and conditioned avoidance among red-winged blackbirds. *Physiology & Behavior, 93*(1–2), 110–117.

Wisse, B. E., Frayo, R. S., Schwartz, M. W., & Cummings, D. E. (2001). Reversal of cancer anorexia by blockade of central melanocortin receptors in rats. *Endocrinology, 142*(8), 3292–3301.

Woods, S. C. (2009). The control of food intake: Behavioral versus molecular perspectives. *Cell Metabolism, 9*(6), 489–498.

Yamamoto, T. (2006). Brain regions responsible for the expression of conditioned taste aversions in rats. *Chemical Senses, 32*, 105–109.

Yamamoto, T. (2008). Central mechanisms of roles of taste in reward and eating. *Acta Physiologica Hungarica, 95*, 165–186.

Yamamoto, T., Shimura, T., Sako, N., Yasoshima, Y., & Sakai, N. (1994). Neural substrates for conditioned taste aversion in the rat. *Behavioural Brain Research, 65*, 123–137.

Zajonc, R. B. (1968). Attitudinal effects of mere exposure. *Journal of Personality and Social Psychology Monographs, 9*(2 p2), 1.

The Development of Eating Behaviors

After reading this chapter, you will be able to

- Understand the effects of prenatal exposure to nutrients and flavors
- Appreciate the impact of early postnatal experience with food and the advantages of breast feeding
- Identify evidence for and against the theory that children can regulate their own energy and nutrient needs

- Understand the influence of external factors (parents, media, portion sizes, etc.) on the eating behaviors of children
- Provide ideas for parents, caregivers, and policy makers for instilling healthy eating behaviors for children

Significant changes in eating behavior occur in the first few years of life—from suckling, to being spoon fed, to eating independently. New tastes and smells are encountered and likes and dislikes are formed. Infants and toddlers learn what foods are socially acceptable, and when and how much should be eaten. Eating patterns established during the early years shape future eating behaviors. Because the obesity rate is increasing in countries around the world, it is important to understand the impact of eating practices established in the first few years of life so that parents, caregivers, and policy makers can improve the food environment of young children, better preparing them for lifelong healthy eating. We know that infants innately like sweet tastes and dislike bitter and sour tastes. This biological predisposition helps us from birth identify and consume foods associated

with more calories and avoid those that could be dangerous. This served our ancestors well in a world with scarce food supplies, but it puts us at an increased risk for obesity in an environment containing an overabundance of sweet-tasting foods with calories exceeding our needs. In this chapter, we explore biological predispositions that we have at birth, and even before birth, and the sociocultural influences (parents, friends, culture, and media) that further shape our eating behaviors during our early years.

THE ONTOGENY OF HUMAN FEEDING: PRENATAL EXPERIENCE

Fetal brain development is impacted by the food, drink, and other substances that the mother ingests, particularly during critical periods.

BOX 6.1   What's the Evidence?

Statistics from the Dutch famine during the winter of 1944–1945 (due to severe food rationing in the Netherlands during World War II) reveal that individuals exposed to famine conditions during early prenatal development were at increased risk for obesity, diabetes, cardiovascular problems, and other health issues later in life (Roseboom, Rooij, & Painter, 2006). Before and after the famine, food was plentiful for most people. It seems that those exposed to energy and nutrient restriction during critical periods of brain organization developed heightened "starvation-resistance" circuitry. So, when these individuals entered an environment with food abundance rather than scarcity, they had increased desire to eat, a reduced ability to regulate energy needs, and more efficient energy storage, making them more likely to overeat and become obese. Similar effects have been found in other human and rodent studies (Levin, 2006).

Maternal malnutrition is correlated with low birth weight, lower intelligence, and reduced motor coordination, among other lifelong impairments (Lechtig et al., 1975). We know that alcohol consumption during pregnancy can result in fetal alcohol syndrome, a condition associated with abnormal facial features, mental retardation, and poor motor coordination (Matson & Riley, 2006). As with the effects of maternal malnutrition, fetal alcohol syndrome and other developmental disorders associated with a toxic uterine environment result in permanent alterations to neurodevelopment. Even disruptions to sodium balance are linked to lifelong changes. It has been shown that early-life sodium depletion (e.g., mothers vomiting often during pregnancy or infants eating a low-salt diet) increases salt preference during adulthood (Crystal & Bernstein, 1995; Curtis, Krause, Wong, & Contreras, 2004). Early sodium depletion increases levels of the circulating hormones aldosterone and angiotensin; these elevations may have permanent or so-called *organizational* effects within the developing nervous system. Also, children born to mothers who are either over- or underweight while pregnant are at increased risk for being overweight, likely because of organizational changes within the developing brain (Black et al., 2008; Cripps, Martin-Gronert, & Ozanne, 2005; Herring, Rose, Skouteris, & Oken, 2012). These are referred to as epigenetic changes, meaning that DNA sequence (building blocks of genes) is unchanged, but *expression* of genes is altered (this and other genetic concepts are reviewed in Appendix 2).

You are probably familiar with the adage that expectant mothers can "eat for two," but is overconsumption during pregnancy a good idea? Until recent decades, food and nutrient scarcity was a threat to the developing child, so pregnant women, with added energy needs, were encouraged to eat heartily. In our current Western environment of food abundance, the advice given to women in earlier decades is no longer applicable. In fact, consuming beyond energy needs puts pregnant women at increased risk for gestational

diabetes, preeclampsia (gestational high blood pressure), and other medical problems that can complicate pregnancy and the health of the child. Further, children born to mothers who gained excessive weight during pregnancy have higher body fat percentages (thus, higher leptin levels) and are at increased risk for obesity later in life compared with children born to mothers who gained a healthy amount of weight during pregnancy (Cripps et al., 2005; Herring et al., 2012).

Results of recent studies indicate that junk food consumption (i.e., foods high in energy and low in nutrients) during pregnancy predisposes children for heightened junk food cravings, which increase the likelihood of unhealthy weight. However, in studies of early human development, it is difficult to distinguish prenatal and postnatal influences. For example, children born to mothers who consume large amounts of junk food during pregnancy are often raised in homes where unhealthy food is eaten, making it difficult for researchers to determine the impact of the prenatal experience only. To address this issue, Bayol, Farrington, and Stickland (2007) conducted a study using a rat model, which allows for greater control over the variables. The design of their study is outlined in Figure 6.1.

The junk food diet included doughnuts, cookies, candy bars, potato chips, cheese, and muffins in addition to standard rat chow. As expected, pregnant rats on the junk food diet consumed more energy and gained more weight compared with rats eating only chow. Although their consumption of sugar, fat, and salt increased, their intake of protein decreased compared with control animals. So, the development of the fetal brains was not only impacted by overconsumption of energy, but also by inadequate consumption of protein. Further, the offspring of dams (mothers) consuming the junk food diet demonstrated enhanced liking of and preference for the junk food diet post-weaning compared with controls. All newly weaned rats demonstrated a liking of the junk food diet, but those exposed prenatally and during lactation selectively preferred foods high in sugar and fat over foods containing protein or fiber. Offspring exposed to the junk food diet during gestation and lactation but then fed only chow after weaning did not demonstrate overconsumption of chow. It seems that early exposure to highly palatable energy-dense food creates an enhanced taste preference for tasty, high-calorie, high-fat food, which serves as a predisposition for obesity.

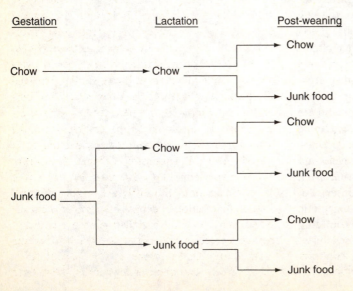

Gestation   Lactation   Post-weaning

Chow ——→ Chow ——→ Chow
                        └——→ Junk food

            Chow ——→ Chow
                        └——→ Junk food

Junk food

            Junk food ——→ Chow
                        └——→ Junk food

FIGURE 6.1 An overview of the "junk food" diet study.

Source: Recreated from Bayol et al. (2007).

BOX 6.2   Can Babies Taste and Smell before Birth?

Mennella Jagnow, and Beauchamp (2001) had groups of pregnant women consume either water or carrot juice during 3 weeks of their last trimester, then water or carrot juice during the first 2 months of breast feeding. When the babies were about 6 months and already eating some baby foods such as rice cereal, they were videotaped as they tried carrot-flavored cereal for the first time. Mennella's group found that babies exposed to carrot juice flavors either prenatally in amniotic fluid or postnatally in breast milk were more accepting of this otherwise novel food than were babies of mothers who consumed only water during these times. These findings indicate that food flavors are detected in amniotic fluid, and that this early exposure influences food preferences after birth. Further, flavor exposure early in life through breast milk also enhances liking of a wider range of foods preparing a baby for the cuisine of his or her environment.

Although it is relatively easy to understand how changes in hormones or nutrients in a mother's blood would be transmitted to the fetus, some questions about prenatal exposure to tastes and other sensory stimuli remain. We know that a fetus can hear, which is why some expectant mothers read stories or play music for their developing babies. The fetus is also exposed to tastes and smells, and these exposures seem to contribute to post-birth preferences. Fetuses show swallowing behavior at approximately 3 months, which becomes more vigorous in the following months. They are swallowing amniotic fluid. The fetus also has mature taste cells at this early time of gestation (~4 weeks; Mistretta & Bradley, 1975), though it is not known when the taste pathway to the cortex for processing of taste information becomes functional.

Menella, Johnson, and Beauchamp (1995) found that amniotic fluid contains food flavors. They asked pregnant women who were undergoing amniocentesis (sampling amniotic fluid) for other reasons to consume either a garlic or placebo pill about 1 hour before the procedure. The researchers then paired up the samples (forming five pairs of garlic and non-garlic samples) and asked a "smell panel" to judge which one of the pair contained garlic. In four of the five pairs, most judges were able to correctly pick out the garlic sample. Smell panels in other studies have similarly detected cumin and curry. This indicates that flavors are transmitted into amniotic fluid and can potentially stimulate smell or taste receptors in the

fetus. This early exposure can actually influence the acceptance of flavors by infants.

EARLY POSTNATAL EATING: FROM SUCKLING TO EATING SOLID FOODS

Infants have an innate preference for sweet tastes: Newborns will suck much more vigorously at a sweet-tasting artificial nipple than at a neutral-tasting nipple. This is even evident in premature infants, although the overall vigor of the response is less (Tatzer, Schubert, Timischl, & Simbruner, 1985). This indicates that detection of and preference for sweet are innate and mature well before birth. Newborns also respond with displeasure to bitter and sour tastes, indicating innate aversions for these potentially dangerous tastes (Birch, 1999). Are all primary taste preferences and aversions innate? Maybe not. Using similar artificial nipple-sucking methods, newborns were indifferent to salt compared to water. Instead, the preference for salt appears at approximately 4 months after birth (Beauchamp, Cowart, Mennella, & Marsh, 1994; Beauchamp, Cowart, & Moran, 1986). Experience does not seem to play a role (after all, amniotic fluid is largely a salt solution). Rather, maturation of central taste systems underlies this effect. Thus, the chemosensory world of newborns, while rich, differs from that of adults presented with the same tastes. Recent findings indicate that chemoreceptors in the enteric nervous system provide important sensory information for infants (see Mayer [2011] for a review of gut-brain communication).

A newborn is able to discriminate his or her mother's breast and underarm odors from those of other mothers (measured by the time spent orienting to the mother for breast feeding). Newborns either by prenatal exposure or, more likely, by rapid postnatal learning are able to learn to seek a complex olfactory stimulus that is predictive of food and shelter. There is evidence that by a few weeks of age infants are able to detect food flavors in their mothers' milk (Beauchamp & Mennella, 2009). Novel flavors (such as garlic and vanilla) produce more vigorous suckling, indicating that the novelty has been detected. Adult smell panels can also detect garlic and vanilla in mothers' milk (Savage, Fisher, & Birch, 2007).

To address early life taste and smell abilities, some researchers have investigated whether or not babies can detect alcohol in breast milk. In one study, mothers drank a test beverage (orange juice) that was normal on one occasion and "spiked" with a small amount of alcohol on another occasion (Menella, 2001). They breast-fed their infants 3 to 4 hours after consuming the beverage. Infants consumed significantly less of their mothers' milk on the alcohol day compared with the non-alcohol day. This indicated that the infants not only detected the alcohol, but also disliked it (alcohol has a bitter taste). It is important to note that this study does not unequivocally prove it is the taste of alcohol in the milk that resulted in a decreased consumption; the mothers' breath or underarm odors could also have been affected, or the mothers' supply of breast milk could have been reduced.

Breast versus Bottle (Formula) Feeding

There is something of a debate among neonatologists (and parents) regarding the benefits of "natural" versus "artificial" milk for infants, and it is our hunch that their positions in the debate reflect complex belief systems that transcend babies and milk! Breast milk has immunological properties, providing some protection from early life illnesses, and it is associated with a reduced

risk for obesity and other health problems (Field, 2005; Gartner et al., 2005; Kramer & Kakuma, 2012); furthermore, breast feeding facilitates an emotional bond between mother and child. The American Academy of Pediatrics currently recommends "exclusive breastfeeding for approximately the first six months and support for breastfeeding for the first year and beyond as long as mutually desired by mother and child" (Gartner et al., 2005, p. 499). However, according to the Centers for Disease Control and Prevention (2009), a survey revealed that fewer than 14% of babies born in the United States were breast-fed exclusively for their first 6 months. Although research unequivocally suggests that breast feeding is advantageous for the infant (and mother), some parents decide to formula feed for a number of reasons, including convenience, health problems, a desire or financial need to return to work, insufficient milk production, or the mother's need to take medication that could be harmful to the baby. Importantly, both breast milk–fed and formula-fed infants grow up fit and well, so a parent's choice about which type of feeding may ultimately come down to personal preference. Let's review some of the main findings around breast versus bottle (formula) feeding.

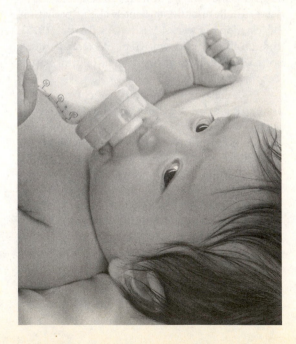

Because breast-fed infants are exposed to flavors from the mother's diet, their chemosensory exposure is more varied than that of formula-fed infants, as the flavor of formula is unchanging. There is some evidence that this better prepares infants for acceptance and liking of novel foods and flavors (Forestell & Mennella, 2007; Hausner, Nicklaus, Issanchou, Mølgaard, & Møller, 2009; Sullivan & Birch, 1994). As previously described in this chapter, Mennella et al. (2001) found that when breast-feeding mothers consumed carrot juice (consequently exposing their infants to that flavor through breast milk), their infants demonstrated increased acceptance and enjoyment of carrot flavor in infant cereal. This is an example of the *mere exposure effect*, meaning that preferences for foods and flavors increase with repeated exposures. Breast-fed infants have the opportunity to learn of a wider variety of flavors and develop more food preferences (and reduced neophobia [fear of new tastes]) than formula-fed infants. And, this experience is correlated with a higher consumption of fruits and vegetables in childhood.

Breast feeding is often done "on demand"; that is, the infant is fed whenever he or she fusses. The infant then suckles for as long (and ingests as much) as desired. This arrangement allows the infant to control both meal size and interval between meals.

In these demand-fed infants, by approximately 2 months of age, meal size (weight gain during a suckling episode) correlates with that of preceding interval since their last suckling. The first nursing episode in the morning is the largest and follows the longest episode (sleep) without feeding (Matheny, Birch, & Picciano, 1990). (Although infants at this age are typically not sleeping through the entire night, they may sleep up to 6 hours, usually their longest bout in a 24-hour period.) In contrast, by about age 6 months, their meal size correlates with the interval that follows the breast feeding. This correlation seems to be driven by the fact that the last nursing episode in the evening is the largest (and these infants do now typically sleep through the night). They *apparently* (but will not be able to tell us this in words for another year or two!) are anticipating the period of deprivation.

In contrast, formula-fed infants are usually not fed on demand; they are fed a "bottle full" (i.e., a fixed maximum meal size) and may not be fed immediately when they start fussing. Parents and caregivers often adhere to a relatively fixed schedule when bottle feeding and, thus, may attempt to delay the onset of a meal. Consequently, meal taking (timing and amount) is relatively more imposed by the parents and/or caregiver. Research reveals no correlation between the intervals before

BOX 6.3 Does Exposure Affect Intake?

Sullivan and Birch (1994) studied the first acceptance of solid foods in infants age 4–6 months. This was an in-home study in which mothers fed their infants a novel vegetable puree on 10 occasions (e.g., one per meal per day). Intake was measured and videotaped. Over the exposure period, infants doubled their intake of novel foods from 30 to 60 g. This was likely both a mere exposure effect and a decline of neophobia. Interestingly, this increase across exposures was much greater in breast-fed compared with formula-fed infants. Sullivan and Birch hypothesized that

breast-fed infants experience an array of food flavors in mothers' milk that enhances their acceptance of other novel foods, as previously discussed, better preparing them to like healthy foods like fruits and vegetables.

or after the meal under these conditions. Perhaps bottle-fed babies are not given the full opportunity to either learn or determine these natural or normal meal size/interval relationships.

The consumption process is more passive for bottle-fed infants (i.e., they have less control over the amount and timing of meals) and requires less effort compared to breast feeding, leading to frequent over-feeding of infants consuming formula. These conditions seem to interfere with their ability to self-regulate calorie consumption and possibly put formula-fed infants at greater risk for obesity (Savage et al., 2007).

Results of several studies indicate that, in general, breast feeding is associated with a decreased risk of being overweight later in life, decreased blood cholesterol and blood pressure, and a reduced risk of developing type 2 diabetes (Arenz, Rückerl, Koletzko, & Von Kries, 2004; Owen et al., 2005; Plagemann & Harder, 2005). Further, longer durations of breast feeding (e.g., 9 months compared with 1 month) are linked to reduced risks of overweight (Gillman et al., 2001; Harder, Bergmann, Kallischnigg, & Plagemann, 2005). The mechanism by which breast feeding may protect from weight-related problems could be its facilitation of early self-regulation of energy intake, which then could persist later in life. Or the mechanism(s) could be related to the nutritional properties (hormones, peptides, or nutrients) of breast milk compared to formula. For example, maternal levels of circulating leptin, a hormone associated with satiety, correlate with levels of leptin in breast milk. Some evidence indicates that this early leptin exposure may contribute to energy and weight regulation (Miralles, Sanchez, Palou, & Pico, 2006). Additionally, formula-fed infants consume larger amounts of protein and generally gain weight more rapidly than breast-fed infants, possibly "programming" them for weight-related problems later in life (Cripps et al., 2005; Singhal & Lanigan, 2007).

Adding Solid Foods to the Diet

Typically, solid foods are introduced to complement breast milk or formula at around 4 to 6 months, the age at which infants have developed

This baby is learning to eat solid foods. It's a messy learning process!

the motor coordination for swallowing food. Rice cereal mixed with breast milk or formula is often a first "solid" food (food is more soggy than solid in the early exposures). Later, pureed meats, fruits, and vegetables are added. Most babies have an innate preference for the sweet-tasting (and more energy-dense) fruits and veggies, such as pureed bananas, sweet potatoes, applesauce, and peaches, and an aversion for the bitter foods such as pureed green beans or spinach. As discussed earlier in this chapter, repeated exposure to initially disliked foods effectively increases the liking and acceptance of those foods. Around 7 to 9 months, finger foods are added, requiring the fine motor coordination of a pincher grasp.

Over time, the ratio of solid food to breast milk or formula increases, and often by age 1 or 2, a child's diet no longer includes breast milk or formula.

So, in a relatively short period of time (from about 6 months in age to 1 year), a baby learns to accept a spoon, move food to the back of the mouth, and safely swallow it (in earlier months, babies reflexively spit food out, which often results in a mess!), then to pick up foods and chew them before swallowing, and lastly to use a spoon independently (or at least start to). These are important developmental milestones that depend on physical ability and readiness, cognitive processing, and guidance from parents or caretakers. It is during this time that children are introduced to cultural norms and also to family norms regarding eating behavior, including meal times, foods associated with particular meals, meal and snack size, table manners, proper use of utensils, and so on. Certainly these are not well understood or mastered at age 1, but a foundation for what will be considered "normal" eating behavior in a particular culture is established. Thus, a parent's role in these early months and years is tremendously influential.

NOT NEEDING A BOTTLE, BUT STILL NEEDING GUIDANCE: EATING IN EARLY CHILDHOOD

One important job that parents and caregivers have is ensuring that infants and young children are receiving proper nutrition (calories and nutrients) to grow well and maintain health. This is sometimes a difficult task because babies and very young children cannot always communicate specific desires or needs. For example, a crying toddler may want more juice or cereal; may be tired, sick, hurt; or may want a particular toy that is out of reach. Parents are often good guessers as to the child's needs, but clearly there is room for error. In our current culture, this error often is overfeeding or feeding comfort foods high in calories and fat when a child cries. These attempts at meeting needs or soothing an upset child can establish an emotional link with food early in life, increasing the likelihood that as the child grows past infancy, he or she will continue to eat for emotional rather than hunger needs. In this section, we explore evidence that infants and children have some ability to regulate their food (energy) needs, but this ability is decreased as children become older and more aware of environmental cues.

Can Infants and Young Children Self-Regulate Energy Needs?

The question of whether or not infants and young children can innately regulate calorie and nutrient needs has been long debated. In the early 1900s, the philosophy among pediatricians was that children should be fed specific and regulated diets. It was assumed that without parental guidance,

children would choose unhealthy ratios of macro- and micronutrients. Thus, parents were advised to exercise an authoritarian approach to eating, leading to commonly used phrases such as "clean your plate." A landmark study by pediatrician Clara Davis (1939) challenged this thinking. She studied 15 newly weaned infants for several months in an institutional setting. Initially, all of the solid foods were novel. In this institution, meals were served at fixed times, but the infants had their choice of what to select (10–12 choices were available at each meal) and how much of each to eat. Davis maintained records of food choices and amounts consumed for several years (up to 4.5 years for two of the children).

An important finding was that children consumed only a few food items at a meal, typically two or three items. Also, children went on what Davis called "food jags," eating only one or two foods for several days in a row. However, over time, those preferences changed so that overall children selected a diet that contained approximately 17% of calories as protein, 35% as fat, and 48% as carbohydrate, healthy ratios of macronutrients for children. Lastly, despite large individual differences in feeding habits, all of the children grew well and were deemed healthy. Davis interpreted her data as support for an "innate self-selection mechanism," which was in striking contrast at the time to the leading philosophy among pediatricians. Davis advocated allowing children to self-select food items and amounts. Following the publication of her findings, pediatricians and parents began loosening controls on children's eating with the new understanding that children had the innate ability to self-regulate energy and nutrient needs.

Are you surprised by Davis's findings? Let's examine some of the details of her study a bit more. The food choices for infants and toddlers in Davis's study included beets, spinach, fruit, oatmeal, potatoes, milk, fish, and meat (liver, brains, beef, kidneys, lamb). Do those menu options sound very appealing to you? Do you think that a typical American 4-year-old would excitedly choose a dinner of liver and beets? Probably not! So, would the results of Davis's study have been the same if she used today's typical kids' menu options? Imagine offering a child all-you-can-eat chicken nuggets, french fries, cookies, pizza, ice cream, and candy every day for years. It is very likely that the child will eat beyond his or her energy needs, and not regulate vitamin and mineral levels. Unfortunately, this scenario is the reality in our current environment. We have easy access to highly palatable foods and a poor ability to self-regulate caloric intake under these conditions. Perhaps if our only options were items like those in Davis's study, we (children and adults) would be much better at maintaining healthy weights. So, despite the groundbreaking results of Davis's study at the time, the innate ability to self-regulate energy seems to work well only in an environment with less palatable and less calorie- and fat-dense foods than those prevalent in modern Western society.

Experimental Studies of Caloric Regulation

Some research suggests that infants and young children (~2 months to 3 years) have internal controls for caloric regulation and that these controls are less effective in older children. For example, Fomon, Filmer, Thomas, Anderson, and Nelson, (1975) found that 6-week-old infants consumed more of dilute (~5 kcal/ml) than dense (~10 kcal/ml) formula. However, over time, they did not achieve perfect caloric compensation. That is, the

A typical meal for American children.

TALKING POINT 6.1

How would you advise parents to monitor children's food choices? Consider both Davis's findings and the rising number of overweight children in Western countries. Revisit this question after you complete the chapter; you may have additional ideas or you may consider some modifications to your initial advice.

volume consumed of the half-strength formula was not double that of the high strength. Recall what you read earlier in this chapter about formula feeding (or bottle feeding) in general: It is an externally imposed regimen of size and time and although these are young infants, they presumably already have had a lot of prior bottle feedings. Thus, these infants may already have learned about portion size and average caloric yield, and so their adaptation to this caloric manipulation may be compromised or limited by prior experience. Other findings indicate that overall energy intake remains constant when solid foods are added to the diets of breast-fed babies, meaning that the infants compensate for the added calories by consuming less breast milk (Savage et al., 2007).

Evidence shows that preschoolers exercise at least short-term (within meal) caloric compensation. A protocol used by Birch and her colleagues in several studies over the past 20 years involved giving a calorically disguised first course (which serves as a preload) followed about 30 minutes later by a self-selected second course (e.g., lunch). Birch found that after a low-calorie preload, the selected meal was calorically larger than after a high-calorie preload. This study design demonstrates short-term caloric adjustment. Interestingly, but perhaps not surprisingly, caloric regulation is poorer in overweight children (Birch & Fisher, 2000; Johnson & Birch, 1994). To quantify the precision of regulation, Birch's group developed the **compensation index**, a measurement of the difference in caloric intake at the second course divided by the caloric difference in the preload. An index of +1 indicates perfect compensation and an index of 0 indicates no effect of the preload (i.e., no compensation). They and others have used the compensation index as a mechanism for quantifying energy compensation in studies of children's eating.

Does caloric compensation occur over a longer period of time? Birch, Johnson, Andresen, Peters, and Schulte (1991) measured 24-hour intakes of children (ages 2–5) over a 6-day period. The children received the same menus each day. Like Davis, Birch found that intake at individual meals was highly variable. In comparison,

BOX 6.4   Do Children Recognize Calories?

Birch, McPhee, Steinberg, and Sullivan (1990) found that children demonstrated conditioned flavor preferences based on caloric density. Novel drink flavors were used in these trials, and the drinks were either high in calories (155 kcal/150 ml) or low (less than 5 kcal/150 ml). (A low-calorie sweetener was used to reduce calories.) The children consumed the beverage and were then allowed to consume additional snacks as desired (milk, cheese, fruit, cookies). The trials actually substituted for the children's regularly scheduled morning snack, thus not interfering with normal meals or routines. At the end of the study, the children reported increased liking of both flavors, a function of the mere exposure effect. However, they had greater liking of the flavor associated with higher calories, both rating it higher and consuming it when given a choice between the flavors. Additionally, the children consumed fewer snacks after consumption of the flavor associated with high calories, indicating learned energy regulation.

24-hour energy intakes were relatively constant. This implies meal-to-meal adjustments of intake for longer-term caloric regulation. However, menu options in this study, as in Davis's, were relatively nutritious items (e.g., turkey sandwiches, fruit, and yogurt) compared to the calorie-dense and nutrient-poor foods found in many restaurants and homes in our current Western culture.

In a subsequent study to directly manipulate this situation, children were again studied over several days, but on some days 14 grams of dietary fat (~130 kcal, which is more than 10% of the total mean caloric intake) were substituted by a zero-calorie fat substitute ("fake fat"—chemically modified fat molecules that cannot be broken down in the gut and absorbed). For example, muffins were baked with fake fat on low-calorie/fat days and with butter on high-calorie/fat days, but the muffins and other manipulated foods were otherwise as similar as possible in appearance and taste. The results again showed high variability between meals, but daily energy intake was constant regardless of whether fake or real fat was offered (Birch, Johnson, Jones, & Peters, 1993). This shows that children are able to compensate for the low-fat version by eating more of other foods, even when they are not aware of the manipulation. What are the implications? This study not only demonstrated caloric regulation in children, it also helped explain the general lack of success that many dieters have when exchanging their regular snacks for low-fat versions. It is likely that dieters compensate the calories and fat grams by consuming more of other foods.

Following a large meal, children tend to regulate calories by eating fewer food items in a second meal, but they do not regulate calories by reducing the amount of each item consumed in the next meal. Children tend to choose their preferred foods in the second meal and eliminate the less preferred, which are typically the more nutritious foods (Birch et al., 1993). And, different children have different preferred foods. Fisher and Birch (1995) found that when children were allowed to self-select their foods (over a 6-day period), their percentage of calories taken from fat varied greatly among them (from 25% to 41%

TALKING POINT 6.2

What type of study could you do to separate genetic from environmental influences on eating behavior and weight?

of calories from fat). Some children consistently chose a high-fat diet and some a low-fat diet, despite having the same choices. Not surprisingly, the children with the highest preference for fat had the highest body mass index (BMI) and also the heaviest parents (Fisher & Birch, 1995; Johnson & Birch, 1994). These results indicate the importance of familial factors in establishing dietary intake and choice in children, although the findings do not discriminate between genetic and environmental influences.

EXTERNAL INFLUENCES ON CHILDREN'S EATING: DISRUPTIONS IN ENERGY SELF-REGULATION

Taken together, studies of caloric and nutrient regulation, from Davis's in the 1930s to many conducted in recent decades, indicate that infants and young children have some ability to regulate energy needs both within and across meals. However, this regulation is imperfect and becomes blunted with age. Self-regulation of energy need is disrupted by the external influences to which older children are exposed, including food attractiveness and palatability, eating behaviors of peers, media, and parental behaviors and attitudes. Thus, with age, children are more likely to eat in response to external cues rather than internal physiological hunger cues.

Parenting Styles, Attitudes, and Weights

Parenting styles and approaches to children's eating have been found to impact food choices and calorie and fat regulation among children. Children of **authoritarian** parents (parents who are controlling, set strict rules, and expect obedience) have a reduced ability to regulate calorie needs (Johnson & Birch, 1994). Further, the more authoritarian the parents, the poorer a child's ability to regulate. This parenting style, in contrast with permissive and authoritative styles, is associated with behaviors such as demanding that the child eat particular foods while forbidding others, without regard for child's needs or preferences. **Permissive parenting** style is associated with few parental regulations or controls. Regarding eating behavior, permissive parents tend to let children have what they want when they want it. These conditions require the child to make his or her own decisions, which typically leads to consumption of the tastiest, most easily available foods (as the child is limited to whatever is in the home or at school).

Authoritative parenting is the happy middle ground between authoritarian and permissive parenting. Authoritative parents provide structure and guidelines but explain the reasons for them and allow flexibility when warranted. This parenting style regarding eating includes behaviors such as encouraging healthy eating and explaining the benefits of a healthy lifestyle, but not forcing children to eat foods that are disliked. Rather, an authoritative parent is likely to offer healthy food options that children can select from. Children of authoritative parents have increased eating of healthy foods (fruits and vegetables) and reduced eating of junk foods, compared with children of authoritarian parents (Patrick, Nicklas, Hughes, & Morales, 2005).

Children of parents who restrict or forbid certain foods, a behavior often associated with the authoritarian style, are more likely to overeat in the absence of hunger, to have higher BMI, and to suffer with body image issues and eating disorders during adolescence. This effect is most pronounced among daughters of restrictive mothers (Birch, Fisher, & Davison, 2003; Johnson & Birch, 1994). When foods are labeled "forbidden," children have reduced ability to control their eating of those foods when given access (perhaps at a friend's house). Researchers have also shown that when food is used as a reward or bribe (e.g., "if you clean your room you can have a cookie"), the liking of that food increases. And, interestingly, promising a treat for eating a disliked food (e.g., "you can have ice cream if you eat your spinach") actually increases the liking of the treat and worsens the aversion for the disliked food (Birch, Birch, Marlin, & Kramer, 1982; Savage et al., 2007). Essentially, all of these examples (restricting, forbidding, using food as a reward) focus attention on **external cues** and decrease a child's responsiveness to internal cues of hunger or satiety.

Homes of authoritative parents have more frequent availability of fruits, vegetables, and dairy, and less availability of junk food compared with homes of authoritarian parents. Thus, children of authoritative parents are more frequently exposed to and offered healthy foods. Further, authoritative parents are more likely to model the consumption of healthy foods. So, in addition to parenting style, children of authoritative parents are influenced by mere exposure and modeling (two learning principles) that further enhance their liking of healthy foods. Researchers have found that children of parents who eat more fruits and vegetables and drink more milk at home are more likely to like and consume the same foods even when they are not at home (see Savage et al. [2007] for a more thorough review).

Parents' food choices and BMIs are also correlated with those of their children (Johnson

TALKING POINT 6.3

Research indicates that children of authoritative parents not only have healthier eating habits, but also tend to have higher self-esteem and greater success in life, compared with children of permissive or authoritarian parents. So, why do you think that the authoritative style is not used by all parents?

& Birch, 1994). Parents who consume more junk food have higher BMIs as do their children. And children of parents who themselves have difficulty controlling their eating also have poorer ability at regulating energy needs. These effects are more pronounced among girls, particularly obese girls. Can you think of explanations for these correlations? Perhaps the effect is due to shared genes. Certainly, genes do predispose individuals to deposit fat in particular places in their body and to metabolize energy at varying rates. But do you think that shared genetics is the only explanation? It is probably not, given the rapid rise in the obesity rate. Shared environment is also a likely explanation. Parents and children in these homes are eating many of the same foods, often those high in fat and calories. Parents model eating of these types of foods, whereas eating of healthy fruits and vegetables is not frequent in these homes.

Obesity is seen among people of all socioeconomic status (SES) levels, but the highest incidence is among people in poverty conditions, or low SES. What is interesting and paradoxical about this situation is that people in this group have both the highest rates of reported hunger and the highest rates of obesity. How could this be? Low SES families often have reduced access to fresh fruits and vegetables, but convenient access to junk food, which is typically high in calories and fat and low in nutritional value. Some low SES communities in Western society have recently been considered to be in "food deserts," areas characterized by limited accessibility to nutritional foods. Limited exposure to healthy

foods (i.e., they are infrequently accessible and their consumption is rarely modeled) increases the likelihood that children will have unhealthy diets and weight problems later in life.

Social Influences

With age, children are increasingly influenced by their peers' behaviors, and this applies to eating behavior, too. Children are more likely to sample a novel food when consumption of that food is modeled by an adult or peer. Studies have shown that children will modify their food preference when they observe that a peer has a different preference (Addessi, Galloway, Visalberghi, & Birch, 2005). As an example, Birch (1980) found that preschool-age children would quickly select the fruit that the other children around them chose, even when the fruit that they typically preferred was available.

The effects of education about food seem to be age related. In a study involving jelly bean flavors, some familiar and others novel (e.g., grape, kiwi, watermelon, coffee, and Dr. Pepper) preschool-age children (3–6 years old) were told positive associations (e.g., "Grape is Winnie the Pooh's favorite flavor") for some flavors and not others. In a second phase, children were asked to rate the hedonic value (using smiley, neutral, or unhappy faces) of the flavors. Exposure to positive information had an effect on the hedonic rating of the flavors, but only for the children older than 4.5 years (Lumeng & Cardinal, 2007). This supports the theory that children are more impacted by external cues with age. It seems that

the maturation of areas of the brain associated with memory (e.g., hippocampus, frontal cortex) contribute to this effect of age.

Food Availability and Portion Sizes

As discussed in other chapters, the current food environment of the Western culture is obesogenic, meaning that food is easily available, energy dense, highly palatable, and heavily (or strategically) marketed. Further, **portion sizes** have increased progressively, leading to increased caloric intake. Studies have shown that children and adults eat more when they are served larger portions and generally do not compensate by eating less of other foods (Fisher, Rolls, & Birch, 2003; Fisher, Liu, Birch, & Rolls, 2007). Significant elevations in energy intake over a 24-hour period were found when portion sizes of entrees and snacks were doubled. Fisher and colleagues (2007) found that portion size and **energy density** have additive effects. Either factor alone increased overall energy intake, but together they had an enhanced impact on energy intake. Although this information is perhaps not surprising, it is important to have this type of empirical evidence, as many of the foods that we are exposed to, particularly in restaurants, are both of large portions and high in energy density.

Total caloric intake is also related to feeding frequency (Garcia et al., 1990a; 1990b). In one study children were fed two scheduled meals per day but additionally could request and receive snacks. They requested food frequently and ate a mean of 13.5 times per day. Children who ate more snacks consumed more calories per day; that is, snacks did not detract from main meal size. (So much for the mother's adage that too much snacking will spoil your appetite for dinner!) Of course, this implies that caloric compensation is weak, contrasting with Birch's findings. These results also indicate that frequent offering of food leads to increased eating. This information, paired with the results of the Fisher et al. (2007) study, illuminates how problematic our modern food environment has become for children. They are exposed to large portions of foods high in energy density and offered foods frequently while they are in the early process of establishing patterns of meal sizes and frequency.

Media

Marketers in the food industry base much of their work on the central tenets of classical conditioning. A seminal aim in advertising is to create positive associations between a branded food item, a store, or restaurant and the customers. It is estimated that more than $7 billion is spent on advertisements for U.S. food products (see Story & French [2004] for a review of marketing directed toward children). Commercials depicting happy children singing and eating a particular food item lead to associations in the minds of children and parents between consumption of that food and positive experiences. As an example, McDonald's has been one of the most successful businesses at associating its brand and food items with positive experiences. Its kids' meal is the "Happy Meal," the Ronald McDonald clown makes appearances at children birthday parties, and the restaurants often have indoor play areas. These are among the powerfully effective marketing tools used by McDonald's (and other food businesses as well) to instill lifelong positive associations with their food items.

Robinson, Borzekowski, Matheson, and Kraemer (2007) demonstrated this effect. Preschool children were asked to taste familiar food items (hamburgers, chicken nuggets, and french fries from McDonald's and carrots, milk, and apple juice from a grocery store). The children tasted two identical samples of each food, one in McDonald's packaging and the other in unmarked wrapping. The children overwhelmingly preferred the food items in the branded packaging, even the carrots, which are not currently offered on McDonald's menu. We should add that it is not our intent to vilify any one brand or even class of foods, because all food companies are engaging in more or less the same behavior.

A recent study similarly demonstrated the preference that 4- to 6-year-old children have for snacks branded with popular cartoon characters (Scooby Doo, Dora the Explorer, or Shrek). Children both selected the cartoon-branded

TALKING POINT 6.4

If children are more likely to eat snacks with popular cartoon characters on the packaging, then don't you think that this type of marketing could help increase consumption of healthy fruits and veggies? Why do you think this tactic is not frequently used? (Hint: Consider costs.) Something else for you to think about: In 2007, the Department of Health and Human Services (HHS) and the Ad Council teamed up with DreamWorks studios to launch a healthy eating ad campaign featuring characters from the *Shrek* movie series.

Within months, members of children advocacy groups objected, some conducting letter-writing petitions in opposition. In the public service advertisements, *Shrek*

characters encouraged children to "get up and play." However, the Ad Council also teamed up with for-profit companies including Kraft Foods, General Mills, Kellogg's, Coca-Cola, and Pepsico among others. So, soon after the initiation of the campaign to combat childhood obesity, the *Shrek* character branding could be found on more than 70 food products, most of which were heavily processed, high in sugar, and low in nutrients, and many containing added green dye for effect. Some of the food products consequently associated with the government's "healthy living" campaign included Snicker's candy bars, pop-tarts, chocolate chip cookies, M&M candies, frozen waffles and pancakes, Twinkies, and several types of sugary cereals.

snacks more often and preferred the tastes of the branded snacks compared with the same snacks in unbranded packaging (Roberto, Baik, Harris, & Brownell, 2010).

Other studies have shown increased food consumption, particularly of sweet snacks, after viewing food advertisements compared with non-food-related advertisements on television (Halford, Gillespie, Brown, Pontin, & Dovey, 2004). Because many nutrient-poor and energy-dense snacks (e.g., candies, fruit roll-ups, cookies, sugary cereals) are frequently marketed to children with popular cartoon characters, instilling preferences for healthier foods is increasingly difficult. A group of researchers analyzed the nutritional content of food depicted in television shows aimed at children age 5 and younger (Radnitz et al., 2009). They found that unhealthy foods were shown about twice as often as healthy foods, and that the characters on these shows frequently endorsed consumption and overconsumption of unhealthy food.

Overweight children are influenced by external influences and marketing to a greater extent than normal weight children. In a study by Forman, Halford, Summe, MacDougall, and Keller (2009), normal weight children consumed

fewer calories when a meal was branded, but overweight children consumed significantly more calories when the meal was branded versus non-branded. Their findings indicate that overweight children are more likely to recognize marketed food items and eat more when food is associated with marketed brands. Halford et al. (2004) also found that obese children were more likely than normal weight children to recognize food advertisements; further, the amount of snacks consumed was correlated with familiarity with the advertisement. This associative learning may put overweight children at a greater risk for obesity and associated health problems in a media-saturated environment.

IMPLICATIONS FOR INSTILLING HEALTHY EATING HABITS IN CHILDREN

Prenatal and early postnatal food and flavor experiences prepare children for the variety of foods that they will encounter in their culture. Exposure to healthy foods during this early time in life enhances children's acceptance of otherwise novel foods. This helps minimize "picky" eating of only heavily processed foods that are high in fat and calories and low in nutrients (e.g., foods often found on restaurant menus for children such as chicken nuggets and hot dogs). Children enter the present food environment with a better predisposition for healthy living when exposed to fruits and vegetables rather than excessive junk food during prenatal (through amniotic fluid) and early postnatal months (through breast milk). When infants begin consuming solid foods, parents should be patient with the process and continue to offer nutritious foods repeatedly, as acceptance and liking of novel foods (especially bitter-tasting vegetables) can take many exposures. Results of a study of children's eating behavior revealed that the most frequently consumed vegetable among toddlers is french fries (Fox, Pac, Devaney, & Jankowski, 2004). Clearly, parents and caregivers too infrequently prioritize the need for early exposure to a healthy variety of foods.

As children grow, parents and caregivers should encourage them to focus on their internal hunger and satiety cues and minimize the focus on external cues by refraining from using phrases such as "you must clean your plate." Parents should also be mindful of their own eating behaviors, both for their own health and as models for their children. Children's consumption of healthy fruits, vegetables, and dairy is correlated with their parents' consumption of the same foods. After extensive research of children's eating behaviors, Birch and Fisher (2000) suggested that parents should provide children with a variety of balanced foods at each meal, but be nondirective about what items and how much are eaten. The argument (like Davis's) is that children will come to focus on their own internal controls ("listen to what their bodies are telling them"), select a nutritionally adequate diet, and be less prone to obesity or eating disorders as teens or adults. This may be especially important in girls, as the loss of internal compensation in obese girls (and the reason that led to their obesity) may reflect this externalization of control by an **authoritarian parenting** style regarding eating.

Finally, as a society, we need to seriously consider the impact that our current food environment has on the health of the current and next generations. The obesity rate has increased dramatically in the past 30 years and unfortunately continues to rise. Childhood obesity rates have also risen, and data from the Centers for Disease Control and Prevention (2007) indicate that one in three children born in the year 2000 or more recently will develop type 2 diabetes (a disorder typically associated with unhealthy eating and weight). The economic burden of the preventable health problems associated with obesity is staggering. Further, obesity (or unhealthy weight) is correlated with psychological dysfunction. Overweight children are at a much greater risk for developing depression during adolescence and adulthood. These mental and physical health issues negatively impact quality of life—and much of this can be prevented by a healthy lifestyle, which includes healthy eating.

So, whereas parents certainly share responsibility for the health of their children, our culture needs to change so that healthy eating is of greater importance. School lunches, for example, should include fresh fruits and vegetables and healthy ratios of micro- and macronutrients. Many children are not provided healthy food options at home; thus, school may be the only environment in which some children have at least one daily exposure to healthy foods. This affords children the opportunity to overcome neophobia of novel foods and increases the likelihood that they will make healthy food choices later in life. Children exposed only to foods such as pizza, burgers, and

TALKING POINT 6.5

Do you think, both at theoretical and practical/ethical levels, that you could use the compensation index as a diagnostic test for children at risk for later eating disorders and try to reeducate them and their parents?

chicken nuggets will continue to choose only those foods later in life, and this is a pattern associated with poor health. Certainly, the inclusion of regular exercise in physical education classes, play time, and sports is another way that schools and communities can promote healthy living. And as shown by the failure of the *Shrek* campaign to reduce childhood obesity, we cannot expect for-profit corporations to regulate healthy eating or lifestyle.

Let's review and apply your knowledge. Take some time to answer these chapter questions

1. Describe at least three pieces of evidence that demonstrate the effects of prenatal experience on eating behavior later in life.
2. How might breast feeding enhance healthy eating among children later in life? Explain.
3. Describe Dr. Clara Davis's study and her conclusions. What do you think about her findings in light of our current food environment?
4. How do parenting styles and parents' eating behaviors and weight influence children's eating behaviors and weight? Are gender or socioeconomic status contributing factors?
5. What is the evidence of the impact of peer influence and media on children's eating behavior? Does weight contribute to this? Explain.

Glossary

Authoritarian parenting   A style characterized by control, strict rules, and expectations of obedience.

Authoritative parenting   A style that encourages a child's independence but provides guidelines and structure.

Compensation index   A measurement of the difference in caloric intake at the second course divided by the caloric difference in the preload; an index of +1 indicates perfect compensation and an index of 0 indicates no effect of the preload (i.e., no compensation).

Energy density   The amount of energy in a given weight of food.

External cues   Stimuli in the environment (e.g., sight and smell of food, eating behavior of others, attractiveness of food).

Permissive parenting   A style characterized by few rules or limits.

Portion size   The amount of allotted food.

References

Addessi, E., Galloway, A. T., Visalberghi, E., & Birch, L. L. (2005). Specific social influences on the acceptance of novel foods in 2–5-year-old children. *Appetite, 45*, 264–271.

Arenz, S., Rückerl, R., Koletzko, B., & Von Kries, R. (2004). Breast-feeding and childhood obesity—a systematic review. *International Journal of Obesity Related Metabolic Disorders 28*, 1247–1256.

Bayol, S. A., Farrington, S. J., & Stickland, N. C. (2007). A maternal "junk food" diet in pregnancy and lactation promotes an exacerbated taste for "junk food" and a greater propensity for obesity in rat offspring. *British Journal of Nutrition*. Doi: 10.1017/S0007114507812037

Beauchamp, G. K., Cowart, B. J., Mennella, J. A., & Marsh, R. R. (1994). Infant salt taste: Developmental, methodological, and contextual factors. *Developmental Psychobiology, 27*(6), 353–365.

Beauchamp, G. K., Cowart, B. J., & Moran, M. (1986). Developmental changes in salt acceptability in human infants. *Developmental Psychobiology, 19*, 17–25.

Beauchamp, G. K., & Mennella, J. A. (2009). Early flavor learning and its impact on later feeding behavior. *Journal of Pediatric Gastroenterology and Nutrition, 48*, S25–S30.

Birch, L. L. (1980). Effects of peer models' food choices and eating behaviors on preschooler's food preferences. *Child Development, 51*, 489–496.

Birch, L. L. (1999). Development of food preferences. *Annual Review of Nutrition, 19*(1), 41–62.

Birch, L. L, Birch, D., Marlin, D. W., & Kramer, L. (1982). Effects of instrumental consumption on children's food preference. *Appetite, 3*, 125–134.

Birch, L. L., & Fisher, J. O. (2000). Mothers' child-feeding practices influence daughters' eating and weight. *The American Journal of Clinical Nutrition, 71*(5), 1054–1061.

Birch, L. L., Fisher, J. O., & Davison, K. K. (2003). Learning to overeat: Maternal use of restrictive feeding practices promotes girls' eating in the absence of hunger. *American Journal of Clinical Nutrition, 78*(2), 215–220.

Birch, L. L., Johnson, S. L., Andresen, G., Peters, J. C., & Schulte, M. C. (1991). The variability of young children's energy intake. *The New England Journal of Medicine, 324*(4), 232–235.

Birch, L. L., Johnson, S. L., Jones, M. B., & Peters, J. C. (1993). Effects of a nonenergy fat substitute on children's energy and macronutrient intake. *The American Journal of Clinical Nutrition, 58*(3), 326–333.

Birch L. L., McPhee, L., Steinberg, L., & Sullivan, S. (1990). Conditioned flavor preferences in young children. *Physiology & Behavior, 47*(3), 501–505.

Black, B. E., Allen, L. H., Bhutta, Z. A., Caulfield, L. E., de Onis, M., Ezzati, M., ... Rivera, J. (2008). Maternal and child undernutrition: Global and regional exposures and health consequences. doi:10.1016/S0140-6736(07)61690-0

Centers for Disease Control and Prevention. (2007). 2007 National Diabetes Fact Sheet. Retrieved from http://www.cdc.gov/diabetes/pubs/figuretext07.htm

Centers for Disease Control and Prevention. (2009). Breastfeeding report card—United States, 2009. Retrieved from http://www.cdc.gov/breastfeeding/pdf/2009BreastfeedingReportCard.pdfON

Cripps, R. X., Martin-Gronert, M. X., & Ozanne, S. X. (2005). Fetal and perinatal programming of appetite. *Clinical Science, 109*(1), 1–12.

Crystal, S. R., & Bernstein, I. L. (1995). Morning sickness: Impact on offspring salt preference. *Appetite, 25*, 231–240.

Curtis, K. S., Krause, E. G., Wong, D. L., & Contreras, R. J. (2004). Gestational and early postnatal dietary NaCl levels affect NaCl intake, but not stimulated water intake, by adult rats. *Journal of Physiology—Regulatory, Integrative and Comparative Physiology, 286*, 1043–1050.

Davis, C. (1939). Results of the self selection of diets by young children. *The Canadian Medical Association Journal, 41*, 257–261.

Field, C. J. (2005). The immunological components of human milk and their effect on immune development in infants. *The Journal of Nutrition, 135*(1), 1–4.

Fisher, J. A., & Birch, L. L. (1995). Fat preferences and fat consumption of 3- to 5-year-old children are related to parental adiposity. *Journal of the American Dietetic Association, 95*, 759–764.

Fisher, J. O., Liu, Y., Birch, L. L. & Rolls, B. J. (2007). Effects of portion size and energy density on young children's intake at a meal. *American Journal of Clinical Nutrition, 86*, 174–179.

Fisher, J. O., Rolls, B. J., & Birch, L. L. (2003). Children's bite size and intake of an entrée are greater with large portions than with age-appropriate or self-selected portions. *American Journal of Clinical Nutrition, 77*, 1164–1170.

Fomon, S. J., Filmer, L. J., Thomas, L. N., Anderson, T. A., & Nelson, S. E. (1975). Influence of formula concentration on caloric intake and growth of normal infants. *Acta Paediatrica Scandanavia, 64*, 172–181.

Formon, J., Halford, J. C. G., Summe, H., MacDougall, M., & Keller, K. L. (2009). Food branding influences ad libitum intake differently in children depending on weight status. *Appetite, 53*, 76–83.

Forestell, C. A., & Mennella, J. A. (2007). Early determinants of fruit and vegetable acceptance. *Pediatrics, 120*, 1247.

Fox, M. K., Pac, S., Devaney, B., & Jankowski, L. (2004). Feeding infants and toddlers study: What foods are infants and toddlers eating? *Journal of the American Dietetic Association, 104* (Supplement 1), S22–S30.

Garcia, S. E., Kaiser, L. L., & Dewey, K. G. (1990a). Self-regulation of food intake among rural Mexican preschool children. *European Journal of Clinical Nutrition, 44*(5), 371–380.

Garcia, S. E., Kaiser, L. L., & Dewey, K. G. (1990b). The relationship of eating frequency and caloric density to energy intake among rural Mexican preschool children. *European Journal of Clinical Nutrition, 44*(5), 381–387.

Gartner, L. M., Morton, J., Lawrence, R. A., Naylor, A. J., O'Hare, D., Schanler, R. J., & Eidelman, A. I.

(2005). Breastfeeding and the use of human milk. *Pediatrics, 115*(2), 496–506.

Gillman, M. W., Rifas-Shiman, S. L., Camargo Jr., C. A., Berkey, C. S., Frazier, A. L., Rockett, H. R., ... & Colditz, G. A. (2001). Risk of overweight among adolescents who were breastfed as infants. *Journal of the American Medical Association, 285*(19), 2461–2467.

Halford, J. C., Gillespie, J., Brown, V., Pontin, E. E., & Dovey, T. M. (2004). Effect of television advertisements for food on food consumption in children. *Appetite, 42*(2), 221–225.

Harder, T., Bergmann, R., Kallischnigg, G., & Plagemann, A. (2005). Duration of breastfeeding and risk of overweight: A meta-analysis. *American Journal of Epidemiology, 162*(5), 397–403.

Hausner, H., Nicklaus, S., Issanchou, S., Mølgaard, C., & Møller, P. (2009). Breastfeeding facilitates acceptance of a novel dietary flavour compound. *Clinical Nutrition, 29*(1), 141–148.

Herring, S. J., Rose, M. Z., Skouteris, H., & Oken, E. (2012). Optimizing weight gain in pregnancy to prevent obesity in women and children. *Diabetes, Obesity, & Metabolism,14*(3), 195–203. doi: 10.1111/j.1463-1326.2011.01489

Johnson, S. L., & Birch, L. L. (1994). Parents' and children's adiposity and eating style. *Pediatrics, 95*(5), 653–661.

Kramer, M. S., & Kakuma, R. (2012). Optimal duration of exclusive breastfeeding. *Cochrane Database of Systematic Reviews*, Issue 8. Art. No.: CD003517. DOI: 10.1002/14651858.CD003517.pub2

Lechtig, A., Habicht, J., Delgado, H., Klein, R. E., Yarbrough, C., & Martorell, R. (1975). Effect of food supplementation during pregnancy on birthweight. *Pediatrics, 56*(4), 508.

Levin, B. E. (2006). Metabolic imprinting: Critical impact of the perinatal environment on the regulation of energy homeostasis. *Philosophical Transactions of the Royal Society B: Biological Sciences, 361*(1471), 1107–1121.

Lumeng, J. C., & Cardinal, T. M. (2007). Providing information about a flavor to preschoolers: Effects on liking and memory for having tasting it. *Chemical Senses, 32*, 505–513.

Matheny, R. J., Birch, L. L., & Picciano, M. F. (1990). Control of intake by human-milk-fed infants: Relationships between feeding size and interval. *Developmental Psychobiology, 23*(6), 511–518.

Mattson, S. N., & Riley, E. P. (2006). A review of the neurobehavioral deficits in children with fetal alcohol syndrome or prenatal exposure to alcohol. *Alcoholism: Clinical and Experimental Research, 22*(2), 279–294.

Mayer, E. A. (2011). Gut feelings: The emerging biology of gut-brain communication. *Nature Reviews Neuroscience, 12*(8), 453–466.

Mennella, J. (2001). Regulation of milk intake after exposure to alcohol in mothers' milk. *Alcoholism: Clinical and Experimental Research, 25*(4), 590–593.

Mennella, J.A., Jagnow, C.P., & Beauchamp, G.K. (2001). Prenatal and postnatal flavor learning by human infants. *Pediatrics, 107*, 88–94.

Menella, J. A., Johnson, A., & Beauchamp, G. K. (1995). Garlic ingestion by pregnant women alters the odor of amniotic fluid. *Chemical Senses, 20*(2), 207–209.

Miralles, O., Sanchez, J., Palou, A., & Pico, C. (2006). A physiological role of breast milk leptin in body weight control in developing infants. *Obesity, 14*, 1371–1377.

Mistretta, C. M., & Bradley, R. M. (1975). Taste and swallowing in utero: A discussion of fetal sensory function. *British Medical Bulletin, 31*(1), 80–84.

Owen, C. G., Martin, R. M., Whincup, P. H., Davey Smith, G., Gillman, M. W., & Cook, D. G. (2005). The effect of breast-feeding on mean body mass index throughout life: A quantitative review of published and unpublished observational evidence. *American Journal of Clinical Nutrition, 82*, 1298–1307.

Patrick, H., Nicklas, T. A., Hughes, S. O., & Morales, M. (2005). The benefits of authoritative feeding style: Caregiver feeding styles and children's food consumption patterns. *Appetite, 44*, 243–249.

Plagemann, A., & Harder, T. (2005). Breast feeding and the risk of obesity and related metabolic diseases in the child. *Metabolic Syndrome and Related Disorders, 3*(3), 222–232.

Radnitz, C., Byrne, S., Goldman, R., Sparks, M., Gantshar, M., & Tung, K. (2009). Food cues in children's television programs. *Appetite, 52*, 230–233.

Roberto, C. A., Baik, J., Harris, J. L., & Brownell, K. D. (2010). Influence of licensed characters on children's taste and snack preferences. *Pediatrics, 126*, 88–93.

Robinson, T. N., Borzekowski, D. L., Matheson, D. M., & Kraemer, H. C. (2007). Effects of fast food branding on young children's taste preferences. *Archives of Pediatric Adolescent Medicine, 161*(8), 792–797.

Roseboom, T., Rooij, S., & Painter, R. (2006). The Dutch famine and its long-term consequences for adult health. *Early Human Development, 82*, 485–491.

Savage, J. S., Fisher, J. O., & Birch, L. L. (2007). Parental influence on eating behavior. *Journal of Law and Medical Ethics, 35*, 22–34.

Singhal, A. A., & Lanigan, J. J. (2007). Breastfeeding, early growth and later obesity. *Obesity Reviews, 8,* 51–54.

Story, M., & French, S. (2004). Food advertising and marketing directed at children and adolescents in the US. *International Journal of Behavioral Nutrition and Physical Activity, 1*(3). doi:10.1186/1479-5868-1-3

Sullivan, S. A., & Birch, L. L., (1994). Infant dietary experience and acceptance of solid food. *Pediatrics, 93,* 271–277.

Tatzer, E., Schubert, M. T., Timischl, W., & Simbruner, G. (1985). Discrimination of taste and preference for sweet in premature babies. *Early Human Development, 12*(1), 23–30.

Social Influences on Eating

After reading this chapter, you will be able to

- Understand the meaning and determinants of cuisine
- Appreciate the influences of "food rules"
- Distinguish indirect versus direct influences on eating

- Recognize and critically consider the direct influences of others on our eating behavior
- Appreciate that the provider (person or company) carries meaning

Food often plays a central role in social gatherings, such as family meals, parties, or holiday events. Imagine attending a friend's birthday or graduation party or visiting a relative for a holiday such as Thanksgiving, and finding that no food was being served. That would likely be a disappointing surprise! Not only is food associated with social gatherings, but specific food items are often linked with particular holidays or occasions. For example, most of us anticipate that cake will be served at a birthday party. What foods do you expect or associate with other holidays or events? Have you ever wondered why this is? For example, why is eggnog often consumed during winter, but not summer, festivities?

In this chapter, we will explore the broader contextual or institutional influences that shape our eating behavior such as cuisine and religion,

and then the more immediate influence of other people on eating and food choice.

CUISINE

What constitutes **cuisine**, and how can we distinguish one cuisine from another? Do particular foods and preparations come to mind when you think of Chinese cuisine? What about when you think of Indian or Mexican cuisine? With each, you probably think of distinctly different foods, flavors, and preparations. According to influential researcher Paul Rozin and Elisabeth Rozin (author and culinary historian), "cuisines are defined by the basic ingredients they employ (e.g., rice, potatoes, fish), the characteristic flavors (flavor principles) employed (e.g., a combination of chili pepper with either tomato or lime for Mexico; a varied

Boy enjoying cake on his first birthday.

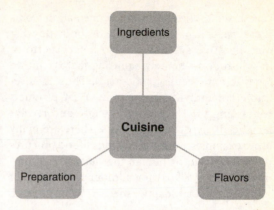

FIGURE 7.1 **Factors that define cuisine.**

mixture of spices called 'curry' for India), and particular modes of food preparation (e.g., stir-frying for China)" (Rozin, 1996a, p. 236; Figure 7.1).

Additionally, cuisine is influenced by cultural rules about which foods should be served with what and when. For example, it is socially acceptable and normal to have cereal with milk, toast with butter, and coffee with creamer for breakfast. However, the serving of this meal at

dinnertime would be considered odd, as would be pairing the foods differently (e.g., coffee with butter instead of creamer). But the serving of the same meal for breakfast at a home in Japan would not be considered the social norm; Japanese people typically eat rice and fish for breakfast.

Anthropologists regard cuisines as a reflection of adaptive (in a Darwinian evolutionary sense) choices for a particular environment. According to this widely accepted view, if a cuisine was maladaptive in some nutritional sense, then the culture practicing it would have become extinct. It is not a goal of the field of psychology to assess the optimality of a given cuisine for the environment in which it evolved; rather, psychology provides an account of human behavioral mechanisms that allow learning and perpetuation of adaptive eating behaviors. An example adaptation is the consumption of milk or milk products in many cultures despite lactose intolerance among adults. Lactase is a digestive enzyme that is required to break down milk sugar (lactose); although all healthy infants express this enzyme, the amount of the enzyme drops to very low levels after infancy in most ethnic groups of the world (e.g., those indigenous to Asia, Africa, the Americas). Lack of this enzyme makes adults lactose intolerant: Lactose is not absorbed from the stomach and this makes you feel ill. These cultures have either largely rejected milk products or use fermented/cultured products (yogurt, cheese, etc.). The reason that fermentation works is that specific bacteria outside the body do what our digestive systems can no longer perform in adulthood—namely, splitting lactose into a digestible molecule (lactic acid). Thus, lactose-intolerant individuals are able to eat products containing this "processed" lactose and receive beneficial energy and nutrients. There are many other examples around the world of food procurement facilitated by human ingenuity. We recommend Rozin (1996a) for additional evidence of cuisine as a social adaptive mechanism of survival.

Determinants of Cuisine

What factors contribute to the determination of ingredients, flavors, and preparation associated with particular cuisines? The first is availability (Figure 7.2). Cuisines largely consist of ingredients and flavors that are accessible and relatively inexpensive in terms of cost and effort to procure. This concept of behavioral economics is explored more thoroughly in other chapters. The mode of preparation typically also depends on what is available in that culture (e.g., tools and technology). Not all available foods and flavors will be adapted as part of a local cuisine; those that are most innately appealing (e.g., energy dense, sweet or salty tasting) are more likely than those that are less attractive (e.g., low in energy yield, bitter or bland tasting) to be incorporated into a cuisine.

A second important determinant of cuisine is the nutritional completeness of the ingredients. Because no natural food source provides all of the nutrients needed for an omnivore's adequate nutrition, combinations of foods are important. For example, served alone, beans, rice, and corn

provide inadequate sources of protein, but when served in pairs (beans and rice, beans and corn), they are complementary and provide adequate protein. This is why these combinations are staples in many Central and South American cultures where they are relatively easily grown and procured.

A third category contributing to the determination of cuisine is beliefs and attitudes, and these require social learning and the direct or indirect influence of others. This category includes religious beliefs and cultural attitudes, cultural food rules, perception of risk associated with particular foods, and attitudes about health. These will be discussed individually.

RELIGIOUS BELIEFS AND CULTURAL ATTITUDES The Hindu reverence of the "sacred cow" stems from the early belief in Indian culture that cows are an important self-renewing source of high-energy food (milk) and a symbol of life that should not be killed (Simoons, 1961). Consequently, beef is not eaten in Hindu cuisine. In fact, most Hindu Indians are vegetarians; none eat beef, and virtually all consider the taste or consumption of beef "disgusting" (Rozin & Fallon, 1987). Anthropologist Marvin Harris theorized that the prohibition of meat eating by Hindus is nutritionally adaptive: Cows are more useful as a dairy resource (in fermented products of course!) than as a meat resource. That is, a cow can provide many more important protein and fat calories in its lifetime from its milk than from its meat (Harris et al., 1966).

Harris also suggested that consumption of dog meat is taboo in Europe and North America because dogs are more useful as hunters or herders or are valuable as companions; in regions with little game and, as a consequence, no need for hunting or herding animals, dogs are considered acceptable as food, and in some areas are even considered delicacies (Harris & Ross, 1987). Regardless of the origin of these beliefs and attitudes about cows or dogs, they are set by the culture and not by any one individual's experience.

How likely are you to eat a sandwich that a bug just crawled across? Despite how unappealing

- Availability
- Nutritional completeness
- Beliefs and attitudes

FIGURE 7.2   **Determinants of cuisine.**

insects may be to you as food (or contaminants of food), they are widely consumed in many non-European cultures (DeFoliart, 1999). Insects such as caterpillars, termites, and locusts are frequently consumed in Africa and Asia, as these contain relatively high amounts of protein and other nutrients. And, importantly for inclusion in a local cuisine, they are easily available in the environment. So, why do we (Westerners) consider them disgusting as food? There is no clear-cut answer, except for the simple explanation that they did not become part of our cuisine.

Our cultural attitude is that insects are not food. Rozin conducted an interesting experiment to demonstrate the pervasiveness of this concept. He asked volunteers to consume juice into which a cockroach had just been dipped. (The juice was previously consumed and liked by the volunteers.)

The volunteers rejected it, despite knowing that the cockroach was dead and sterilized, thus could not actually contaminate the drink. Would you drink the juice if it were offered to you? What would be your rationale if you refused the drink? Rozin reported that volunteers' explanations included "it's a cockroach!" (Rozin, 1996a; Rozin, Millman, & Nemeroff, 1986). In other words, the *idea* of roach or insect, despite its cleanliness following sterilization, elicits a feeling of disgust that is a result of social learning. (Trust us, this attitude is not innate. Just ask any parent and you will be assured that 1- and 2-year-olds have no qualms about picking up and putting in their mouths nearly anything, including insects!)

CULTURALLY DETERMINED FOOD RULES

Cultural food rules dictate the time of day at which specific foods are considered appropriate, which foods should be served with which other foods, and how they should be eaten (e.g., with fingers, a fork, chopsticks). As previously mentioned, cereal for breakfast is considered normal according to American food rules, but it is generally unacceptable for dinner (or, at least, unexpected). We will highlight a few other cross-cultural comparisons of food rules. In the United States, salad is often served as a first course for dinner, whereas it is usually served after the main dish, as a third course, in France. In Japan, the dishes, or courses, of the dinner meal are

TALKING POINT 7.1

What are some of the food rules that you follow? Have you ever had cereal or oatmeal for dinner? Would you order such items for dinner if you were with others at a restaurant? Consider this: It is acceptable to have a donut, but not cake, for breakfast despite their similar macronutrients and tastes, and it would be considered odd to serve your dinner guests donuts for dessert, whereas cake is a typical dessert. Why do you think we follow these social food rules?

traditionally all served at once rather than in the sequential process that is typical in Western cultures. Americans typically consume french fries by picking them up with fingers. However, it is regarded as inappropriate to do the same with other potato preparations, such as roasted or baked potatoes. None of these food rules (and there are many) is inherently superior to any others, as they all allow for healthful eating. They are the result of social learning, and not biological necessity.

PERCEPTION OF RISK   You may recall mass media concern about mad cow disease, technically called bovine spongiform encephalopathy (BSE). This is a progressive and fatal neurological disease in cattle; neurological problems can result among people who consume contaminated beef, particularly if it contains nervous system tissue. In the United States, although no human health problems have been linked to contaminated beef, consumption of beef declined significantly for a few months in 2003 following the first report of an infected cow. This occurred nationwide (not just in areas near the location of the infected cow in the United States) and was accompanied by increased consumption of other meats such as chicken and pork (Schlenker & Villas-Boas, 2009). In cases like this and others, when the perception of risk associated with a particular food is high, the incorporation of it in the diet of that society decreases. Of course, this often makes good sense, particularly when other food options exist with fewer perceived risks. In the case of beef, the perceived risk was short lived, so it was not removed from the American cuisine. However, if risk associated with a particular food persists, whether it's actual or simply perceived, that food is eliminated from a culture's cuisine. Presumably, this is an explanation for the relative absence of dairy in Asian cuisine (as a result of lactose intolerance among that population).

Another example of a societally inflicted risk involves medication and juice. In today's world, health-promoting drugs are frequently taken, for example, to stabilize mood or reduce blood pressure. Many drugs are inactivated and

Example of a warning label on a container of prescription medication.

broken down in the intestine and liver by a particular enzyme (in the P450 family). Grapefruit juice contains compounds called *furanocoumarins* that can interfere with this enzyme's actions. Thus, the metabolism and hence effectiveness of many drugs (including statins, antidepressants, and many more) are potentially affected by grapefruit. Prescribing physicians routinely recommend that patients do not eat grapefruit, even though these drugs do not have a uniformly high risk of adverse interaction (see Bailey, Dresser, & Arnold [2012] for a review). The risk is sometimes that the drug would be more effective, but the idea of taking lower doses of the drug with grapefruit does not seem to have caught on. As a result of this risk that is passed down by physicians, sales of grapefruit juice have dropped, and grapefruit hybrids (e.g., pomelos) are being developed that have lower levels of furanocoumarins.

ATTITUDES ABOUT HEALTH   In modern Western cultures with food abundance, concerns about appearance and in particular thin appearance are common. Attitudes about food and health are also different in these cultures compared with more traditional cultures and less "Westernized" cultures. Nonetheless, despite the obesity epidemic, Americans are more likely than people in European countries and Japan to rate all fats as "harmful to health," despite known benefits of some fats (e.g., omega-3 fatty acids) in moderation. Americans also exhibit more anxiety

TALKING POINT 7.2

In 2012, three people in the United States died after eating contaminated cantaloupe. In 2006, five people died, including a 2-year-old boy, after consuming spinach tainted with E. coli. Did these stories have an effect on your food choices? What other food "scares" have you experienced? Have other perceived risks influenced your behavior? For example, have you ever changed travel plans after hearing of a plane crash or other disaster?

and guilt about eating (Rozin, Fischler, Imada, Sarubin, & Wrzesniewski, 1999). Rozin and colleagues have theorized that this heightened concern with healthy eating contributes to stress- and emotion-related eating and thus actually reduces our ability to moderate our food intake.

DIRECT VERSUS INDIRECT INFLUENCES

Eating behaviors, including food combinations, portion sizes, and timing of meals or snacks, are a culmination of a lifetime of experience. Starting in infancy, our parents and caregivers teach us what items are appropriate as food, how much we should eat, and when. Some of this teaching is direct or explicit (e.g., a parent's directive to "clean your plate"), and other teaching is more incidental or passive (e.g., modeling of parents' eating behaviors or exposure to flavors through breast milk). We will discuss other examples of the direct influence of others on our eating behavior in the next section, but first we will consider the combination of direct and indirect factors that shape cuisine and adherence to the associated food rules within a culture.

Indirect Influences

Indirect influences are those that are effective even in the absence of other people, although they most likely first developed in the presence of others. As a case in point, most of you are unlikely to consume the beverage with the roach previously discussed, regardless of whether or not other people are around. This is because you learned at an early age that roaches are not food, that they contaminate food and should be avoided. Likewise, as a consequence of social learning, Hindu Indians neither consume, nor want to consume, beef either when alone or in the presence of others.

What about portion sizes? How do you know how much of any particular food item to choose or consume when making your own selections? We typically consume food in amounts with which we are familiar. For example, you might have a sandwich, apple, and can of soda for lunch because this is a meal with which you have had prior positive experiences (e.g., no one laughed at you because this is a socially "normal" meal in Western culture, you felt appropriately satiated, and you didn't get sick). The sandwich may be relatively low in fat and calories, the apple quite small, and the soda calorie free; or the sandwich could be dense in fat and calories, the apple large, and the soda more than 100 calories. Yet, people typically consume such items in their entirety. Food and portion selections such as these occur with or without the presence of others, though earlier in life we learned of them from others (Nestle et al., 1998).

Availability, as previously discussed, is an important influence on our food selection, and this is largely an indirect influence. Availability of food is both a *determinant* and a *consequence* of cuisine. Upon being adopted as a staple in a particular cuisine, that food becomes much more accessible than foods that are not part of the cuisine. For instance, if you were to crave fish and rice for breakfast while visiting Japan, you would be in luck, because those are the items you are most likely to find in restaurants, markets, and

A typical Japanese breakfast and a typical American breakfast.

perhaps in the home in which you are a guest. You would be less fortunate, though, if you desired pancakes and bacon, as those items are not as frequently available. And the converse would be true in the United States: Pancakes and bacon are often on the menus for breakfast at restaurants and the ingredients are available in most grocery stores. Our desire for particular foods is shaped by experience, but our consumption of those foods is limited by our access, and this applies whether or not others are around us.

Direct Influences of Others

Direct influences are those that require the actual presence of others. It is known that people tend to eat more when in a group (de Castro, 1990). However, overconsumption including binge eating often occurs in isolation (Stice, Telch, &

Rizvi, 2000). Thus, whereas social gatherings often facilitate food consumption, social constraints may at the same time encourage healthy eating behavior. This has even been demonstrated in laboratory rats. Rats normally avoid novel foods but are more likely to consume a novel food and choose healthy ratios of macronutrients in the presence of a rat who is demonstrating these behaviors compared to rats tested alone (Galef, Kennett, & Stein, 1985; Galef, Attenborough, & Whiskin, 1990; Galef & Wright, 1995).

As omnivores, we are able to consume an incredibly wide range of food items, and we need to consume a variety of foods to obtain optimal nutrition. However, our natural attraction to new foods (neophilia) juxtaposes with our fear of potential dangers of new foods (neophobia); this is known as the **omnivore's paradox** (Fischler, 1980). Cultural beliefs, traditions, and rules provide guidance around which foods to eat, how much, and when, allowing a society to manage the omnivore's paradox. Thus, group or **commensal food consumption** allows for the sharing of these practices and the continuance of them among generations, keeping societies safe from danger and adequately nourished. Evidence suggests that cultures in which meals are consumed in group (e.g., family) settings have lower obesity rates and longer life expectancies than cultures in which individuals eat alone (e.g., Veugelers & Fitzgerald, 2005).

Renowned French sociologist Claude Fischler and others have surveyed people from the United States and several Western European

TALKING POINT 7.3

Let's explore some explanations for the link between poor management of the omnivore's paradox and obesity. Describe some of the reasons you think people tend to eat more when alone and free of food rules? Have you heard of the expression "mindless eating"? Have you experienced it? Do you eat alone when engaging in some other activity? Compare your list with those of your peers. Studies have indicated that we eat more when we are districted and less mindful of our food consumption (e.g., Wansink, 2006).

countries regarding attitudes about food, meals, and health (see Rozin's [2005] review of this research). French people, compared with Americans, feel that the quality of the food, drink, and company of others (essentially the meal *experience*) is more important than the quantity of the food. Further, the French spend more time per day consuming their meals (2 hours compared to 1 hour for Americans), consume a diet higher in fat, *and* have lower obesity rates. This is considered the "French paradox" (Drewnowski et al., 1996; Renaud & de Lorgeril, 1992). It seems that in postindustrial societies, such as the United States, rules of eating are loosening, and even vanishing, perhaps because meals are often eaten in isolation, reducing the opportunity for the sharing of food rules and healthy practices. Further, portion sizes are typically larger in countries like the United States. Fischler (1980, 1988) and others (e.g., Rozin, Kabnick, Pete, Fischler, & Shields, 2003) consider this lack of proper management of the omnivore's paradox to be a contributing factor to rising obesity.

It is known that we tend to copy the intake of others, closely matching the amount that the people around us are eating; this trend persists despite either extreme hunger or fullness (Herman, Koenig-Nobert, Peterson, & Polivy, 2005; Herman, Roth, & Polivy, 2003). We also tend to eat more when served food in large containers (Wansink & Sobal, 2007). Wansink and colleagues have demonstrated that we are largely unaware of the impact of these external factors, and we consequently underestimate our daily food consumption (see Vartanian, Herman, & Wansink [2008] and Wansink [2006] for more

on this). These findings support Fischler's (2011) belief that commensal eating helps maintain or constrain food consumption to appropriate levels. Eating in groups reduces the risk of overconsumption because of the awkwardness associated with deviation from social norms and may in some cases promote healthier food choices.

Why Do We Eat Previously Disliked Foods?

Children develop many food preferences on the basis of social-affective context; for example, foods eaten by parents, older siblings, peers or food items associated with fictional superheroes, smiling faces, and so on are often preferred. The acquired chili pepper preference in some cultures is an example of this socially mediated food liking. Spicy "hot" foods are innately disliked because they activate pain receptors in the mouth (Caterina et al., 1997). However, as children are slowly introduced to chili peppers with adult approval and encouragement, they come to like them (this is particularly evident in the Mexican culture; Rozin, 1996a).

You may have had a similar experience with coffee. Can you recall your first sip of black coffee? It probably tasted bitter and gross. The addition of sweetener and creamer made it taste much more appealing. Typically, the amount of sweetener and creamer preferred by coffee drinkers decreases, and over time people enjoy a beverage that they previously disliked. The role of associative learning in changing this type of food or flavor preference is discussed in other chapters. However, if coffee tasted disgusting to you on

your first exposure and you had no other positive associations with it, then why would you ever try coffee again? The fact is that coffee has many appealing associations in our culture—the smell of the kitchen on a relaxed morning, the vibe at popular coffee houses, studying with friends late into the night, and so on. Thus, we have a social motivation to overcome our innate dislike of the bitter taste, and we are reinforced for doing so, all resulting from the direct influences of others.

FOOD ASSOCIATIONS WITH THE PROVIDER

Most of us have fondness for foods made by familiar people (especially loved ones), served at particular restaurants, or associated with certain brands. Can you think of any examples of this that apply to your food preferences? Perhaps your grandmother's apple pie is your favorite. We feel connections to the handlers, providers, or brand associations of the food we eat. Grandma's pie is better because it was made by Grandma; particular cookies are better than others because they are branded in packaging for which we have positive associations. These associations are emotionally and psychologically rooted. Rozin (1996b) and anthropologists before him refer to this as the **law of contagion**, meaning that once two things have been in physical contact, that contact remains an influence even after the physical bond is broken (even to the point of nostalgia!). So, food prepared by people whom we like carries their "essence" and is preferred; conversely, food prepared by enemies or people we find unappealing will not be desired or enjoyed. In other cultures, such as the Hindu Indian culture, the law of contagion pertaining to human handlers is more evident as people are often acutely aware of the handler's identity and social status. In Western culture, we are often detached from the original sources of our food; thus, many of our food associations are with companies and logos rather than with individuals. We prefer food branded with the essence of companies with which we have positive associations to those with which we have unpleasant associations. Even at very young ages, children prefer branded over non-branded foods (Roberto, Baik, Harris, & Brownell, 2010; Robinson, Borzekowski, Matheson, & Kraemer, 2007), and this certainly persists into adulthood. Interestingly, our perception that certain branded foods taste better is associated with altered neural activity in areas of the brain associated with memory (McClure et al., 2004).

BOX 7.1   Are We Neurologically Affected By Labels?

Coke and Pepsi sodas are chemically nearly identical; however, many soda drinkers have strong allegiance to and preference for one over the other. McClure et al. (2004) used fMRI technology to compare brain activity of people who consumed Coke and Pepsi in a blinded condition (i.e., the participants didn't know which soda they were receiving) to people who were "brand-cued" (i.e., they were exposed to the familiar Coke or Pepsi labeling before consuming the beverage). In the blinded condition, brain activity was most intense in areas of the prefrontal cortex associated with decision making and reward. However, in the cued condition, increased activity was seen in the hippocampus (associated with memory) and part of the prefrontal cortex associated with bias. These results help explain why food or drink from liked sources (people or companies) seems to taste better; altered brain activity affects perception.

CONCLUDING REMARKS

Despite our largely similar biologically predisposed taste preferences, aversions, and physiology, eating behaviors vary widely around the world. Cuisines and food rules, both of which have tremendous influence on our eating, endure within a culture only if they allow for the survival of its population. We learn of what is normal in our culture and establish our eating behaviors early in life with the guidance of parents and caregivers. As we age, the influence of others on our eating continues. In fact, most of our eating occurs in the presence of others. Research indicates that if the food consumption of those around us is healthy (appropriate portions and ratios of macronutrients), our eating is likely to be healthy as well. Conversely, when eating alone without the healthy model, societal food rules loosen and we are likely to consume beyond our energy needs. Further, as Wansink's group has demonstrated, we are largely unaware of the direct and indirect influences on our eating (e.g., bowl size) and can consequently be easily fooled into consuming excess calories at restaurants, for example. The issues discussed in this chapter are important for policy makers and advocates of a healthier society to consider as they illuminate some of the challenges in improving eating behaviors.

Glossary

Commensal food consumption   Eating in groups.

Cuisine   A style of cooking usually associated with a particular culture.

Law of contagion   Contact between two people or objects results in a lasting connection.

Omnivore's paradox   The contradiction between omnivores' liking of new food and fear of new food.

References

Bailey, D. G., Dresser, G., & Arnold, J. M. O. (2012). Grapefruit-medication interactions: Forbidden fruit or avoidable consequences? *Canadian Medical Association Journal*. DOI: 10.1503/cmaj.120951

Caterina, M. J., Schumacher, M. A., Tominaga, M., Rosen, T. A., Levine, J. D., & Julius, D. (1997). The capsaicin receptor: A heat-activated ion channel in the pain pathway. *Nature, 389*(6653), 816–824.

De Castro, J. M. (1990). Social facilitation of duration and size but not rate of the spontaneous meal intake of humans. *Physiology & Behavior, 47*, 1129–1135.

DeFoliart, G. R. (1999). Insects as food: Why the Western attitude is important. *Annual Review of Entomology, 44*(1), 21–50.

Drewnowski, A., Henderson, S. A., Shore, A. B., Fischler, C., Preziosi, P., & Hercberg, S. (1996). Diet quality and dietary diversity in France: Implications for the French paradox. *Journal of the American Dietetic Association, 96*(7), 663–663.

Fischler, C. (1980). Food habits, social change, and the nature/culture dilemma. *Social Science Information, 19*(6), 937–953.

Fischler, C. (1988). Food, self, and identity. *Social Science Information, 27*(2), 275–292.

Fischler, C. (2011). Commensality, society and culture. *Social Science Information, 50*, 528–548.

Galef Jr, B. G., Attenborough, K. S., & Whiskin, E. E. (1990). Responses of observer rats (Rattus norvegicus) to complex, diet-related signals emitted by demonstrator rats. *Journal of Comparative Psychology, 104*(1), 11–19.

Galef Jr, B. G., Jr., Kennett, D. J., & Stein, M. (1985). Demonstrator influence on observer diet preference: Effects of simple exposure and presence of a demonstrator. *Animal Learning & Behavior, 13*, 25–30.

Galef, B. G., Jr., & Wright, T. J. (1995). Groups of naive rats learn to select nutritionally adequate foods faster than do isolated naive rats. *Animal Behaviour, 49*(2), 403–409.

Harris, M., Bose, N. K., Klass, M., Mencher, J. P., Oberg, K., Opler, M. K., ... Vayda, A. P. (1966). The cultural ecology of India's sacred cattle. *Current Anthropology*, (7), 51–66.

Harris, M., & Ross, E. B. (1987). *Food and evolution: Toward a theory of human food habits*. Philadelphia: Temple University Press.

Herman, C. P., Koenig-Nobert, S., Peterson, J. B., & Polivy, J. (2005). Matching effects on eating: Do individual differences make a difference? *Appetite, 45*, 108–109.

Herman, C. P., Roth, D. A., & Polivy, J. (2003). Effects of the presence of others on eating: A normative interpretation. *Psychological Bulletin, 129*, 873–886.

McClure, S. M., Li, J., Tomlin, D., Cypert, K. S., Montague, L. M., & Montague, P. R. (2004). Neural correlates of behavioral preference for culturally familiar drinks. *Neuron, 44*, 379–387.

Nestle, M., Wing, R., Birch L., DiSogra, L., Drewnowski, A., Middleton, S., … Economos, C. (1998). Behavioral and social influences on food choice. *Nutrition Reviews, 56*(5), S50–S74.

Renaud, S., & de Lorgeril, M. (1992). Wine, alcohol, platelets, and the French paradox for coronary heart disease. *The Lancet, 339*(8808), 1523–1526.

Roberto, C. A., Baik, J., Harris, J. L., & Brownell, K. D. (2010). Influence of licensed characters on children's taste and snack preferences. *Pediatrics, 126*, 88–93.

Robinson, T. N., Borzekowski D. L., Matheson, D. M., & Kraemer, H. C. (2007). Effects of fast food branding on young children's taste preferences. *Archives of Pediatric Adolescent Medicine, 161*(8), 792–797.

Rozin, P. (1996a). Social influences on food preferences and feeding. In E. D. Capaldi (Ed.), *Why we eat what we eat: The psychology of eating* (pp. 233–263). Washington, DC: American Psychological Association.

Rozin, P. (1996b). Towards a psychology of food and eating: From motivation to module to model to marker, morality, meaning, and metaphor. *Current Directions in Psychological Science (Wiley-Blackwell), 5*(1), 18–24.

Rozin, P. (2005). The meaning of food in our lives: A cross-cultural perspective on eating and well-being. *Journal of Nutrition Education and Behavior, 37*, S107–S112.

Rozin, P., & Fallon, A. E. (1987). A perspective on disgust. *Psychological Review, 94*(1), 23–41.

Rozin, P., Fischler, C., Imada, S., Sarubin, A., & Wrzesniewski, A. (1999). Attitudes to food and the role of food in life in the U.S.A., Japan, Flemish Belgium and France: Possible implications for the diet-health debate. *Appetite, 33*, 163–180.

Rozin, P., Kabnick, K., Pete, E., Fischler, C., & Shields, C. (2003). The ecology of eating smaller portion sizes in France than in the United States help explain the French paradox. *Psychological Science, 14*(5), 450–454.

Rozin, P., Millman, L., & Nemeroff, C. (1986). Operation of the laws of sympathetic magic in disgust and other domains. *Journal of Personality and Social Psychology, 50*(4), 703–712.

Schlenker, W., & Villas-Boas, S. B. (2009). Consumer and market responses to mad cow disease. *American Journal of Agricultural Economics, 91*(4), 1140–1152.

Simoons, F., J. (1961). *Eat not this flesh: Food avoidances in the Old World*. Madison: University of Wisconsin Press.

Stice, E., Telch, C. F., & Rizvi, S. L. (2000). Development and validation of the Eating Disorder Diagnostic Scale: A brief self-report measure of anorexia, bulimia, and binge-eating disorder. *Psychological Assessment, 12*(2), 123–131.

Vartanian, L. R., Herman, C., & Wansink, B. (2008). Are we aware of the external factors that influence our food intake? *Health Psychology, 27*(5), 533–538.

Veugelers, P. J., & Fitzgerald, A. L. (2005). Prevalence of and risk factors for childhood overweight and obesity. *Canadian Medical Association Journal, 173*(6), 607–613.

Wansink, B. (2006). *Mindless eating: Why we eat more than we think*. New York: Bantam Books Dell.

Wansink, B., & Sobal, J. (2007). Mindless eating: The 200 daily food decisions we overlook. *Environment and Behavior, 39*(1), 106–123.

Mood and Food, Cravings, and Addiction

After reading this chapter, you will be able to

- Describe the connections between mood and eating behavior
- Understand the role of stress on eating
- Provide the biological and psychological explanations of food cravings
- Appreciate and understand a basis for an addiction model of overeating

Have you ever headed straight to the freezer for some ice cream after a particularly stressful day? Have you ever eaten far more chips than you intended to eat while nervously studying for an upcoming exam? Mood plays an interesting role in eating behavior, which can be problematic, leading to unhealthy eating habits. Some people report cravings for the foods that seem to comfort them or, at least temporarily, improve their mood. A *craving* is characterized by an intense and prolonged desire or yearning. Food cravings are very common (especially among women; Weingarten & Elston, 1991), but some people claim that these cravings are intrusive and are resolved only by the consumption, and at times overconsumption, of the craved food. The cycle of powerful craving followed by compulsive consumption is similar to that seen among drug addicts. The idea that food can be addictive has received much attention and has also spawned debate. Perhaps, as with drug addiction, some people are more prone

to becoming addicted to food and, consequently, have a difficult time regulating their intake. In this chapter, we explore the mood-food connection and the neurobiological evidence for food addiction.

THE MOOD-FOOD CONNECTION

Which types of foods do you typically prefer when you are feeling down or stressed? Frequently craved "comfort foods" include cookies, chips, pasta, pizza, ice cream, and candy (especially chocolate!) (Wansink, Cheney, & Chan, 2003). What do these foods have in common, and why are they among the most desired foods when we're depressed or tense? These foods are quite diverse, but one common feature is that they contain a lot of carbohydrates; we often refer to these foods as "high carb," although they often also contain quite a lot of fat. Maybe the commonality in macronutrient composition is what makes these

foods craved. Or maybe these foods are just the tastiest, so of course they would be preferred. It could instead be that these foods were our favorites during childhood, and we feel comforted by them when we're having a bad day. All of these are reasonable explanations for our comfort food preferences associated with a depressed mood. Let's first consider the explanation that relates to post-ingestive consequences—macronutrients—because this is not as intuitive as the taste or experience explanations.

TALKING POINT 8.1

Do you eat differently when you're feeling down? What foods do you tend to consume more or less of when your mood is low? Compare your list with your classmates' lists.

A Biological Explanation for Carbohydrate (Sugar) Craving?

Depression is believed to be associated with reduced activity of the neurotransmitter **serotonin** (e.g., Parsey et al., 2006), although other neurotransmitters may also be involved. One of the pillars of this theory of depression is that the most effective antidepressant medications work primarily by increasing synaptic levels of serotonin in the brain. Carbohydrate consumption also boosts serotonin activity in the brain, though the mechanism is different from that of antidepressants. **Tryptophan** (a diet-derived amino acid) is the raw material for a two-step synthesis of **serotonin (5-HT)** in the neuron. It is one of six large neutral amino acids (LNAAs) that all compete for the same molecular carrier to get across the blood-brain barrier and into the brain. So, 5-HT synthesis in the brain ultimately depends on the ratio of tryptophan to all LNAAs in the blood. (If you think of the molecular carriers as boats, and the LNAAs as potential passengers, and there are many more passengers than seats in the boats, then you'll get the picture.) It turns out that **insulin** in the bloodstream increases the tryptophan/LNAA ratio and so increases the net amount of tryptophan getting into these molecular "boats."

Because carbohydrates increase insulin secretion to a greater extent than proteins or fats, carbohydrate consumption has the greatest impact on 5-HT synthesis relative to the other macronutrients. The theory is, then, that carbohydrate-dense foods elevate 5-HT, so have an antidepressant or mood-elevating effect, at least among people who identify themselves as "carbohydrate cravers" (this is the *medicine effect*; Corsica & Spring, 2008; Lieberman, Wurtman, & Chew, 1986; Wurtman & Wurtman, 1995). This association is probably learned very early in life, leading some people to continue to desire these types of foods when mood is low, using food as a form of self-medication (Wurtman & Wurtman, 1995). The effect of carbohydrate consumption on 5-HT activity may take hours, whereas the mood-elevating effect is very rapid. This evidence supports the impact of learning of the medicine effect and also the idea that the *expectation* that our mood will be enhanced actually enhances our mood.

Stress and Eating

Most people eat differently when they are "stressed" (Zellner et al., 2006). Stress has diverse causes and descriptions, so more precise terms have been introduced. *Eustress* is stress that is associated with positive experiences, and *distress* is stress associated with negative experiences; these can be thought of as on opposite ends of a stress continuum. However, despite our polar opposite reasons for feeling stressed (from encountering a bear in the woods, to hearing your professor announce a pop-quiz, to walking into a surprise party), our bodily response is quite similar. When we perceive a situation as stressful, our **hypothalamic-pituitary-adrenal (HPA) axis** is activated, triggering an increase in

> ### TALKING POINT 8.2
>
> Do you think that you eat more when you're "stressed"? What types of foods do you typically consume more or less of in this state?

blood pressure, heart rate, breathing, and also the release of the hormones adrenaline and cortisol that perpetuate the elevated physiological state. Typically, hunger is suppressed with short-term exposure to a severe stressor (like the bear in the woods). However, longer-term exposure to non-life-threatening stressors (e.g., preparing for final exams) is more associated with increased eating.

The foods that we eat more of when we are stressed are "comfort" or "junk" foods, and not healthy foods (Dallman, Pecoraro, & la Fleur, 2005; Zellner et al., 2006). It has been demonstrated that even people who feel less hungry when stressed eat more of their calories as high-energy and high-fat comfort foods. So, for some people, overall eating may decrease, but the ratio of unhealthy to healthy foods consumed increases (Gibson, 2006). Further, most increased food consumption associated with stress is in the form of snacks rather than meals. Most students tend to snack on high-energy fat foods such as chips and candy when studying, and many adults report similar junk food preferences when stressed (e.g., Dallman et al., 2005; Oliver & Wardle, 1999). Cantor, Smith, and Bryan (1982) found that humans working on an information-processing (tracking) task consumed more snacks than when they were not performing the task. And the more difficult the task (presumably, the more stressful), the more snacks consumed.

Other research indicates that women are more prone than men to this type of stress-induced palatable food consumption (e.g., Zellner, Saito, & Gonzalez, 2007). Rats and mice, like humans, also selectively consume more energy- and fat-dense food when experiencing stress (Foster et al., 2009). When we (humans and rodents) are stressed, it seems that external factors, particularly the attractiveness and palatability of food,

serotonin activity. It seems that stress-induced glucocorticoid release and the cascade of other chemical changes work to additively alter eating behaviors, including the desire to eat, the motivation to obtain and consume food, and the pleasure experience of eating the food (Dallman et al., 2005; Dallman, 2010). Eating behavior then reduces stresses, at least temporarily, reinforcing the behavior. This can become a habitual pattern for some people. And because the foods preferred when we are stressed are palatable high-energy junk or comfort foods rather than more healthful foods such as fruits and veggies, this habit is likely to lead to unhealthy weight gain (Dallman, 2010).

FOOD CRAVINGS

Elsewhere in this book we have talked about specific appetites. For example, salt appetite is well documented and is triggered initially by a physiological need for sodium. However, most of the substances that we crave are not specific molecules; for example, it would sound odd to say, "I really need some tryptophan today." Further, craved foods are rarely single macronutrients (e.g., pure sugar) but are instead specific food commodities that are mixtures of many ingredients. So a critical question is whether or not cravings for specific commodities have an underlying need basis. Surveys indicate that most people experience cravings—about 70% of young men and nearly 100% of young women (Weingarten & Elston, 1991). Cravings vary in intensity but are typically characterized by a strong desire for a particular food (Wansink et al., 2003). Often, but certainly not always, cravings are followed by the consumption of the desired food. The availability or proximity of the commodity and/or an individual's level of dietary restraint contribute largely to whether or not the food will be consumed, but typically the craving is satisfied only by consumption of the craved food item. Physiological hunger is not a necessary precondition for food craving. Often foods craved and consumed (or overconsumed) are high in carbohydrate and fat and are neither essential nor high in nutritional quality (e.g., chocolate is the most frequently craved

have an increased influence on our food intake. Like eating associated with a depressed mood, stress-induced eating may also be explained by the pleasurable and mood-enhancing activity of serotonin, dopamine, opioids, and other chemicals, which reinforce the eating behavior (Gibson, 2006). Thus, people living in environments with chronic stress are more likely to overeat in the absence of physiological hunger, making them more likely to become overweight or obese.

Stress seems to impact eating for another reason. Activation of the HPA axis also triggers secretion of **glucocorticoids**, which are hormones with several associated functions including elevated emotional state, increase in insulin secretion, and changes in dopamine and

TALKING POINT 8.3

How might a downturn in the economy affect eating behaviors? Might the effects of feeling stuck in a bad job, dealing with a divorce, or grieving a loved one be similar?

TALKING POINT 8.4

Do you ever experience food cravings? Which foods do you most often crave? Do your cravings occur more often when you are alone or in social situations? Does time of day contribute? Do you typically consume the foods that you crave?

food in Western society). In contrast, when we are physiologically hungry, we tend to desire more nutritious and savory-tasting foods, such as a pasta dish, a turkey sandwich, or steak and potatoes. And when truly hungry, we are more accepting of a variety of foods.

One group of researchers (Pelchat & Schaeffer, 2000) found that participants on a monotonous but nutritionally complete diet for several days had large increases in cravings. (They consumed a nutritional supplement beverage and water only.) This further supports that food craving and unhealthy snacking are not necessarily due to hunger or nutritional need. Rather, mood and desire for dietary variety have more documented links with cravings than with physiological hunger. Cravings are also influenced by age (they decrease with advanced age), culture, and hormone fluctuations (particularly among women; Pelchat, 1997; Zellner, Garriga-Trillo, Rohm, Centeno, & Parker, 1999).

Craving-related eating, particularly when it occurs frequently, increases the risk of binge eating, which in turn is associated with bulimia nervosa, binge eating disorder, and obesity. The pattern of craving, consuming, overconsuming, feeling good, then feeling guilty, leading to repetition of the cycle is similar to that seen among drug abusers. Drug and food cravings can both be powerfully triggered by exposure to associated stimuli (e.g., sight of drug paraphernalia or a candy bar wrapper). The shared neurobiology involved in food craving and drug abuse is discussed later in this chapter.

Is Chocolate Special?

Many desired and craved snacks contain chocolate, which is carbohydrate (sugar) dense but

also contains fat and protein and some bioactive ingredients and micronutrients. In light of the fact that chocolate is the most craved food in Western society (Weingarten & Elston, 1991; Zellner et al., 1999), two questions have arisen: Is chocolate special, and if so, why? Some researchers believe that the bioactive substances in chocolate (specifically in cocoa, a major ingredient in chocolate) trigger a mood-enhancing release of neurotransmitters within the brain. Among the proposed mood-elevating, and possibly addictive, substances are caffeine (a stimulant), theobromine (structurally similar to caffeine but with a far lower stimulating effect), anandamide (binds pleasure-inducing cannabinoid receptors), phenylethylamine (similar to amphetamine, triggers dopamine activity within the brain reward pathway), and tryptophan (increases serotonin synthesis).

In a study of chocolate craving (Michener & Rozin, 1994), self-identified chocolate cravers were given five small sealed boxes that appeared identical but in fact each contained a different item: milk chocolate, white chocolate (similar in texture to milk chocolate, but without the bioactive substances found in cocoa), cocoa capsules (these have the bioactive ingredients, but none of the sensory aspects of chocolate), placebo capsules, or nothing. Participants were told to open one box at random whenever they craved chocolate and consume the contents. (Which box would you hope to open if you were a participant?) They were asked to rate perceived intensity of the chocolate cravings before and 90 minutes after eating the contents. The results showed that only dark or milk chocolate consumption reduced the craving for chocolate. The finding that cocoa alone did not reduce craving indicates that the bioactive substances have little or no role in chocolate craving (i.e., no specific biological deficit caused the craving and alleviation of which reduced craving). In fact, participants preferred the white chocolate to the cocoa capsules, indicating that the taste, smell, and additional sensory components of chocolate consumption are more important than bioactive ingredients. Additional evidence against the role of chemical-enhancement as the basis for chocolate craving or addiction comes from food-use studies that show that dark chocolate (which contains the highest amounts of cocoa and, thus, the highest levels of the bioactive substances) is less preferred and less consumed than either milk chocolate or chocolate-coated sweets that contain lesser amounts of the chemicals. Furthermore, the amounts of the bioactive compounds mentioned previously that actually cross the blood-brain barrier and have any effect within the brain are likely very small.

There could be other bioactive ingredients in chocolate that make it special. For example, chocolate contains significant amounts of riboflavin (vitamin B_2), magnesium, and antioxidants, all which enhance health. Perhaps deficiencies for these vitamins and minerals contribute to chocolate craving. For example, women tend to have increased cravings for chocolate when experiencing premenstrual syndrome, a time associated with reduced levels of magnesium (Bruinsma & Taren, 1999). However, many infrequently craved foods contain much higher amounts of magnesium (including barley, spinach, and pumpkin seeds). And riboflavin deficiency is an unlikely explanation for chocolate craving because riboflavin concentrations in chocolate are some 20-fold lower than they are in less preferred foods such

as liver. So, despite some possible health benefits of chocolate, these are implausible as the basis for chocolate craving.

Chocolate, especially milk chocolate, has an appealing taste, smell, and creamy texture. It seems that the pleasurable orosensory aspects of chocolate and the innately reinforcing qualities of the macronutrients in chocolate (carbohydrate and fat), rather than any particular chemical or micronutrient are the bases for chocolate craving. Exposure to the sight or smell of chocolate can trigger intense and difficult-to-ignore cravings, particularly among people who claim to be "chocolate lovers" or chocolate cravers. You have probably heard these people referred to as "chocoholics," and maybe you've used this term to characterize your own affection for chocolate. The idea of chocolate addiction compares the intense cravings for chocolate to the cravings drug addicts have for particular substances of abuse. In support of this, fMRI studies have revealed that exposure to the sight and/or taste of chocolate triggers different brain activity for chocolate cravers compared to non-cravers (Rolls & McCabe, 2007). Specifically, areas associated with pleasure and reward show enhanced activity in the chocolate cravers' brains much like drug addicts' brains show increased activity upon exposure to drug paraphernalia.

Psychological and Sociocultural Explanations for Chocolate Craving

Despite the fact that chocolate is the most frequently craved food, it is not the most consumed food. In fact, some people, despite their reported liking of chocolate, refrain entirely from eating it or consume it infrequently and/or in small amounts. In our society, chocolate is considered an indulgence. Perhaps the belief that chocolate is "nice but naughty" actually makes it more desired. In cultures where chocolate is not considered as forbidden as it is in ours, chocolate craving is actually much lower (Zellner et al., 1999). However, in many of these cultures, dark chocolate is the most prevalent type of chocolate consumed. This form has higher concentrations of the bioactive ingredients but lower levels of fat and sugar, and

TALKING POINT 8.5

Do you think that people had food cravings before the global availability of sweet chocolate? If so, what food cravings do you think they might have had?

consequently it may not have the same reinforcing properties as does the milk chocolate more widely consumed among Americans. In evolutionary terms, the availability of chocolate is a recent event for most of the world's population. The first record of cultivation of cacao dates from Aztec civilizations and was imported to Europe by the conquistadors. Cacao itself is bitter and the word *chocolate* derives from the Nahuatl words for "bitter drink."

Can Someone Actually be a "Food Addict"?

The mood-food connection is well supported by both anecdotal and empirical evidence. Perhaps, extending the idea, some people actually self-medicate using food to improve mood and become dependent on certain foods to feel good. This is the cycle in which drug addicts find themselves: intense cravings and need for the drug in order to function and feel normal or good. Addiction is also associated with uncontrolled consumption. Is it plausible that certain foods can be addictive like cocaine, heroin, and nicotine can be? One problem with this line of thinking is that we all need food to survive, but we do not need recreational drugs. Another caveat is that we are all exposed to food (we all consume food from the day that we are born), whereas not everyone ingests recreational drugs. So, if food can be problematically addictive, why doesn't everyone suffer in this way? There are two ways to think about this. The first is that only some individuals are genetically and physiologically predisposed to become food addicts. Another way is to consider that we are all predisposed, but some of us have mechanisms and strategies to resist food; this is referred to as **dietary restraint**.

People with high levels of restraint can resist the temptation to consume delicious looking and smelling foods (e.g., freshly baked cookies) despite their liking of such food. Conversely, people with low restraint are unable to resist similar temptations, regardless of a possible desire to avoid unhealthy foods, and are more likely to consume more than intended (Lawson et al., 1995). Many factors contribute to the different levels of dietary restraint that people have, including a desire to lose weight or maintain a low or healthy weight, religion (e.g., fasting during the days of Ramadan or giving up chocolate for Lent), ethics (e.g., many vegans and vegetarians refrain from eating meat because of personal conviction that animal consumption and/or poor treatment of animals is unethical), and for other health-related issues (e.g., avoiding high-sodium foods in an effort to lower blood pressure). An individual's personality also contributes; people with impulsive personalities typically have lower levels of dietary restraint. As discussed in other chapters, low dietary restraint can result in overeating and obesity (Van Strein & Van de Laar, 2008); however, high restraint is often associated with the eating disorder anorexia nervosa (Bulik, Sullivan, Fear, & Pickering, 2000).

Our current food environment is quite different from that of our ancestors, with palatable and energy-dense foods easily available. Some evidence supports a link between our obesogenic environment and food addiction. People with low dietary restraint have a more difficult time in today's food environment resisting the temptation

of overconsuming appealing food, but perhaps they would be able to resist bland food. In a recent study (Johnson & Kenny, 2010), one group of rats was given rat chow *ad libitum* plus extended (nearly unlimited) access to a cafeteria or junk food diet including foods commonly found in our environment, such as bacon, sausage, chocolate, and cheesecake. Another group of rats had rat chow *ad libitum* with 1 hour of access to the cafeteria diet, and the control group had rat chow *ad libitum* only. After 40 days of the assigned diet, the rats experienced foot shock in the presence of a particular light stimulus, thus quickly developing a conditioned fear of the light. On test day, all rats had access to the cafeteria diet, and all demonstrated interest in the food. However, the presence of the feared light stimulus (this time it was not paired with a foot shock) suppressed eating of the cafeteria food in the control and 1-hour access groups, but not in the extended access group. It is interesting that even in a sated state, the cafeteria-fed rats had such an apparent liking of highly palatable food that they were willing to risk experiencing the unpleasant foot shock. Drug-addicted rats similarly lever press for injections of particular drugs even in the presence of cues associated with punishment.

The rats on the cafeteria diet in the Johnson and Kenny study gained twice the weight of the rats in the other two conditions; they apparently enjoyed our Western diet! They also showed behavioral and biological markers that characterize drug addiction (discussed later). They were willing to risk an aversive stimulus to get the cafeteria food and routinely ate far more calories compared with control rats when given the palatable food, but not when given regular chow. These findings parallel data from human studies indicating that obese individuals (compared with lean individuals) have more intense cravings for palatable high-energy foods and demonstrate reduced restraint when exposed to these foods (Stice, Spoor, Bohon, Veldhuizen, & Small, 2008). In the Johnson and Kenny study, rats were not "addicted" to the cafeteria diet right from the start. It was not until they had been exposed to it for some time that these characteristics of addiction became apparent. All rats tested in the extended-access group showed signs of addiction,

TALKING POINT 8.6

Have you ever gone to great lengths to obtain any of the types of foods in the cafeteria diet that the rats were so fond of? Perhaps a late night or early morning trip across town for pancakes and bacon? Maybe a special outing for ice cream or chocolate? Do you think these behaviors support the idea that palatable foods can be addictive? Why or why not?

and although they were all from a similar genetic background, the evidence suggests that the addiction is a result of environmental exposure more than biological predisposition.

Neurobiology of Food Addiction

Interest in brain reward circuitry stems from the finding in the 1950s by Olds and Milner (1954) that rats will lever press for intracranial brain stimulation in lieu of food, water, or sleep. The **mesolimbic dopamine system** (Figure 8.1), including the ventral tegmental area (VTA), nucleus accumbens, and several cortical regions, and the **endogenous opioid system** are particularly associated with reward and pleasure. Exposure to pleasurable stimuli, such as food, water, sex, drugs, roller coaster rides, and so on, activates brain "reward" circuitry, reinforcing our experiences and leading us to want to repeat them. These mechanisms presumably evolved so that our ancestors would enjoy food, water, and sex enough that they would seek them out, despite the risks and efforts required. The pathways, though, did not evolve so that we would enjoy and possibly become addicted to drugs or so that we would stand in line again and again to repeat the ride on a thrilling roller coaster. Drugs of abuse, in particular, can be considered super-stimuli, activating our reward pathways more powerfully than do naturally reinforcing stimuli. Recent evidence

(e.g., Johnson & Kenny, 2010) indicates that the extremely palatable food in our environment may also be a super-stimulus. This could explain the addiction-like behaviors and neurobiological changes of the cafeteria-diet fed rats and perhaps the overconsumption of energy-dense food by many people in Western culture.

Reports of people feeling unable to resist sweet snacks or people experiencing a depressed mood when they are deprived of the palatable food they are accustomed to consuming at a particular time every day are well established. These symptoms—compulsion to consume the palatable food and mood change or withdrawal when the craved food is not consumed—resemble symptoms of drug addiction. Dr. Bart Hoebel of Princeton University and colleagues were among the first to formally propose the idea of sugar addiction, at least in rats. They found that rats intermittently fed sugar demonstrated the hallmark signs of addiction, including withdrawal, bingeing when receiving access, craving, and increased interest in other drugs (cross-sensitization; Avena, Rada, & Hoebel, 2008). It has also been demonstrated that rats will lever press for saccharin over cocaine, suggesting that the sweet taste is a powerful reinforcer (Lenoir, Serre, Cantin, & Ahmed, 2007). The cafeteria-diet study by Johnson and Kenny further supports these claims. We recommend Kenny (2011) for a thorough review of research surrounding the

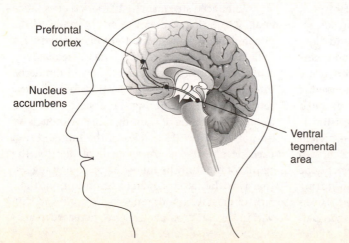

Prefrontal cortex

Nucleus accumbens

Ventral tegmental area

FIGURE 8.1 The mesolimbic dopamine system. *Source:* National Institute on Drug Abuse

neurobiology of obesity and drug addiction. The following is an overview of some key findings of the neural mechanisms that could underlie sugar or palatable food addiction.

DOPAMINE SYSTEM   **Dopamine** release in the **nucleus accumbens (NAc)** upon exposure to sugar and other palatable foods or drugs of abuse has been well documented (Kenny, 2011). Each exposure to sugar or addictive drugs triggers release of dopamine in the NAc, and over time this leads to changes in the availability or function of dopamine receptors. Drug abusers tend to need more of their drug with repeated exposures for it to have its initial effect; this is referred to as **tolerance**. Tolerance is explained, in part, by the down-regulation of dopamine receptors, therefore, blunted dopamine activity. Higher doses of a drug are needed in order to activate more of the functional dopamine receptors. Perhaps this also happens with sugar or palatable food addiction, so that people need to consume increasingly more palatable food over time to experience the good, or "comforted," feeling they recall having with that food.

It would be easy to assume that sugar, because it is associated with calories, is innately reinforcing and consequently always triggers dopamine release. However, modifications to the neurobiological response can be made based on post-ingestive consequences. For example, dopamine activity within the NAc increases when rats ingest a sweet-tasting saccharin solution (an innately liked taste) for the first time. However, in rats with a conditioned taste aversion to saccharin produced by pairing nausea-producing lithium chloride injections with saccharin ingestion, dopamine activity is reduced when they are given oral saccharin infusions (Mark, Blander, & Hoebel, 1991). (Note that they will actively avoid *drinking* saccharin; hence, the oral infusion is used to expose them to the taste for a sufficient period for the dopamine measurements. Rats with a conditioned aversion will actively reject—the rat equivalent of spitting out—saccharin during this test.) Further, dopamine release after a positive association has been made with sugar, palatable food, or addictive drug, is actually higher

on *anticipation* of its delivery than the actual receipt of it (Pelchat, Johnson, Chan, Valdez, & Ragland, 2004; Small, Jones-Gotman, & Dagher, 2003; Volkow et al., 2003). So, although dopamine release is initially in response to a pleasurable or rewarding stimulus, after conditioning, its release is shaped by learned expectations about the consequences of the anticipated stimulus.

The binding of dopamine to its D2 receptor subtype in the striatum, a brain region associated with pleasure and motivated behaviors, is elevated by palatable food consumption or addictive drug use. A reduction of D2 receptors in the striatum, sometimes referred to as **striatal dysfunction,** is associated with drug abuse. Some theorists believe that this indicates that drug addicts have a blunted "reward" response and thus seek drugs as a way to boost their sluggish reward systems (Stice, Yokum, Blum, & Bohon, 2010). Similarly, obese humans and rats have reduced D2 receptor expression in the striatum. Johnson and Kenny (2010) discovered that striatal D2 receptor expression in the cafeteria-diet rats was inversely related to weight gain after about 1.5 months on the palatable diet. It seems that a decrease in D2 receptors is a response to overactivation of the reward pathway. This consequently leads to increased desire for activation of the pathway through pleasurable stimuli such as palatable food or addictive drugs.

Interestingly, despite the reduction of striatal D2 receptors, the brains of obese individuals show enhanced striatal activity to food cues (Stice et al., 2010). Some researchers believe that obese people have heightened activity associated with anticipated food reward, but a decreased activity to the actual receipt of food. This could underlie intense food craving and wanting, but blunted satisfaction on consuming the desired food, and a continued feeling of wanting more. Although we do not yet know if changes in the human brain precede obesity or are a result of obesity, the results of the study by Johnson and Kenny suggest that it is the latter: Overconsumption, particularly of palatable food, reduces dopamine activity within the striatum eliciting an increased yearning for more palatable food.

BOX 8.1   Does Weight Affect Brain Reactivity To Food Cues?

Stice and colleagues (2008) conducted an fMRI study to assess brain activity associated with anticipation compared with receipt of a palatable food by obese and lean adolescent girls. Particular cues preceded the delivery of a palatable chocolate milkshake, a tasteless solution, or nothing while the girls were in the MRI scanner. Obese girls (compared to lean girls) showed greater activation when anticipating and receiving the "rewarding" taste of the milkshake in areas of the cortex associated with food taste, reward, and craving, including the gustatory cortex, insular cortex, and anterior cingulate cortex. The researchers also found that BMI was inversely correlated with activity in the caudate (a part of the striatum) in response to food consumption. These findings support the theory that food "wanting" is enhanced with increased body weight, but enjoyment or satisfaction on food consumption is inversely correlated with weight. In another fMRI study, the activity in reward-associated brain regions was modulated by the *label* of the palatable food. Brain activation was higher in anticipation of the regular milkshake compared with anticipation of the milkshake labeled "low fat," supporting the idea that obese individuals are more responsive to external food cues such as anticipated palatability (Ng, Stice, Yokum, & Bohon, 2011).

ENDOGENOUS OPIOID SYSTEM   Activity of the **endogenous opioid system** is associated with pleasurable stimuli, including addictive drug ingestion. Opioid drugs, including heroin, morphine, and oxycontin, work as direct agonists of the opioid system by binding to endogenous opioid receptors. Other drugs of abuse activate the system indirectly, but also powerfully. For example, drugs such as alcohol, nicotine (in cigarettes), and cocaine activate other neurotransmitter systems directly but trigger indirect activity of the opioid system. We know this because opioid antagonist drugs can effectively reduce alcohol, cigarette, and cocaine use by addicts, seemingly because the drugs are no longer as pleasurable when activity of the opioid system is blocked.

Certainly, consumption of sweet and palatable food is pleasurable, so the opioid system is likely involved. Naloxone and naltrexone, two opioid receptor blockers used in drug addiction research and therapy, reduce the hedonic ratings of sweet and palatable tastes and smells and can reduce binge consumption associated with binge eating disorders (Drewnowski, Krahn, Demitrack, Nairn, & Gosnell, 1995). Naloxone, in particular,

has been shown to reduce sugar consumption in rats conditioned to receive sugar following a cue (Grimm, Manaois, Osincup, Wells, & Buse, 2007). The opioid blocker seems to negate the sugar craving induced by the conditioned stimulus. Further, injections of an opioid receptor stimulant (DAMGO) into the nucleus accumbens of rats have been shown to increase consumption of palatable solutions (water with sucrose, saccharin, or salt) but not water alone (Zhang & Kelley, 1997, 2002). The endogenous opioid system seems to be involved in selective preferences for palatable tastes and perhaps palatable food addiction and overconsumption.

OREXIN SYSTEM   An increasing amount of evidence indicates a role of the **orexin** (also referred to as *hypocretin*) system in drug abuse and palatable food consumption. Orexin receptors have been found in the hypothalamus (associated with maintaining homeostasis and motivation) and mesolimbic regions (associated with reward). Orexin signaling seems to modulate dopamine activity within the mesolimbic region, enhancing the reward of pleasurable stimuli and increasing the motivation to seek out such stimulation. However, orexin antagonists do not block food-deprived rats' consumption of chow, indicating that orexin activity is involved in hedonic food consumption and drug use, but not hunger-induced food consumption (Choi, Davis, Fitzgerald, & Benoit, 2011).

Direct administration of orexin into rat brains triggers selective eating of palatable high-fat food. Findings also indicate that when rats are conditioned to receive palatable food, such as chocolate, at regular intervals or on particular cues, orexin signaling increases when rats "expect" the treat. Additionally, orexin antagonists have been shown to reduce impulsivity, a problem associated with drug abuse and binge eating. Orexin activity, thus, seems to facilitate eating for pleasure rather than for physiological need, which can drive overconsumption of high-fat and high-calorie palatable foods.

CANNABINOIDS   Marijuana smoking has for centuries been linked with increased food consumption, particularly of snack or junk food. Tetrahydrocannabinol (THC), the psychoactive substance in marijuana, activates the cannabinoid system, stimulating hunger for and palatability of hedonic foods. Much of the information about marijuana and increased hunger and eating has been in the form of anecdotal reports from marijuana users. However, in the 1990s, researchers discovered that THC administration in rats and mice triggered hyperphagia and that blockage of the cannabinoid system prevented the overconsumption. This empirical evidence of the hyperphagic effects of cannabinoid stimulation led to attempts to better understand its role in eating behavior and possibilities of the use of antagonist drugs for the treatment of obesity.

THC and other cannabinoids work by binding endogenous cannabinoid receptors (primarily the CB1 receptor subtype) in the brain and periphery. Cannabinoid receptors have been found in areas of the brain associated with eating regulation and motivation (e.g., regions of the hypothalamus), areas associated with reward or pleasure (e.g., nucleus accumbens), and peripheral regions involved in digestion (e.g., intestines;

Kirkham, 2009). Researchers realized that if endogenous receptors exist, there must be some natural chemicals within the body that bind to them. This awareness led to the discovery of endocannabinoids, the brain's endogenous THC-like neurotransmitters. Endocannabinoid release is activated by pleasurable experiences and this neural activity enhances their hedonic value. This system apparently works in conjunction with the orexin, dopamine, and opioid systems within the hypothalamic and reward pathways of the brain to additively enhance reward associated with palatable food consumption and the memories associated with such consumption. Endocannabinoids seem to play a particular role in appetite stimulation and the motivation to seek out and consume food, particularly palatable food (Abel, 1975; Foltin, Fischman, & Byrne, 1988).

Recent evidence helps explain the "munchies" (selective eating of high-energy foods) associated with marijuana use. Antagonists of this system effectively result in reduced eating and weight loss in humans and animals. However, cannabinoid antagonist drugs are currently not used as weight-loss medication because they are associated with an increased risk for depression (Izzo & Sharkey, 2010).

CONCLUDING REMARKS

The idea of "food addiction" is supported by a growing number of studies including human anecdotal reports and empirical human and animal evidence. Many overweight people claim that their favorite foods are too irresistible, and this issue likely underlies the failure of many diet or weight-loss efforts. In the documentary film *Super Size Me* (2004), Morgan Spurlock exclusively consumed food from fast-food restaurants for 30 days in an effort to explore the health risks, if any, of frequent consumption of heavily processed foods high in carbohydrate and fat (e.g., soda, cheeseburgers, french fries, and milkshakes). He gained a large amount of weight (about 25 lbs.) in a very short period of time, which is perhaps not surprising considering his significant increase in daily energy consumption. More surprising to

Morgan, and of interest to us, were his reported mood swings, depression, and lethargy while on the fast-food diet. Further, his depressed mood was relieved by the consumption of his palatable and energy-dense meals. His cycle of craving, bingeing, and having associated mood swings is consistent with that described by drug addicts. Anecdotal reports such as Morgan's support the notion that food can have profound effects on mood and can have addictive-like qualities.

Recent fMRI studies indicate that the brain regions associated with taste and pleasure are more intensely activated in obese compared with lean people when exposed to food cues. This is consistent with evidence showing that drug addicts have increased activity in pleasure-associated regions when exposed to cues such as pictures of drug paraphernalia. As previously discussed in this chapter, other behavioral and biological markers are similar for drug addicts and obese people or animals (perhaps "food addicts"). The neural mechanisms that underlie food liking and craving and the motivation to seek out and consume food are consistent with those that underlie drug abuse. It seems that the palatable high-energy foods so prevalent in our society overactivate our reward pathways, resulting in neurophysiological and behavioral symptoms of addiction. Importantly, the addiction model of overeating is likely an insufficient explanation of the complex reasons for disordered or unhealthy eating behaviors among our diverse population; however, the parallels between addiction to drugs and overconsumption of palatable foods warrant consideration and continued investigation.

Let's review and apply your knowledge. Take some time to answer these chapter questions

1. How may serotonin activity impact carbohydrate craving?
2. Describe the impact that stress has on eating behaviors.
3. What is the evidence that cravings are usually not need based?
4. What are the leading explanations for chocolate cravings?
5. Provide at least four pieces of evidence supporting the idea that palatable food can be addictive.
6. Which neurotransmitter systems seem to underlie food addiction? What is the supporting evidence for their involvement?
7. How does our current food environment impact cravings for comfort or junk foods, which can lead to binges (behaviors associated with addiction)?

Glossary

Dietary restraint   The extent to which food is resisted.

Dopamine (DA)   A monoamine neurotransmitter associated with reward, motivation, and movement.

Endogenous opioid system   The brain system involved with pain relief.

Glucocorticoid   A class of steroid hormones released in response to stress. In humans, cortisol is the principal glucocorticoid.

Hypothalamic-pituitary-adrenal (HPA) axis   The interaction among the hypothalamus, pituitary gland, and adrenal glands to regulate the body's response to stress.

Insulin   A hormone released from the pancreas that allows cells to absorb glucose from the blood.

Mesolimbic dopamine system   A brain pathway extending from the ventral tegmental area in the midbrain to forebrain regions associated with pleasure and reward.

Nucleus accumbens (NAc)   A forebrain region associated with pleasure and reward.

Orexin   A neurotransmitter involved with appetite and arousal.

Serotonin (5-HT)   A monoamine neurotransmitter involved with mood, appetite, and sleep. Some 14 receptor subtypes have been identified; the 2c receptor is most implicated in appetite and feeding.

Striatal dysfunction   Altered activity of dopamine in the striatum.

Tolerance   The reduced effect of a drug after repeated use, so that a higher dose is needed for it to have its initial effect.

Tryptophan   The amino acid from which serotonin is synthesized.

References

Abel, E. L. (1975). Cannabis: Effects on hunger and thirst. *Behavioral Biology, 15,* 255–281.

Avena, N. M., Rada, P., & Hoebel, B. G. (2008). Evidence for sugar addiction: Behavioral and neurochemical effects of intermittent, excessive sugar intake. *Neuroscience & Biobehavioral Reviews, 32,* 20–39.

Bruinsma, K., & Taren, D. L. (1999). Chocolate: Food or drug? *Journal of the American Dietetic Association, 99*(10), 1249–1256.

Bulik, C. M., Sullivan, P. F., Fear, J. L., & Pickering, A. (2000). Outcome of anorexia nervosa: Eating attitudes, personality, and parental bonding. *International Journal of Eating Disorders, 28*(2), 139–147.

Cantor, M. B., Smith, S. E., & Bryan, B. R. (1982). Induced bad habits: Adjunctive ingestion and grooming in human subjects. *Appetite, 3,* 1–12.

Corsica, J. A., & Spring, B. J. (2008). Carbohydrate craving: A double-blind, placebo-controlled test of the self-medication hypothesis. *Eating Behaviors, 9*(4), 447–454.

Choi, D. L., Davis, J. F., Fitzgerald, M. E., & Benoit, S. C. (2010). The role of orexin-a in food motivation, reward-based feeding behavior and food-induced neuronal activation in rats. *Neuroscience, 167,* 11–20.

Dallman, M. F. (2010). Stress-induced obesity and the emotional nervous system. *Trends in Endocrinology and Metabolism, 21*(3), 159–165.

Dallman, M. F., Pecoraro, N. C., & la Fleur, S. E. (2005). Chronic stress and comfort foods: Self-medication and abdominal obesity. *Brain, Behavior, & Immunity, 19*(4), 275–280.

Drewnowski, A., Krahn, D. D., Demitrack, M. A., Nairn, K., & Gosnell, B. A. (1995). Naloxone, an opiate blocker, reduces the consumption of sweet high-fat foods in obese and lean female binge eaters. *American Journal of Clinical Nutrition, 61*(6), 1206–1212.

Foltin, R. W., Fischman, M. W., & Byrne, M. F. (1988). Effects of smoked marijuana on food intake and body weight of humans living in a residential laboratory. *Appetite, 11,* 1–14.

Foster, M. T., Warne, J. P., Ginsberg, A. B., Horneman, H. F., Pecoraro, N. C., Akana, S. F., & Dallman, M. F. (2009). Palatable foods, stress, and energy stores sculpt corticotropin-releasing factor, adrenocorticotropin, and corticosterone concentrations after restraint. *Endocrinology 150*(5), 2325–2333.

Gibson, E. L. (2006). Emotional influences on food choice: Sensory, physiological and psychological pathways. *Physiology and Behavior, 89,* 53–61.

Grimm, J. W., Manaois, M., Osincup, D., Wells, B., & Buse, C. (2007). Naloxone attenuates incubated sucrose craving in rats. *Psychopharmacology, 194*(4), 537–544.

Izzo, A. A., & Sharkey, K. A. (2010). Cannabinoids and the gut: New developments and emerging concepts. *Pharmacology & Therapeutics, 126,* 21–38.

Johnson, P. M., & Kenny, P. J. (2010). Dopamine D2 in addiction-like reward dysfunction and compulsive eating in obese rats. *Nature Neuroscience, 13,* 635–641.

Kirkham, T. C. (2009). Cannabinoids and appetite: Food craving and food pleasure. *International Review of Psychiatry, 21,* 163–171.

Kenny, P. (2011). Common cellular and molecular mechanisms in obesity and drug addiction. *Nature Reviews Neuroscience, 12,* 6538–6651.

Lawson, O. J., Williamson, D. A., Champagne, C. M., DeLany, J. P., Brooks, E. R., Howat, P. M., ... & Ryan, D. H. (1995). The association of body weight, dietary intake, and energy expenditure with dietary restraint and disinhibition. *Obesity Research, 3*(2), 153–161.

Lenoir, M., Serre, F., Cantin, L., & Ahmed, S. H. (2007). Intense sweetness surpasses cocaine reward. *PLoS ONE 2*(8), 1–10. doi:10.1371/journal.pone.0000698

Lieberman, H., Wurtman, J., & Chew, B. (1986). Changes in mood after carbohydrate consumption among obese individuals. *American Journal of Clinical Nutrition, 45,* 772–778.

Mark, G. P., Blander, D. S., & Hoebel, B. G. (1991). A conditioned stimulus decreases extracellular dopamine in the nucleus accumbens after the development of a learned taste aversion. *Brain Research, 551*(1), 308–310.

Michener, W., & Rozin, P. (1994). Pharmacological versus sensory factors in the satiation of chocolate craving. *Physiology & Behavior, 56*(3), 419–422.

Ng, J., Stice, E., Yokum, S., & Bohon, C. (2011). An fMRI study of obesity, food reward, and perceived caloric density. Does a low-fat label make food less appealing? *Appetite, 57*(1), 65–72. doi: 10.1016/j.appet.2011.03.017

Olds, J., & Milner, P. (1954). Positive reinforcement produced by electrical stimulation of septal area and other regions of rat brain. *Journal of Comparative Physiological Psychology, 47*(6), 419–427.

Oliver, G., & Wardle, J. (1999). Perceived effects of stress on food choice. *Physiology & Behavior 66*(3), 511–515.

Parsey, R. V., Oquendo, M. A., Ogden, R. T., Olvet, D. M., Simpson, N., Huang, Y. Y., … & Mann, J. J. (2006). Altered serotonin 1A binding in major depression: A [carbonyl-C-11] WAY100635 positron emission tomography study. *Biological Psychiatry, 59*(2), 106–113.

Pelchat, M. L. (1997). Food cravings in young and elderly adults. *Appetite, 28*(2), 103–113.

Pelchat, M. L., Johnson, A., Chan, R., Valdez, J., & Ragland, J. D. (2004). Images of desire: Food-craving activation during fMRI. *NeuroImage, 23,* 1486–1493.

Pelchat, M. L., & Schaefer, S. (2000). Dietary monotony and food cravings in young and elderly adults. *Physiology & Behavior, 68*(3), 353–359.

Rolls, E. T., & McCabe, C. (2007). Enhanced affective brain representations of chocolate in cravers vs. non-cravers. *European Journal of Neuroscience, 26*(4), 1067–1076.

Small, D. M., Jones-Gotman, M., & Dagher, A. (2003). Feeding-induced dopamine release in dorsal striatum correlates with meal pleasantness ratings in healthy human volunteers. *Neuroimage, 19,* 1709–1715.

Stice, E., Spoor, S., Bohon, C., Veldhuizen, M., & Small, D. (2008). Relation of reward from food intake and anticipated food intake to obesity: A functional magnetic resonance imaging study. *Journal of Abnormal Psychology, 117,* 924–935. doi: 10.1037/a0013600

Stice, E., Yokum, S., Blum, K., & Bohon, C. (2010). Weight gain is associated with reduced striatal response to palatable food. *The Journal of Neuroscience, 30*(39), 13105–13109.

Van Strien, T., & Van de Laar, F. A. (2008). Intake of energy is best predicted by overeating tendency and consumption of fat is best predicted by dietary restraint: A 4-year follow-up of patients with newly diagnosed Type 2 diabetes. *Appetite, 50*(2), 544–547.

Volkow, N. D., Wang, G. J., Maynard, L., Jayne, M., Fowler, J. S., Zhu, W., … Pappas, N. (2003). Brain dopamine is associated with eating behavior in humans. *International Journal of Eating Disorders, 33,* 136–142.

Wansink, B., Cheney, M. M., & Chan, N. (2003). Exploring comfort food preferences across age and gender. *Physiology & Behavior, 79*(4), 739–747.

Weingarten, H.P., & Elston, D. (1991). Food cravings in a college population. *Appetite, 17*(3), 167–175.

Wurtman, R., & Wurtman, J. (1995). Brain serotonin, carbohydrate craving, obesity, and depression. *Obesity Research, 3*(4), 477S–480S.

Zellner, D. A., Garriga-Trillo, A., Rohm, E., Centeno, S., & Parker, S. (1999). Food liking and craving: A cross-cultural approach. *Appetite, 33,* 61–70. doi: 10.1006/appe.1999.0234

Zellner, D. A., Loaiza, S., Gonzalez, Z., Pita, J., Morales, J., Pecora, D., & Wolf, A. (2006). Food selection changes under stress. *Physiology & Behavior, 87*(4), 789–793.

Zellner, D. A., Saito, S., & Gonzalez, J. (2007). The effect of stress on men's food selection. *Appetite, 49,* 696–699.

Zhang, M., & Kelley, A. E. (1997). Opiate agonists microinjected into the nucleus accumbens enhance sucrose drinking in rats. *Psychopharmacology, 132*(4), 350–360.

Zhang, M., & Kelley, A. E. (2002). Intake of saccharin, salt, and ethanol solutions is increased by infusion of a mu opioid agonist into the nucleus accumbens. *Psychopharmacology, 159*(4), 415–423.

9

Hunger, Satiety, and the Brain

After reading this chapter, you will be able to

- Understand the concept of motivation and its application to theories of feeding behavior

- Describe allostasis and its application to feeding behavior and weight regulation

- Identify signals from adipose tissue and weight regulation

- Understand the role of the arcuate nucleus and NTS in biological signaling of hunger

- Describe reward systems and feeding and other higher-order brain processes

CENTRAL ORIGIN OF HUNGER

Earlier in this book we discussed conditions in the environment that might affect the timing and the amount of food consumed and indicated that foraging was an important factor. Foraging requires effort, so there has to be a mechanism internal to the animal or person that will initiate and sustain that foraging effort. That mechanism is **motivation**. What is it that motivates us to seek or select food? And what is it that causes motivation to diminish as we eat and eventually cease pursuing or eating? Again, as introduced in previous chapters, the psychological states underlying this alternation of interest and disinterest in food are referred to as **hunger** and **satiety**, respectively. **Satiation** refers to the end of an ongoing eating episode. The terms *satiation* and *satiety* are often confused in usage: To be clear, satiation is mediated by internal states that start during an eating bout, whereas satiety is mediated by internal states that occur after the bout has ended. These states and signals, some of which we will review, overlap in time (Figure 9.1; Blundell, 1991).

Hunger is usually an unpleasant state and satiety a pleasant state. Imagine that you are feeling very hungry, perhaps because you haven't been able to eat all day. Where in your body do you feel hungry? For example, is it in your stomach (growling), your muscles (fatigued), or your brain? Conversely, if you have eaten recently and are feeling sated, where does that sensation come from—can you localize it? Questions such as these were asked by early investigators in the field, and their studies failed to find any compelling evidence that signals from outside the brain and of which we

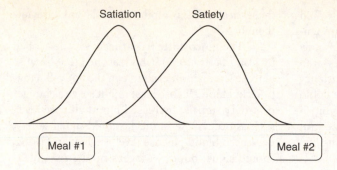

FIGURE 9.1   Schematic representation of the rise and fall of satiation and satiety signals in relation to meals.

are consciously aware—such as stomach sensations of emptiness or fullness—are necessary for us to experience hunger. It has thus been considered that hunger and satiety are central (brain) constructs. However, as we will see, there are many signals from the periphery of which we are not consciously aware that profoundly influence eating behavior.

The human brain is an extraordinary energy consumer—up to 20% of the energy that adults consume is used to fuel the brain. You'd like to think this was a useful investment, right? From a "selfish brain" perspective, one of the critical things that the brain does is to ensure that our physiology and behavior are adequate to keep itself in business. We organize this chapter into two categories of executive brain control. It is convenient to treat them separately, but we emphasize this is merely a conceptual convenience rather than a neurobiological reality; indeed, their seamless integration is what orchestrates the many facets of feeding behavior. The categories are *allostasis* and *reward/decision making*.

We recognize that some readers will have little background in neurobiology; the present chapter will assume only a few basic concepts, at a level comparable to that covered in general psychology texts. A brief primer of these concepts can be found in Appendix 1.

ALLOSTASIS

Many physiological variables have to be maintained within certain limits compatible with survival. An example with which you are probably familiar is body temperature. If your temperature goes up just a little, for example, because you are exercising or have a fever, you start sweating; this provides evaporative cooling to lose heat. Conversely, if you are cold, one of the physiological mechanisms for heat production is shivering. Behavioral actions such as taking off or putting on clothes amplify these physiological changes. The variations in body temperature are normally very small and occur around an average that does not change across your lifetime

---

BOX 9.1   What's the Evidence? Origins of Hunger or Satiation

In an early study (Cannon & Washburn, 1912), Washburn (a medical student) swallowed a balloon that was attached to a tube through which the balloon could be inflated once in the stomach. By measuring the air pressure through this tube, Cannon was able to record when the stomach was contracting (i.e., squeezing the balloon). They reported that contractions were most vigorous when Washburn felt hunger pangs. However, subsequent observations failed to corroborate this "stomach" theory of hunger, including the fact that people whose stomachs have been removed for medical reasons still experience hunger (Woods, Schwartz, Baskin, & Seeley, 2000).

Many other studies (e.g., Nicolaidis & Rowland, 1976) have infused nutrients at different levels of the gastrointestinal tract or directly into the bloodstream to examine the origin of satiation. A simplified summary is that partial satiation can be achieved by many classes and locations of nutrient delivery: Natural foods and eating use most of these mechanisms together or sequentially.

and is the same as that of everyone else. It would be impossible for us to have a "temperature epidemic" parallel to the obesity epidemic. If our body temperature changed even by a few degrees, we'd literally burn up or freeze to death. Such constancy and uniformity of a physiological variable could not occur by chance; Walter Cannon (1929) introduced the term **homeostasis** to describe the process including the active regulatory mechanism(s) by which constancy could be maintained.

Figure 9.2 shows the essentials of a homeostatic mechanism for energy and feeding. Key to this model is a mechanism by which a **set point** can be maintained. Temperature control in your house or apartment works like this: Set point is the room temperature that you select with a thermostat and the output mechanisms are heaters and air conditioners. To what extent are homeostatic principles such as these applicable to regulation of energy balance and body weight? If you think about this for a moment, you'll recognize that two key facts about body temperature (lifetime constancy and uniformity across individuals) are not remotely close to being true for body energy regulation. Nonetheless, perhaps because homeostasis was the only viable physiological model of the mid-to-late twentieth century, early theorists emphasized "stasis" models. These had a profound impact on the field and because elements of

those theories persist today, it is relevant to review them briefly.

The **glucostatic hypothesis** was developed by Jean Mayer (1953), who reasoned that because glucose is a major fuel source in the body, fluctuations in blood glucose level might serve as hunger or satiety signals. Increased blood glucose level, such as occurs after a meal, should signal satiety; decreased blood glucose level, such as in fasting, should signal hunger. Mayer's model requires is a biological mechanism to detect blood glucose level. Such a mechanism was unknown at the time he proposed the theory, but subsequent work has revealed many types of *glucose sensors* or *receptors* that measure glucose level in several organs of the body (e.g., Levin, 2006).

The **lipostatic hypothesis** was developed by Gordon Kennedy (1953), who reasoned that because adipose tissue is the major energy store in the body, fluctuations in fat stores might produce signals related to fat content that influence hunger and satiety. As body fat is stored in several depots around the body, the only mechanism that seemed viable would be blood-borne chemicals secreted from each depot. This led to a search for such a molecule, but it was not until 40 years later that a candidate, **leptin**, emerged (Halaas et al., 1995; see also our chapter on genes and obesity). Leptin belongs to a chemical class of cell-to-cell signaling molecules

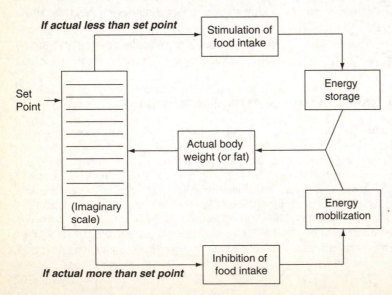

FIGURE 9.2   Diagram of a homeostatic system for energy with a set point.

The actual value (in this case of body weight or a correlate thereof) is compared with the desired or set point using an imaginary scale or comparison device. The direction of any difference is then used to engage a change in eating behavior that will tend to reduce that difference toward zero.

TALKING POINT 9.1

Low blood glucose levels often are associated with symptoms of fatigue. Have you ever felt as if you had low blood sugar? What did you do that made you feel more energetic? Why are snacks that are high in simple sugars often called *cytokines*; it is now known that adipose tissue secretes several cytokines that collectively are known as *adipokines*. Some cytokines promote and some attenuate inflammatory responses in several tissues, and for this reason many people now consider that high levels of adipokines in obesity constitute an **inflammatory disorder** (Odegaard & Chawla, 2013). Fat stores fluctuate slowly, so adipokines are considered to be long-term regulators of food intake, at least within a homeostatic scheme.

There are more fundamental challenges to the concept of homeostasis as applied to body weight. First, weight per se cannot be the critical variable. If it were, weightless astronauts should experience uncontrollable hunger—but they don't. (In its defense, the lipostatic theory does not refer to weight, but rather to the derivative concept of fat content or adiposity.) Second, the occurrence of an obesity epidemic refutes the idea of constancy at a population level. Third, the large variability between individuals in their fat content is completely unlike the small variance in variables such as body temperature.

A more flexible concept, **body weight settling point,** was proposed by Wirtshafter and Davis (1977). According to this theory, given a particular set of conditions such as type and cost of food and energy expenditure, food intake would stabilize at a particular level and body weight and adiposity would correspondingly but passively settle at an equilibrium value. This model correctly predicts that if food were made cheaper or higher in fat content (i.e., gross energy gain increased), then caloric intake and the resultant settling point for body weight would increase. Neither of these outcomes is predicted by the simplest form of the body weight set point model. The concept of set point is thus largely historical and is used sparingly frowned on by schoolteachers? From an evolutionary perspective, do you think it would be adaptive to have hunger occur *only* when blood glucose was low?

by modern researchers. However, it is a seductively simple concept insofar as it provides a culprit if we weigh more than we would like. The term still can be found in many readings as if it was an established fact—reader or Internet surfer, beware!

Some theorists have noted these and other shortcomings of homeostasis, perhaps none more forcefully than Schulkin (2003) and Sterling (2012), who argue that the premise of homeostasis is fundamentally flawed. They propose that the goal of internal regulation is *not* constancy but is continual adjustment to optimize survival. Integral to this flexible concept called **allostasis** is the idea that regulation will involve anticipation of needs, rather than simply reacting to them as implied by a simple homeostatic model. The goal of the concept of *allostasis* is in many ways similar to that of settling point, namely that intake and weight will change adaptively to environmental conditions. You should also recognize the similarity of these concepts to the flexibility required by optimal foraging theory.

HYPOTHALAMUS, TRANSMITTERS, AND FEEDING

More than 100 years ago, Austrian neurologist Alfred Fröhlich described patients who quite suddenly developed a voracious appetite, known as **hyperphagia**, and gained large amounts of body weight (fat). When these patients died, it was found that they had tumors growing in the ventral hypothalamus (the hypothalamus is a small but important region near the middle of the ventral or bottom surface of the brain). Some years later, this dramatic hyperphagia and weight gain (often reaching two to three times normal body weight!) was observed in laboratory rats in which experimental damage (or lesion) to the **ventromedial**

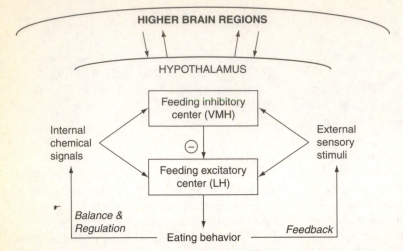

FIGURE 9.3 Dual center neural model of feeding.

(Redrawn and simplified from Stellar (1954).)

hypothalamus (VMH) was produced. An apparently opposite syndrome of **aphagia** (lack of eating) or hypophagia (reduced eating) and associated weight loss followed lesions of the **lateral hypothalamus** (LH). These and other findings led Eliot Stellar (1954) to propose a *dual center* model for feeding (Figure 9.3). This model was the first formal brain-based theory of feeding and emphasized the interactions between a feeding-excitatory center (LH) and a feeding- inhibitory center (VMH). (The terms *excitatory* and *inhibitory* in this context refer to behavioral outcome and should not be confused with electrical potentials and neural activation. The reason is that the brain detects change, so a decrease in the firing rate of a neuron conveys as much information as an increase.)

The study of lesions such as these has been superseded by more selective research methods that interfere with or damage a specific class of cell, gene, transmitter, or receptor. We now talk of feeding-excitatory and feeding-inhibitory neurons or clusters of neurons in a particular brain region all of which express similar genes and proteins. At a conceptual level, the interaction between "on" and "off" systems remains much as proposed by Stellar.

The most studied feeding-excitatory system is anchored by a subpopulation of neurons in the **arcuate nucleus** of the hypothalamus that use neuropeptide Y (NPY), agouti-related peptide (AgRP), and γ-amino butyric acid (GABA)

as co-transmitters (Figure 9.4). These neurons directly inhibit adjacent feeding-inhibitory neurons in the arcuate nucleus that express the

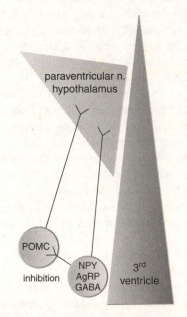

FIGURE 9.4 Schematic diagram of two groups of neurons.

The neurons are in the arcuate nucleus of the hypothalamus (near the fluid-filled third ventricle—only one side of the brain is shown) projecting axons to the paraventricular nucleus of the hypothalamus. The NPY/AgRP (feeding excitatory neurons) also project to and inhibit the feeding inhibitory (POMC) neurons via the inhibitory transmitter GABA.

BOX 9.2	What's the Evidence? Spotlight on NPY and AgRP as a Feeding Peptides

In the 1980s, it was discovered that injection of minute amounts of NPY into the brain of well-fed rats immediately caused them to eat a very large meal. Repeated administration led to sustained overeating and weight gain. The PVN was the most sensitive region of the brain for this effect. Food deprivation was found to increase the endogenous synthesis and release of NPY. The NPY cells also express AgRP. The AgRP story originates with a spontaneous mutation of yellow (*agouti*) coat color in a stock of normally dark-coated mice. Mice with yellow coats all developed obesity relative to their dark-coated siblings. It was then found that *agouti* mice express high levels of a peptide that was named agouti-related peptide (AgRP). AgRP is an natural antagonist of receptors for **melanocortins** receptors: The normal ligand at melanocortin receptors is alpha-melanocyte stimulating hormone, a product from the POMC gene. The yellow coat color is due to blockade of melanocortin receptors (type 1) involved in pigmentation, whereas obesity is due to blocking type 3 and/or 4 melanocortin receptors that are expressed in the brain. Some neurons in the arcuate nucleus express the POMC gene and are part of an inhibitory system for feeding.

The two systems mutually interact to "buffer" overall activity in the PVN, although there is no set point as such. Recently, Aponte, Atasoy, and Sternson (2011) used a new technique, **optogenetics**, to shed light on the role of AgRP. By genetically engineering AgRP cells in mice to express a light-sensitive ion channel (called channel rhodopsin), they were able to selectively activate these cells when they pulsed light down a tiny optical fiber targeted at the arcuate nucleus. Mice ate vigorously each time the light was turned on, even when they were required to work to obtain the food.

---

pro-opiomelanocortin (POMC) gene. These feeding-excitatory and inhibitory neurons project to several locations in the brain, including the paraventricular nucleus of the hypothalamus (PVN). These connections show neuroplasticity, such as modification by metabolic events that are consistent with the adaptability of an allostasis framework.

Meals

A well-known proverb says that any journey begins (or ends) with a single step, and in the same way, internal factors that control food intake ultimately must operate at the level of a single bite or mouthful. A collection of bites in time defines an eating episode. As we noted in an earlier chapter, eating in most animals including humans is intermittent or episodic. For the moment neglecting snacks (see Talking point 9.2), intake occurs

in defined episodes called *meals* and, across the day, in a species-typical sequence or pattern. To maximize the chance of identifying internal factors underlying hunger and satiety, meal patterns are generally measured when plenty of food is available all of the time; this is called an ***ad libitum* feeding** condition (translation—"at one's pleasure"). Many humans eat three meals per day. The timing of these meals is dictated largely by the structure of the workday and/or by habits learned by exposure to the adult food culture during early life and normative external constraints on meal size such as portion size (Herman & Polivy, 2008).

Cultural factors can be minimized by using animals in a laboratory setting in which no structure is imposed, except any that may be dependent on an artificial day-night cycle (often 12 hours light and 12 hours dark). Most studies use individually housed rodents. A typical graph of food intake across a 24-hour period for a rat is

TALKING POINT 9.2

When you eat something, what factors make you categorize that as either a meal or a snack? Wansink, Payne, and Shimizu (2010) asked students and staff at a U.S. university to numerically rate the degree to which imaginary eating situations were considered a meal or a snack. Some environmental factors that emerged were eating with family or alone, ceramic or paper plates, and sitting or standing. Some food-related factors were large or small portion size, low or high cost, and prepared or packaged food. Did you include these? Can you think of others that would be important (or unimportant)?

shown in Figure 9.5 and reveals that eating is episodic, meals are easily identifiable, and (beyond this text) precise mathematical criteria have been applied (e.g., Tolkamp et al., 2011; Zorilla et al., 2005).

These meals are not all the same size—some are bigger than others (taller steps in the graph), and the interval between them is variable (the horizontal distance between steps). If you were to observe a particularly large spontaneous meal, you might reasonably infer that this occurs because the rat has not eaten for a long time and might be particularly hungry. But if this were true, then the sizes of meals should correlate positively with length of non-feeding intervals *preceding* the meals; this is not the case. Indeed, in some studies, the sizes of meals correlate instead with the intervals *after* the meals (i.e., the time until the next meal). This means that eating a certain amount of food predicts a certain average duration of satiety

or that the onset of a meal is caused by the decay of satiety from the previous meal, not by a separate hunger mechanism (LeMagnen, 1985).

This conclusion has exerted a profound influence on research over the past 50 years by fueling a search for internal satiation/satiety signals rather than hunger signals. Ultimately, satiety signals will impinge on the brain, which in turn organizes behavior—for example, "should I eat now or later"? Smith (1996) argued that there are two classes of satiety signals: direct and indirect. Direct signals are those internal signals that arise from eating food and have an effect on metabolism or behavior by action in the brain. Indirect signals are those that modulate the effectiveness of these direct cues (e.g., whether the food is tasty, the social context, current body fat content), also by acting in the brain. The direct signals are the short- and long-term mechanisms we introduced earlier. Most short-term signals are thought to be

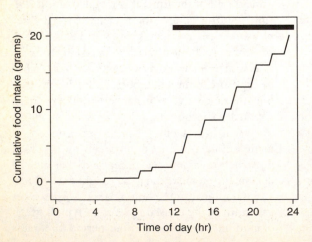

FIGURE 9.5   **Idealized cumulative graph of** *ad libitum* **food intake across a 24-hour period by a rat.**
Each upward step represents food removed from a bowl. Episodes of eating (meals) are clearly distinguishable from non-eating periods; most eating occurs at night (indicated by horizontal black bar).

BOX 9.3   Food for Thought: This is (or was) Your Brain on Fat!

You've probably all seen or heard of the "this is your brain on drugs" campaign from some years ago, in which the brain was depicted as a fried egg. It turns out that obesity might be frying your brain as well! As mentioned earlier, obesity has some characteristics of inflammatory illness. Recent findings suggest that, in contrast to the relatively slow onset of markers of inflammation in adipose tissue, these reactions occur in the brain within a few days of starting to feed mice a high-fat diet (Thaler et al., 2012). Within several weeks, neuronal death was observed in or near the arcuate nucleus. After 8 months, the number of POMC cells in the arcuate of mice was reduced by 30%; evidence for comparable damage in obese humans was obtained from fMRI analysis. Thus, a chronic high-fat diet could be destroying the very parts of the brain that are designed to receive food-related signals that inhibit food intake! Further, high-fat diets induce neuroplasticity in mice within specific brain regions (e.g., Bouret, Bates, Chen, Myers, & Simerly, 2012; Koch et al., 2010), potentially altering—possibly permanently—how memory, perception, and other higher brain processing occurs.

enteroendocrine hormones such as CCK (refer to chapter on chemical senses) and most long-term signals are thought to be adipokines (see previous discussion).

Recall from earlier in the book that increased levels of insulin in obesity lead to a state of insulin resistance in which insulin receptors no longer respond fully. A comparable phenomenon occurs with leptin: Obesity is associated with **leptin resistance**. This means that leptin and insulin may operate as inhibitory signals for food intake within only a relatively narrow range—too little and there's next to no signal, too much and the receptors don't respond any more. Professionals treating obese people often ask them to "listen to your body's signals"—but if those signals are out-of-range (or a critical part

of the brain is damaged), they can't possibly be heard! If we make the reasonable assumption that food intake is controlled by both internal (e.g., adipokines) and external (e.g., cost, appearance, taste) factors, then, at best, the internal factors will have only partial control over eating. It follows that if obese people have receptor resistance that impairs their ability to respond to some or all internal signals, their behavior will be more under the control of external factors such as normative and social factors, conditioning, or stress (see later chapters) than is the case in lean individuals. Schachter's (1968) **externality theory** of obesity is consistent with this reasoning. Conversely, after fasting, when internal signals may have a strong effect, we should be less sensitive to external factors such as taste or cost, and that often is true.

TALKING POINT 9.3

How do your food choices change as a function of time since you last ate or even within a meal? Have you ever been *really* hungry, for example, on a strict diet or stranded without food for some time? Can you recall any changes in your thinking or behavior during that time?

Estrogens

Estrogens, usually in the form of estradiol, which is the main estrogen in humans and rats, suppress food intake. After puberty, female rats generally have 4-day estrous cycles and food intake is ~20% lower on the day of estrous when estradiol levels are highest than on other days of the cycle. Conversely, removal of estradiol in female rats (e.g., by surgical removal of ovaries or after they reach the rat equivalent of menopause) causes an increase in food intake resulting in higher body weight, and replacement of estradiol reverses this condition. The magnitude of this effect can be seen in female compared with male rats fed chow *ad libitum* through their lives (Figure 9.6).

Males approach their maximum weight (and fat content) by about age 6 months, whereas females plateau at a much lower and leaner level between about 3 and 12 months. But at about 1 year or mid-life, estrous cycles stop and average estradiol levels drop. At that point, these middle-aged females eat more and their body weight (almost all as fat) rises rapidly. The mechanism by which estradiol reduces food intake is primarily via receptors of the ERα subtype that are found in several hypothalamic brain nuclei, with multiple effects on feeding systems (Brown & Clegg, 2010).

Now that we know about some more signal molecules, let's ask how these nutrition-related signals cause altered activation of NPY/AgRP or POMC cells in the arcuate nucleus. The arcuate nucleus, like the area postrema in the hindbrain, is one of a few brain structures that have a weak blood-brain barrier. This allows hormones such as leptin and insulin that are in the bloodstream to

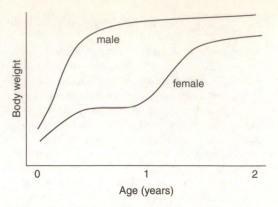

FIGURE 9.6 **Mean body weights of *ad libitum*–fed rats of the Sprague-Dawley strain across their life span.** *Source:* Drawn by the authors from data Keenan et al 2005.

reach the arcuate nucleus. Importantly, there are receptors for both of these hormones on neurons in the arcuate nucleus and both trigger the same intracellular message system. That is, the short- and long-term controls to which we referred earlier actually have the same effect on these cell types; both leptin and insulin have an inhibitory effect on POMC neurons (Williams et al., 2010) and an excitatory effect on AgRP/NPY neurons (Yang, Atasoy, Su, & Sternson, 2011). But do insulin and leptin effects occur in exactly the same cell? Maybe not: Williams et al. (2010) showed that only about one-third of all POMC cells in the arcuate were inhibited by insulin (the rest were unaffected), whereas a different one-third of POMC cells were inhibited by leptin. This finding will require analysis of functional implications, but it serves to illustrate the complexity of organization of brain circuits and feeding.

TALKING POINT 9.4

Hormone (estrogen) replacement therapy is now used quite commonly in postmenopausal women to prevent potentially adverse health effects such as osteoporosis. Middle age is a period of special vulnerability to weight gain in women and often has been linked to menopause. However, estrogen replacement therapy does not reliably prevent weight gain in women (Augoulea, Mastorakos, Lambrinoudaki, Christodoulakos, & Creatsas, 2005). Why do you think that is the case?

Other factors will certainly influence the activity of the AgRP and POMC systems. For example, many of these cells seem to be sensitive to ATP (energy) production from glucose and other metabolic fuels (Belgardt, Okamura, & Bruning, 2009) and may contain specific energy-sensitive regulatory proteins (Blouet, Liu, Jo, Chua, & Schwartz, 2012; Dietrich et al., 2010). Drugs that influence the activity of these systems are potential targets for novel appetite suppressants. Another modulator is the monoamine transmitter **serotonin (5-HT)**. Serotonin has many different receptors distributed throughout the brain, but the most likely candidate for a role in energy homeostasis is the serotonin 2C (*5-HT$_{2C}$*) receptor subtype, and specifically in the hypothalamus. There is evidence that some 5-HT$_{2C}$ receptors are located on POMC cells in the arcuate nucleus (e.g., Sohn & Williams, 2012). Several appetite suppressant drugs work though the serotonin system and will be discussed in a subsequent chapter.

We have so far offered a taste of neural systems that confer some degree of orderliness and stability to food intake. Additional known transmitters, and probably many yet to be discovered, are involved in feeding that we do not have room to discuss. Regardless of how many transmitters and pathways or systems are discovered, we must always return to *the* basic question and ask ourselves which features of this ensemble were selected to confer an adaptive advantage during evolution. It seems that the stasis models for energy regulation significantly miss the point that we are opportunistic feeders, and although the physiology has to match that lifestyle (e.g., feast and famine), it probably is not a major determinant of behavior. In other words, feeding control systems must and do exist, but they have relatively weak control over behavior. That means that something else has stronger control over behavior—we will consider what that might be in the next section.

REWARD AND DECISION MAKING

One of the difficulties with asking people to eat less food, which would certainly cure obesity, is that they like food; in fact, they like it a lot!

Psychologists refer to this as the rewarding or pleasurable aspect of food. It is now believed that a reward system, for foods and probably other things that we find pleasurable, operates independently of or in addition to a regulatory or allostasis-based system.

The first evidence for a reward system in the brain came from work by Olds and Milner (1954), who found that delivering very small electric currents through electrodes to specific regions of rats' brains seemed to be pleasurable because the rats would keep on coming back for more. In fact, they would completely give up food for the electrical stimulation. It is now known that drugs of abuse engage the same brain system. A group of neurons in the **ventral tegmental area** (VTA) of the midbrain that use **dopamine** as their transmitter are known to be the principal component of a reward system (Figure 9.7).

These neurons project to both the nucleus accumbens and the frontal cortex; the systems so formed are called mesolimbic and mesocortical, respectively, although in this text we will not make a functional distinction between them.

There are, of course, circumstances under which ingestion can alleviate a physiological need, such as eating after a long fast or a specific appetite such as for sodium. You might think that

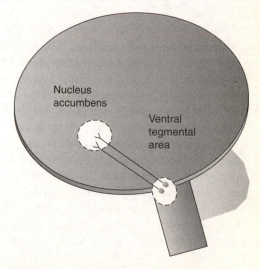

FIGURE 9.7   A representation of the mesolimbic dopamine (reward) system in a human brain.

| BOX 9.4 | What's the Evidence? The Mesolimbic System is Activated by Food |

In a laboratory technique called *in vivo* **microdialysis**, most usually performed in rats, a small double-barreled probe is precisely lowered into a brain region of interest (e.g., the nucleus accumbens), and artificial extracellular fluid is pumped very slowly down one barrel of the probe and is withdrawn up the other. (Brain tissue has no pain receptors, so rats seem quite unaware of this sampling procedure.) At the tip of the probe, a special membrane allows neurotransmitters (and other small molecules) released in the vicinity of its outside surface to diffuse inside and be carried away in the fluid flow. The fluid is collected and subjected to a sensitive chemical assay to determine the amount of each substance (e.g., dopamine) that was released. To obtain enough for analysis, samples are usually collected in 5- to 20-minute epochs. Bassareo and Di Chiara (1999) were among the first to show that eating a palatable food caused an increase in dopamine release that started when food was presented and continued for up to 1 hour afterward. They found that this was restricted to novel palatable foods—preexposure to the test food abolished the dopamine release. Using a technique (voltammetry) that allows continuous sampling, it appears that dopamine may be released in anticipation of rather than a consequence of food delivery in a predictable environment (Roitman, Stuber, Phillips, Wightman, & Carelli, 2004). These aspects of dopamine release parallel the drug abuse literature: we address craving for food in another chapter.

dopamine should be released in these conditions, and insofar as it has been studied, this indeed seems to be the case. The microdialysis study cited in Box 9.4 used well-fed rats, so there was no obvious survival-related benefit to eating the palatable treat.

If the temptation to eat is driven by excess dopamine, you might ask whether giving drugs that block dopamine receptors would reduce eating or motivation. They do, but there are clinical and procedural problems. The clinical problem is that blocking dopamine receptors causes slowness of movement, similar to those caused by **Parkinson's disease** (this is mediated through another dopamine system, distinct from the reward pathways). The procedural problem is that if an animal or human eats less under the action of such a drug, is that effect because reward is attenuated or because they can't move very well? Salamone, Correa, Farrar, and Mingote (2007) described an ingenious way to tease this apart. In their studies, food-deprived rats were given the choice between working for a palatable food and receiving regular chow at no cost. Normally, rats were prepared to work quite hard for the palatable food and ate relatively little chow. Pretreatment with a low dose of a dopamine receptor antagonist (haloperidol) produced a shift in intake from the expensive food to chow, but without any change in the total number of calories consumed. Thus,

the reward of the palatable food can be blunted without impairing the rat's physical ability to consume food.

The brain systems involved in decision making, notably economic decisions including foraging, are more difficult to study. Natural foraging implies mobile subjects making decisions over time in a complex environment, whereas most techniques to study the active brain involve a person or an animal to be relatively physically inactive or even immobile. For example, functional magnetic resonance imaging (fMRI) used in contemporary human studies requires the subject to lie perfectly still in a noisy environment for many minutes. A few studies have used drugs to address foraging in a restricted laboratory setting. One example was cited previously (Salamone et al., 2007) in which animals altered food choice when treated with haloperidol. Day and Bartness (2004) devised a two-compartment burrow system for Siberian hamsters, a small rodent with pouches in its cheeks. In one compartment, they worked for small food pellets by running in a wheel with a fixed unit price. At low unit prices, the hamsters ran to obtain far more pellets than they consumed; they pouched the rest and took them down a tube to a second and dark compartment that simulated their burrow. There, they deposited the extra pellets and formed a food hoard. At high unit prices, they earned fewer pellets and hoarded less. When

BOX 9.5	**What's the Evidence? Interaction of Reward Systems and Energy Regulation**

As mentioned earlier, a GLP-1 projection from hindbrain to forebrain constitutes a potential direct link between internal food-related signals and reward (Figure 9.8) The GLP-1 neurons are activated by meal-related signals, including CCK and gastric distension, and project to the nucleus accumbens (Dossat, Lilly, Kay, & Williams, 2011; Hayes, De Jonghe, & Kanoski, 2010). Further, neurons in the nucleus accumbens that use the transmitter *orexin* (Latin *orexis* = longing, appetite) project caudally to the NST (Figure 9.8).

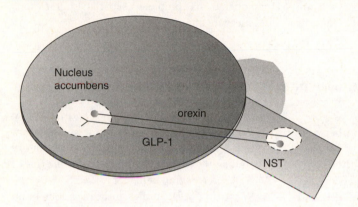

FIGURE 9.8   Representation of the reciprocal interaction in a rat brain between a reward area (n. accumbens) and visceral processing region (NST).

Injection of orexin into some brain regions increases food intake (hence its name). But, contrary to the idea that all orexin pathways increase food intake, injections into the NTS of a drug that blocks orexin receptors also increased food intake (Parise et al., 2011). This suggests that when orexin cells in the nucleus accumbens are activated, feeding-contingent satiation signals in the NTS are less effective. This constitutes a direct and bidirectional interface between a system implicated in reward and afferent signals related to meals and eventually energy regulation.

AgRP was injected into the cerebral ventricles, consistent with its orexigenic action, food intake was stimulated but hoarding was stimulated to an even greater extent—up to 10-fold more than intake. It was concluded that AgRP preferentially stimulates appetitive/foraging behavior over feeding.

Aside from the unfortunate patients with Fröhlich's syndrome, most recent studies of the human brain in relation to food have used fMRI. Patients have to be immobile for these scans, so natural eating is not possible with the current technology although some experiments have been conducted with participants sipping beverages such

TALKING POINT 9.5

If many drugs or transmitters that have been shown to increase (or decrease) food intake instead, as in the Day and Bartness (2004) example, turned out to have a preferential effect on food acquisition and storage, would

that change your view of the distinction between appetitive and consummatory behavior? Would this change (if so, how) the way in which you apply the concept of net energy gain to foraging studies?

as milkshakes through straws, so they are able to ingest liquid food without the movement of chewing. Instead, to simulate a more natural environment, subjects in the scanners may be shown food and non-food pictures and the brain's response to each compared. Some studies have examined decision making, for example, when a subject is asked to play a game or make a choice related to food. In all of these studies, the frontal cortex is a common region of activation (Plassmann, O'Doherty & Rangel, 2010). Recall this is the general region to which olfactory and taste information is channeled, and it also receives a dopamine input via the mesocortical system mentioned earlier, although fMRI is not able to specify the transmitter(s) involved. In summary, at the present time, it appears that foraging and other food-related decisions may engage both nutrient and reward-related systems rather than operate via completely separate brain regions and mechanisms.

Let's review and apply your knowledge. Take time to answer these chapter questions

1. Briefly explain how communication between neurons occurs.
2. Which brain regions are particularly important in homeostatic regulation of eating? Explain the roles of NPY, leptin, AgRP, and α-MSH.
3. Explain the role of dopamine in brain reward processing.
4. What is foraging? Why might it be important to mimic naturalistic conditions in laboratory studies of eating? What seems to be the role of AgRP in foraging behavior?
5. What do fMRI studies indicate about brain activity associated with decision making and cognitive processing regarding food?

Glossary

Ad libitum **feeding**   Food is available for consumption at all times.

Allostasis   A mode of regulation that encompasses anticipation of needs.

Aphagia   Lack or absence of feeding (when food is available) over an extended period.

Arcuate nucleus   The most ventral part of the hypothalamus; has a weak blood-brain barrier allowing penetration of blood-borne hormones. This region is involved with eating behaviors.

Body weight settling point   The concept that in any particular set of environmental conditions, such as availability or palatability of food, body weight will stabilize or settle at a particular value.

Dopamine (DA)   A monoamine neurotransmitter associated with reward, motivation, and movement.

Externality theory   Individuals who are obese or are predispose to obesity are more influenced than non-obese individuals by appetite-stimulating external factors such as sight or smell of food.

Glucostatic hypothesis   Historically important hypothesis that blood glucose concentrations can be used as a signal for hunger and satiation when levels are low and high, respectively.

Homeostasis   Mode of regulation that implies constancy of internal variables. Most versions or models of homeostasis react to rather than anticipate biological needs.

Hunger   Internal (unpleasant) sensation that diverts our thoughts and actions to acquiring and eating food; hunger is a motivating force.

Hyperphagia   Overeating relative to a normal or control condition.

Inflammatory disorder Inflammation is a response by the body to remove a harmful stimulus or to heal. It is therefore a signal of bodily distress, often associated with release of cytokines.

Lateral hypothalamus (LH) Region on the lateral edges of the hypothalamus, a roughly round nucleus at the bottom of the brain. Lesions of the LH produce a variety of neurological disorders including lack of eating (aphagia).

Leptin Peptide hormone, released into the bloodstream primarily from fat cells (adipocytes) in proportion to their fat content. Leptin receptors are found in several brain regions suggesting leptin concentration serves as a signal to the brain about body fat content.

Leptin resistance The phenomenon whereby sustained high concentrations of leptin cause the receptors to desensitize and therefore become resistant to leptin signaling.

Lipostatic hypothesis Historically important hypothesis that a blood-borne factor related to body fat content can be used as a signal for hunger and satiation when levels are low and high, respectively.

Melanocortins A family of neuropeptide transmitters and their receptors. Relative to feeding, α-melanocyte stimulating hormone (MSH) may be the principal ligand, and type 3 and/or 4 receptors the most prominently activated.

Microdialysis Technique to measure release of transmitters; in the present context, the release in specific brain region(s) of alert animals in food-related conditions.

Motivation The driving force that causes an organism to act to obtain a desired goal and/or sustains goal-directed behaviors; for example, hunger elicits food-directed behaviors.

Optogenetics Genetic engineering technique that modifies cells that normally are not photosensitive (e.g., neurons) to be electrically excited by light of a specific wavelength.

Parkinson's disease Neurodegenerative process in which dopamine neurons (in the substantia nigra) degenerate, producing severe and ultimately fatal problems including tremor and difficulty initiating movement.

Satiation The processes that terminate an ongoing eating bout. Satiation can also be viewed as an early phase of satiety.

Satiety The absence of hunger between eating episodes.

Serotonin (5-HT) A monoamine neurotransmitter involved with mood, appetite, and sleep. Some 14 receptor subtypes have been identified; the 2c receptor is most implicated in appetite and feeding.

Set point Hypothetical mechanism for specifying a constant or optimal value for an internal variable within a homeostatic control system.

Settling point The concept that external conditions affect the level at which a controlled system equilibrates.

Ventral tegmental area (VTA) A small group of dopamine-containing cell bodies, near the base of the midbrain, with axons projecting to the nucleus accumbens (mesolimbic) and frontal cortex (mesocortical) regions of the forebrain.

Ventromedial hypothalamus (VMH) Region near the midline of the hypothalamus, a roughly round nucleus at the bottom of the brain. Lesions of the VMH induce overeating and consequent obesity (hyperphagia).

References

Aponte, Y., Atasoy, D., & Sternson, S.M. (2011). AGRP neurons are sufficient to orchestrate feeding behavior rapidly and without training. *Nature Neuroscience, 14,* 351–355.

Augoulea, A., Mastorakos, G., Lambrinoudaki, I., Christodoulakos, G., & Creatsas, G. (2005). Role of postmenopausal hormone replacement therapy on body fat gain and leptin levels. *Gynecological Endocrinology, 20,* 227–235.

Bassareo, V., & Di Chara, G. (1999). Modulation of feeding-induced activation of mesolimbic dopamine transmission by appetitive stimuli and its relation to motivational state. *European Journal of Neuroscience, 11,* 4389–4397.

Belgardt, B. F., Okamura, T., & Bruning, J. C. (2009). Hormone and glucose signaling in POMC and AgRP neurons. *Journal of Physiology, 587,* 5305–5314.

Blouet, C., Liu, S. M., Jo, Y. H., Chua, S., & Schwartz, G. J. (2012). TXNIP in AgRP neurons regulates adiposity, energy expenditure, and central leptin sensitivity. *Journal of Neuroscience, 32,* 9870–9877.

Blundell, J. E. (1991). Pharmacological approaches to appetite suppression. *Trends in Pharmacological Sciences, 12,* 147–157.

Bouret, S. G., Bates, S. H., Chen, S., Myers, M. G., & Simerly, R. B. (2012). Distinct roles for specific leptin receptor signals in the development of hypothalamic feeding circuits. *Journal of Neuroscience, 32,* 1244–1252.

Brown, L. M., & Clegg, D. J. (2010). Central effects of estradiol in the regulation of food intake, body weight, and adiposity. *Journal of Steroid Biochemistry and Molecular Biology, 122,* 65–73.

Cannon, W. B. (1929). Organization for physiological homeostasis. *Physiological Reviews, 9,* 399–431.

Cannon, W. B., & Washburn, A. L. (1912). An explanation of hunger. *American Journal of Physiology, 29,* 441–454.

Day, D. E., & Bartness, T. J. (2004). Agouti-related protein increases food hoarding more than food intake in Siberian hamsters. *American Journal of Physiology: Regulatory Integrative Comparative Physiology, 286,* R38–R47.

Dietrich, M. O., Antunes, C., Geliang, G., Liu, Z.-W., Borok, E., Nie, Y., ... Horvath, T. L. (2010). AgRP neurons mediate Sirt1's action on the melanocortin system and energy balance: Roles for Sirt1 in neuronal firing and synaptic plasticity. *Journal of Neuroscience, 30,* 11815–11825.

Dossat, A. M., Lilly, N., Kay, K., & Williams, D. L. (2011). Glucagon-like peptide 1 receptors in nucleus accumbens affect food intake. *Journal of Neuroscience, 31,* 14453–14457.

Halaas, J. L., Gajiwala, K. S., Maffei, M., Cohen, S. L., Chait, B. T., Rabinowitz, T., ... Friedman, J. M. (1995). Weight-reducing effects of the plasma protein encoded by the obese gene. *Science, 269,* 543–546.

Hayes, M. R., De Jonghe, B. C., & Kanoski, S. E. (2010). Role of the glucagon-like-peptide-1 receptor in the control of energy balance. *Physiology and Behavior, 100,* 503–510.

Herman, C. P., & Polivy, J. (2008). External cues in the control of food intake in humans: The sensory-normative distinction. *Physiology and Behavior, 94,* 722–728.

Keenan, K. P., Hoe, C. M., Mixson, L., McCoy, C. L., Coleman J. B., Mattson, B. A., ..., Soper, K. A. (2005). Diabesity: A polygenic model of dietary-induced obesity from ad libitum overfeeding of Sprague-Dawley rats and its modulation by moderate and marked dietary restriction. *Toxicologic Pathology, 33,* 600–608.

Kennedy, G. C. (1953). The role of depot fat in the hypothalamic control of food intake in rats. *Proceedings of the Royal Society, Series B, 140,* 578–592.

Koch, C., Augustine, R.A ., Steger, J., Ganjam, G. K., Benzler, J., Pracht, C., ... Tups, A. (2010). Leptin rapidly improves glucose homeostasis in obese mice by increasing hypothalamic insulin sensitivity. *Journal of Neuroscience, 30,* 16180–16187.

LeMagnen, J. (1985). *Hunger.* New York: Cambridge University Press.

Levin, B. E. (2006). Metabolic sensing neurons and the control of energy homeostasis. *Physiology and Behavior, 89,* 486–489.

Mayer, J. (1953). Glucostatic mechanism of regulation of food intake. *New England Journal of Medicine, 249,* 13–16.

Molon-Noblot, S., Hubert, M.-F., Hoe, C.-M., Keenan, K. & Laroque, P. (2005). The effects of ad libitum feeding and marked dietary restriction on spontaneous skeletal muscle pathology in Sprague–Dawley rats. *Toxicological Pathology, 33,* 600–608.

Nicolaidis, S., & Rowland, N. (1976). Metering of intravenous versus oral nutrients and regulation of energy balance. *American Journal of Physiology, 231,* 661–668.

Odegaard, J. I., & Chawla, A. (2103). Pleiotropic actions of insulin resistance and inflammation in metabolic homeostasis. *Science, 339,* 172–177.

Olds, J., & Milner, P. (1954). Positive reinforcement produced by electrical stimulation of septal area and other regions of rat brain. *Journal of Comparative and Physiological Psychology, 47,* 419–427.

Parise, E. M., Lilly, N., Kay, K., Dossat, A. M., Seth, R., Overton, J. M., & Williams, D. L. (2011). Evidence for the role of hindbrain orexin-1 receptors in the control of meal size. *American Journal of Physiology: Regulatory Integrative Comparative Physiology, 301,* R1692–1699.

Plassmann, H., O'Doherty, J. P., & Rangel, A. (2010). Appetitive and aversive goal values are encoded in the medial, orbitofrontal cortex at the time of decision making. *Journal of Neuroscience, 30,* 10799–10808.

Roitman, M. F., Stuber, G. D., Phillips, P. E. M., Wrightman, R. M., & Carelli, R. M. (2004). Dopamine acts as a subsecond modulator of food seeking. *Journal of Neuroscience, 24,* 1265–1271.

Salamone, J. D., Correa, M., Farrar, A., & Mingote, S. M. (2007). Effort-related functions of nucleus accumbens dopamine and associated forebrain circuits. *Psychopharmacology, 191,* 461–482.

Schachter, S. (1968). Obesity and eating. *Science, 161,* 751–756.

Schulkin, J. (2003). Rethinking homeostasis: Allostatic regulation in physiology and pathophysiology. Cambridge, MA: The MIT Press.

Smith, G. P. (1996). The direct and indirect controls of meal size. *Neuroscience and Biobehavioral Review, 20,* 41–46.

Sohn, J.-W., & Williams, K.W. (2012). Functional heterogeneity of arcuate nucleus pro-opio-melanocortin neurons: Implications for diverging melanocortin pathways. *Molecular Neurobiology, 45,* 225–233.

Stellar, E. (1954). The physiology of motivation. *Psychological Review, 61,* 5–22. [Reprinted in 1994, *Psychological Review, 101,* 301–311.]

Sterling, P. (2012). Allostasis: A model of predictive regulation. *Physiology & Behavior, 106,* 5–15.

Thaler, J. P., Yi, C. X., Schur, E. A., Guyenet, S. J., Hwang, B. H., Dietrich, M. O., ... Schwartz, M. W. (2012). Obesity is associated with hypothalamic injury in rodents and humans. *Journal of Clinical Investigation, 122,* 153–162.

Tolkamp, B. J., Allcroft, D. J., Barrio, J. P., Bley, T. A. G., Howie, J. A., Jacobsen, T. B., ... Kyriazakis, I. (2011). The temporal structure of feeding behavior. *American Journal of Physiology: Regulatory Integrative and Comparative Physiology, 301,* R378–R393.

Wansink, B., Payne, C. R., & Shimizu, M. (2010). "Is this a meal or a snack?" Situational cues that drive perceptions. *Appetite, 54,* 214–216.

Williams, K.W., Margatho, L.O., Lee, C.E., Choi, M., Lee, S., Scott, M. M., ... Elmquist, J. K. (2010). Segregation of acute leptin and insulin effects in distinct populations of arcuate proopiomelanocortin neurons. *Journal of Neuroscience, 30,* 2472–2479.

Wirtshafter, D., & Davis, J. D. (1977). Set points, settling points, and the control of body weight. *Physiology and Behavior, 19,* 75–78.

Woods, S. C., Schwartz, M. W., Baskin, D. G., & Seeley, R. J. (2000). Food intake and the regulation of body weight. *Annual Review of Psychology, 51,* 255–277.

Yang, Y., Atasoy, D., Su, H. H., & Sternson, S. M. (2011). Hunger states switch a flip-flop memory circuit via a synaptic AMPK-dependent positive feedback loop. *Cell, 146,* 992–1003.

Zorilla, E. P., Inoue, K., Fekete, E. M., Tabarin, A., Valdez, G. R., & Koob, G. F. (2005). Measuring meals: Structure of prandial food and water intake of rats. *American Journal of Physiology: Regulatory Integrative Comparative Physiology 288,* R1450–1467.

10

Eating Disorders and Treatment

After reading this chapter, you will be able to

- Understand the clinical conditions of anorexia nervosa and bulimia nervosa
- Recognize personality and behavioral differences and similarities associated with anorexia nervosa and bulimia nervosa

- Know the leading biological, psychological, and sociocultural explanations for eating disorders
- Describe the most effective contemporary treatments for eating disorders and the issues surrounding treatment
- Appreciate animal models of eating disorders

Estimates indicate that between 1% and 3% of the American population (roughly 8 million people) suffer with a diagnosed eating disorder, and many more suffer from subclinical (less severe) disordered eating (Hudson, Hiripi, Pope, & Kessler, 2007). In comparison with the percentage of the population that is overweight or obese (~65%), the incidence of these eating disorders may seem low; however, eating disorders are severely debilitating and have the highest death rate of any psychiatric illness. Further, the frequency of eating disorders is much higher among certain groups of people, including college students, actors, models, and athletes participating in "appearance sports" (sports with an emphasis on appearance, weight, speed, or diet, e.g., dance, gymnastics, swimming, running, and wrestling; Prouty, Protinsky, & Canady, 2002; Sundgot-Borgen & Torstveit,

2004; Zucker, Womble, Williamson, & Perrin, 1999). The *Diagnostic and Statistical Manual for Mental Health Disorders* (5th ed.; DSM-5) provides criteria for the diagnosis of anorexia nervosa and bulimia nervosa (American Psychiatric Association [APA], 2013). The diagnosis of binge-eating disorder was added to the most recent edition of the DSM, with estimates that this disorder affects twice the number of people compared with anorexia or bulimia. Disordered eating behavior that does not meet the criteria for a specific diagnosis in the DSM is identified as an eating disorder not otherwise specified (EDNOS). This diagnosis, as are the other eating disorder diagnoses, is associated with emotional distress and reduced quality of life (Turner, Bryant-Waugh, & Peveler, 2010).

It is important to bear in mind that the distinction between disordered eating and normal eating is often unclear. We all at times have "peculiar" eating habits and food preferences or aversions. Dieting and being concerned about weight are considered normal in our society. So, when does "normal" behavior become "abnormal"? The important difference with clinically disordered eating is the extreme persistence regarding ritualistic or restrained eating behaviors, and this is associated with particular personality types and ways of thinking. In this chapter, we discuss the symptoms associated with anorexia nervosa and bulimia nervosa, risk factors, leading explanations for these disorders, and best current treatments.

ANOREXIA NERVOSA

Anorexia nervosa (AN) is characterized by extreme thinness and a desire to lose weight or maintain an abnormally low weight. According to the DSM-5 criteria (see Table 10.1), a diagnosis of AN can be made if an individual is considerably underweight and fears gaining weight; thus, the diagnosis does not apply to sufferers of metabolic disorders or other illnesses that cause weight loss, if those individuals hope to return to a healthy weight. The psychology and distorted body image associated with AN are significant aspects of the illness and its diagnosis (APA, 2000; 2013).

Katie

When Katie started high school, kids occasionally teased her about being "chubby," and a friend suggested that she would probably be more popular if she lost a little weight. She decided to cut out desserts and candy from her diet in hopes of shedding a few pounds. After several months of dieting and increasing her exercise, she started receiving compliments from friends and family members. Her mom proudly took her out shopping for some new cute clothes, and the boy she had a crush on asked her out. Liking her success, Katie eliminated bread and meat from her diet. She also increased her exercise regimen from every other day to every day. Within 2 years, the compliments turned to looks of concern. Katie, 5 feet 4 inches in height, now weighed 85 pounds. (Weights between 110 and 145 pounds are considered healthy for someone of her height [Division of Nutrition, Physical Activity, and Obesity, National Center for Chronic Disease, 2011].) She was an excellent student, made straight As, and thought she looked great, although she believed she could look better if she lost a little more weight. Katie assumed the people questioning her weight and health were just jealous of her looks and ability to control her diet so well. Her parents became concerned about her shrinking appearance and her obsession with her exercise regimen, but they assumed she was going through a teenage girl "phase" and would soon return to normal eating habits. However, when she visited her family physician for an annual checkup, she was asked about her menstrual cycle. Katie happily answered that she hadn't had a period in more than a year. Her physician realized that Katie's low weight, denial of its seriousness, amenorrhea (cessation of menses), and refusal to gain weight were symptoms of anorexia nervosa. Her parents were consulted, and she spent the next 3 months in an inpatient facility focused on helping her restore weight and develop healthier eating habits and body image. We will return to Katie's story a little later in this chapter.

TABLE 10.1   **DSM-5, Diagnostic Criteria for Anorexia Nervosa**

1. Restriction of food intake leading to significantly low body weight.
2. Intense fear of gaining weight.
3. Disturbed body perception and/or denial of the seriousness of the current low weight.

Source: Based on APA, 2000

BOX 10.1   How Can Body Perception Be Measured?

Several techniques have been used by different groups of researchers to assess perceived body size. Results of these studies consistently indicate that people with AN overestimate their body size and are more dissatisfied with their body size compared to peers without eating disorders (e.g., Farrell, Lee, & Shafran, 2005). In one such study, photographed images of the participants were projected in front of them adjacent to a full-length mirror allowing them to simultaneously see their actual reflection (Shafran & Fairburn, 2002). The participants were asked to have the experimenters adjust the projected image until it matched what they saw in the mirror. The participants with eating disorders significantly overestimated

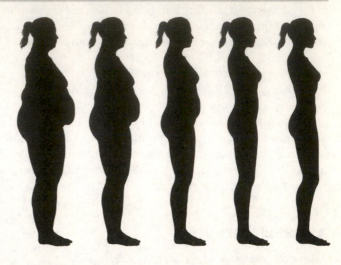

their body size compared with those without eating disorders. This study was one of the first to allow the participants to actually see their own reflection as they estimated body size; most studies require participants to recall their size from memory.

Katie's story is typical of how many eating disorders begin—with an effort to lose some weight. AN has an average age of onset between 14 and 18 years, a time of hormonal fluctuation and heightened social pressures (APA, 2000). Individuals with AN are often characterized as perfectionists and are usually competitive and high achieving. They view their weight loss as success and become fixated on losing more weight and being the "thinnest" person in their peer group. Frequently, as with Katie, their weight loss is initially met with praise and reinforcement. Thus, severe calorie restriction, meal rituals, and excessive exercise become obsessions. They hold distorted thoughts about their body size and appearance, usually estimating themselves to be much larger and less attractive than they actually are (Farrell, Shafran, & Lee, 2005).

Two patterns are associated with AN: The restricting type is characterized by severe and persistent calorie restraint, and the binge-eating/purging-type involves efforts to eliminate consumed food (e.g., self-induced vomiting, excessive exercise, or laxative or diuretic misuse).

AN is considered the most severe psychological disorder, with 15% to 20% of sufferers dying within 20 years of the onset of their disorder (Birmingham, Su, Hlynsky, Goldner, & Gao, 2005; Lucas, Beard, O'Fallon, & Kurland, 1991). Suicide and cardiovascular problems are the leading causes of deaths among anorexics (Herzog et al., 2000). As discussed, people with AN are rarely sufficiently pleased with their weight or appearance and are severely distressed by issues surrounding food. Anorexics often isolate themselves socially: They avoid the unwanted comments or concerned looks from friends or family members. Further, people with AN are preoccupied with food (reading recipe books, planning and preparing food for others, learning how to disguise their minimal intake and food regimens, etc.). So, over time they withdraw from others, which contributes to a sense of loneliness, despair, and self-loathing. Depression and anxiety are often co-morbid with AN (Silberg & Bulik, 2005).

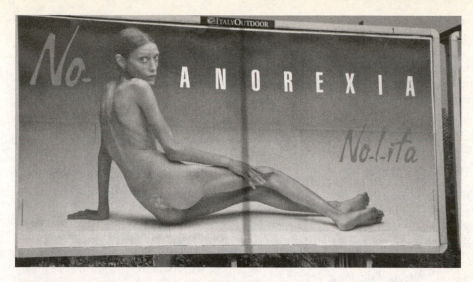

FIGURE 10.1 Isabelle Caro, a French model and actress, struggled with anorexia and died in 2010 at age 28 as a result of medical complications associated with AN. Her picture was used as part of an anorexia awareness campaign in Italy and other countries. (bajootraluz.blogspot.com)

Medical Problems Associated with AN

The medical problems associated with AN are consistent with those associated with starvation (Katzman, 2005). With energy intake below its needs, the body attempts to conserve its resources and preserve its vital functions. Medical consequences include low blood pressure, heart rate, and body temperature; amenorrhea (absence of the menstrual cycle in females of menstruation age); dry and brittle skin, hair, and nails; and lanugo (fine, downy hair normally present on third trimester fetuses) on the face and extremities. The reduced body temperature results in heightened sensitivity to cold temperatures, something anorexics often complain about (Brown, Mehler, & Harris, 2000).

The amenorrhea associated with AN is due to a decrease in levels of several hormones including estrogen. (Klibanski, Biller, Schoenfeld, Herzog, & Saxe, 1995). Estrogen helps support bone density in females; consequently, low levels increase the likelihood of early-onset osteoporosis, a disorder associated with bone fractures and reduced height. Estrogen disturbances can also result in reproductive difficulties and infertility. People with AN have increased risks for electrolyte imbalances and cardiovascular problems, particularly if vomiting, diuretics, or laxatives are used as methods of purging. Cardiac arrest as a result of electrolyte and fluid imbalance can result in sudden death. Anorexics also commonly suffer sleep disturbances, perhaps because of an imbalance of serotonin (a neurotransmitter associated with the homeostatic regulation of eating and sleep) or a persistent desire to burn calories, thus a need to busy themselves even during nighttime hours (Haleem, 2012).

Let's return to Katie: In the years that followed in-patient treatment, Katie remained underweight and continued to use excessive exercise as a means of purging the food she ate. She became increasingly rigid with her eating and exercise routines, isolating herself from close relationships with others. Now at age 35, Katie's thin hair and hunched posture (a result of early onset osteoporosis) make her appear much older than she actually is. Katie has realized the unfortunate consequences of her years of starving herself, but much of the damage is irreversible.

Generally, the more chronic the symptoms of AN, the more resistant they are to treatment. The rigid personality, fear of weight gain, and long-term medical consequences associated with AN contribute to the difficulties in treating and preventing relapse in this population, as with Katie. Thus, early identification and treatment of AN symptoms are critical for recovery.

BULIMIA NERVOSA

Bulimia nervosa (BN) is more prevalent than AN, affecting between 1% and 3% of the population (AN affects less than 1% of the population; Hudson et al., 2007). BN is characterized by cycles of food binges and purges (getting rid of the excessive food consumed during a binge).

A *binge* is an excessive amount of food eaten within a limited amount of time (less than 2 hours) (APA, 2013). Binges cause uncomfortable fullness and feelings of shame and guilt; thus, purges serve as compensatory behavior. Commonly used purging methods include vomiting; misusing laxatives, diuretics, or enemas; and excessive exercising. (The term *excessive exercise* refers to exercise performed not for enjoyment, and not because of participation on a sports team or training for an athletic event, or even for health, but rather as a means of burning off calories recently consumed. This type of exercise involves a psychology that differs in key ways from exercise performed for enjoyment, health, or sport.)

Binges usually occur when the individual is alone and are done secretly. The eating is beyond physiological needs, and hunger is not a necessary prerequisite for a binge—psychological factors such as stress, loneliness, or depressed mood can prompt binge eating (Mathes, Brownley, Mo, & Bulik, 2009). Foods consumed during binges are normally soft textured and require little or no chewing (e.g., cookie dough, ice cream, breads and sandwiches, milkshakes, juices and sodas, cookies, and cake) and are frequently sweet tasting, high in calories and fat (Latner & Wilson, 2000), and considered "forbidden." Binges usually contain more than 1,000 calories (often more than 4,000; Kaye et al., 1992). In

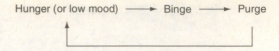

FIGURE 10.2 The cycle associated with BN.

other words, in a single "sitting" or bout, bulimics may consume more than the recommended caloric intake for an entire day. Bulimics describe their binges as numbing, pleasurable, and even euphoric. However, the "high" is quickly followed by a "low." After bingeing, bulimics feel guilty, ashamed, worried about weight gain, and often experience self-hatred and depression (Hayaki, Friedman, & Brownell, 2002). Bulimics are concerned about their appearance and are fearful of gaining weight. Purging helps alleviate the guilt and discomfort associated with the out-of-control bingeing and eliminate some of the food consumed, but it also causes guilt and shame. Further, because purging empties the stomach, hunger follows and the cycle of binge-eating and purging continues (Figure 10.2).

Bulimics are typically within 10 pounds of the expected or healthy weight for their height. It is often assumed that they should be underweight because purging "undoes" the binge; however, purging methods do not allow 100% compensation. Vomiting, for example, results in the elimination of only about half of the calories consumed in a binge (Latner & Wilson, 2000). Further, recurrent purging disrupts the body's ability to regulate hunger and satiety, leads to more frequent feelings of hunger, and alters digestion and metabolism of food consumed. The diagnosis of BN requires that bingeing and purging behaviors occur at least once a week (see Table 10.2), but these behaviors are usually far more frequent; for some sufferers, episodes occur more than 30 times per week (Kaye et al., 1992).

Medical Problems Associated with BN

The medical problems associated with BN are generally related to the means of purging. People who use forced vomiting as a frequent purging method risk damage to their teeth, gums, and

TABLE 10.2	DSM-5, Diagnostic Criteria for Bulimia Nervosa

1. Recurrent episodes of binge-eating.
2. Recurrent inappropriate purging behavior to prevent weight gain.
3. The symptoms occur, on average, at least once a week for 3 months.
4. Inappropriate focus on shape and weight.

Source: Adapted from APA (2013).

esophagus. Gastric acids cause erosion of tooth enamel, making teeth prone to cavities and decay. It is not uncommon for a dentist or dental hygienist to be among the first to identify symptoms of BN (DeBate, Tedesco, & Kerschbaum, 2005). Acids can also cause ulcerations of the esophagus and swallowing difficulty. Frequent forced vomiting can result in reflexive, unwanted vomiting (this is called *reverse peristalsis*). Misuse of laxatives and diuretics can cause kidney damage, bowel control problems, and electrolyte imbalances that can be fatal.

Andrea

Andrea, a bright and ambitious college student, had interests in opera, foreign languages, human rights, and a desire to "save the world." She was fluent in Spanish, was studying German, and planned to tackle the Japanese language next. She was an ardent supporter of human rights and planned to use her degree in international business and politics to improve the lives of others around the world. Andrea was a loving daughter, sister, and friend. Unfortunately, she suffered with bulimia nervosa. Her mother beautifully describes her and shares entries from her journals written during high school and college in the book *Andrea's Voice* (Smeltzer, Smeltzer, & Costin, 2006). Andrea's mood swings, self-hatred, and frustration elevated during the months she battled bulimia. She wrote in her journal about her desire to "win" the battle and described her disappointment and resentment when she had setbacks. In one entry, she wrote that she feared she needed to cut back on her purging (vomiting) because she was starting to experience reflexive vomiting and was unable to keep food down (reverse peristalsis). Despite her tremendous accomplishments in life and promising future,

Andrea felt imprisoned by her illness, angry at her captor, and alone. Tragically, after a 13-month battle with bulimia, an electrolyte imbalance caused her heart to fail and she died in her sleep at age 19.

Risk Factors for Eating Disorders

People with eating disorders are considered the most homogeneous of all psychiatric populations (Kaye, Fudge, & Paulus, 2009). About 90% of people with AN or BN are females; most are white, of middle or upper socioeconomic status, and between ages 14 and 35. Until recently, eating disorders were considered Western problems, reported primarily among people in North America and Western Europe. However, rates of eating disorders are now rising in industrialized countries around the world. In Japan, for example, a culture that values thinness particularly among women, eating disorders are among the fastest-growing psychiatric problems for females in adolescence and early adulthood (Pike & Borovoy, 2004). Rates of eating disorders have likewise risen among Hispanic and African American females and among young white males, groups of people in our culture that until recently did not emphasize extreme thinness (Gentile, Raghavan, Rajah, & Gates, 2005; Miller & Pumariega, 2001).

The average age of onset of eating disorders is during adolescence or early adulthood (most often between ages 15 and 21, with AN usually occurring at younger ages than BN; Hoek & Van Hoeken 2003; Hudson et al., 2007). Depression, anxiety, and substance abuse are frequently comorbid with AN and BN (Hudson et al., 2007; Kaye, 2008). These may contribute to the onset of eating disorders or they could be consequences of them; however, recent evidence indicates that other factors underlie eating disorders and the co-morbid disorders (e.g., personality, serotonin imbalance, genetics; Kaye et al., 2009; Stice, Burton, & Shaw, 2004). Stimulants (e.g., cocaine, methamphetamine, nicotine), which speed up metabolism and reduce feelings of hunger, are often abused by people with eating disorders. People with BN are more likely than people with AN to additionally abuse alcohol and marijuana (as these can contribute to weight gain; Root et al., 2010).

Different personality characteristics are associated with AN and BN. As discussed previously, anorexics are typically perfectionists, exercising high levels of self-control and harm avoidance, and hold themselves to idealistic standards (Kaye, 2008). Consequently, they tend to be very self-critical. They are paradoxically obsessed with food and eating rituals, yet steadfast in their restraint from eating in their pursuit of weight loss. Many have symptoms of obsessive-compulsive personality disorder. Because they tend to isolate themselves so that they can pursue their eating and exercise rituals without receiving negative attention, they can exhibit symptoms of avoidant personality disorder (Diaz-Marsá, Luis, & Sáiz, 2000).

Bulimics are less controlling and restrained than anorexics. Rather, bulimics tend to be more impulsive and have more erratic mood swings. Some people with BN have symptoms of borderline personality disorder, which is characterized by emotional instability and impulsiveness. Bulimics tend to be highly concerned with pleasing and being attractive to others, whereas anorexics are more focused on meeting their own goals and adhering to their stringent standards. These personality traits seem to differentially increase an individual's risk of either AN or BN (Tyrka, Waldron, Braber, & Brooks-Gunn, 2002).

BIOPSYCHOSOCIAL EXPLANATIONS OF EATING DISORDERS

Eating disorders are found primarily in industrialized societies that emphasize a thin appearance. Media and marketing contribute to the pervasiveness of particular attractiveness ideals. In the 1960s, super-thin models, such as Twiggy, were glamorized. Some theorists postulate that this idealization of a thin body type led people (women, in particular) to hold themselves to this standard and judge themselves harshly, resulting in restrained and disordered eating for some. Another poignant example of the influence of media occurred in Fiji. Eating disorders and body image issues were minimal among the Fijian population (with only one reported case of AN) prior to the 1995 introduction of television. Rates of body dissatisfaction and disordered eating increased significantly within just a few years of media exposure and had a particularly negative impact among adolescent girls (Becker, Burwell, Gilman, Herzog, & Hamburg, 2002).

However, it is important to consider this: Media messages idealizing the thin body image are pervasive; yet only between 1% and 3% of our population has a diagnosable eating disorder. If media or other social influences bear full responsibility for disordered eating, then, theoretically, everyone within that culture would suffer, and clearly that is not the case.

Historical investigation reveals that disordered eating occurred in ancient Greek, Roman, and Egyptian cultures, among early Christians, and during the Renaissance, usually for ritualistic or religious reasons (Miller & Pumariega, 2001). For example, it is well documented that bingeing and purging occurred during Roman festivals or events (particularly among the wealthy). Early Christians are known to have restrained from food as a demonstration of selflessness and purity (the psychology behind their restraint is clearly different from that associated with AN, but the behaviors can appear similar). And similar self-imposed food restriction occurs today in non-Western cultures (e.g., fasting among Buddhists as a practice of self-control).

Whereas it is quite clear that sociocultural influences contribute to distorted body image and eating behaviors, other factors must additionally contribute. In this section, we explore the **biopsychosocial model** to explain eating disorders. According to this model, biological, psychological, and sociocultural factors are

A Buddhist monk at a place of worship.

separate but have additive or synergistic effects increasing an individual's risk for developing an eating disorder.

Biological Factors

Eating disorders occur at much higher rates within families than among the general population, and the closer someone is related to an individual with an eating disorder, the greater the risk that person has of developing an eating disorder as well even when raised in a different environment (Klump, Suisman, Burt, McGue, & Iacono, 2009). Studies of identical (monozygotic) and fraternal (dizygotic) twins indicate a 50% to 80% genetic contribution to the vulnerability for

TALKING POINT 10.1

Could there be alternative explanations for the higher rates of eating disorders within families other than biological factors? Explain.

AN or BN (Bulik et al., 2006; Kaye, 2008; Kendler et al., 1991; Kendler et al., 1995; Klump, Miller, Keel, McGue, & Iacono, 2001). It seems that some people may have shared genetic liability for the development of eating disorders. Of particular interest to researchers are genes, neurotransmitters, and brain pathways associated with appetite, impulse control, motivation, and reward.

SEROTONIN   Several groups of researchers have found evidence implicating a role of the genes involved in the synthesis of the neurotransmitter **serotonin** and its receptors in eating disorders (Haleem, 2012; Kaye, 2008). Serotonin activity is associated with satiety, mood, and inhibition. People with AN or BN are at increased risk for co-morbid depression, which is also associated with irregular serotonin activity (Haleem, 2012). However, it seems that serotonin activity associated with AN differs from that associated with BN. For example, people with AN exercise high levels of dietary restraint and inhibition, whereas people with BN have impulse control difficulties, indicating that serotonin activity may be high in the brains of people with AN and low in those with BN. Further, symptoms of BN are typically reduced by antidepressant medications that increase serotonin activity, but these medications are unreliable in the treatment of AN (Ferguson, La Via, Crossan, & Kaye, 1999; Kaye, 2008). This further supports the theory that serotonin activity is lower than normal for bulimics, but higher for people with anorexia.

People with AN have reduced brain volume, particularly in chronic cases. Thus, in studies of their brain irregularity, it is difficult, and often impossible, to determine which factors are *causal* versus *consequential* of the disorder (Kaye et al., 2009). With AN, a cycle of below normal consumption of food and weight loss drives a continued effort to restrict calories and lose more weight. Some evidence supports the theory that anorexics have higher than normal levels of serotonin activity *prior* to the onset of their symptoms, which contribute to their feelings of satiety, nervousness about food consumption, and drive for thinness and perfection. Further, food consumption elevates the already high levels of serotonin, whereas starvation serves to reduce levels and stabilize mood. So, people with AN may actually avoid food as an attempt reduce their anxiety. (We recommend Kaye et al. [2009] for a review of the neurobiology of AN.)

DOPAMINE AND THE ENDOGENOUS OPIOID SYSTEM   Individuals with AN have blunted enjoyment of palatable food (along with decreased enjoyment of other typically rewarding or enjoyable stimuli; Kaye et al., 2009) whereas people with BN frequently report euphoric-like feelings associated with binge episodes. These dissimilar emotional states associated with the two eating disorders indicate that the brain's reward pathways may respond in different ways to food-related stimuli. Most people have elevated neural activity on seeing or consuming appetizing food (e.g., brownies, pizza, candy) in areas of the brain associated with reward, but these stimuli have the converse effect on the brain activity of people with AN, indicating disturbances within the **dopamine** system, which persist after recovery from

symptoms (Kaye, Frank, & McConaha, 1999). Dopamine dysfunction could contribute to the diminished reward response associated with food-related stimuli in the brains of people with AN and their reduced motivation to consume food.

In contrast, heightened responsiveness of the reward pathways (involving dopamine and endogenous opioids) is linked to the binge-eating aspect of BN. One group of researchers found that naloxone, a drug that blocks opioid receptors in the brain, reduced palatable food consumption among people with BN (or with binge-eating problems) but not among normal weight or obese non-bingeing individuals (Drewnowski, Krahn, Demitrack, Nairn, & Gosnell, 1995). Along with the reduced activity of serotonin, the neurobiological alterations of reward circuitry may help explain the impulse-control problems and overconsumption associated with binge eating.

Psychological Factors

People with eating disorders have distorted attitudes about eating and body weight. They have frequent negative thoughts about their appearance and their eating behaviors. From the **cognitive perspective** in the field of psychology, their maladaptive and negative thoughts lead to attempts to restrain eating and lose weight. In other words, the thoughts precede the behaviors. Further, the cycle of negative thinking coupled with unhealthy eating behaviors is reinforcing, and the person becomes more convinced of his or her distorted thoughts about weight and eating and is increasingly compulsive about his or her eating behaviors (more restraining with AN or more frequent bingeing and purging with BN).

Theorists from the **psychodynamic perspective** in psychology posit that disordered eating behaviors stem from misuse of food by parents during an individual's childhood (Bruch, 1973; Zerbe, 2008). Parents sometimes use food as a means of soothing children. This can lead to a lifelong emotional association with food. Children parented in this way learn to seek food for comfort, rather than nutrition, which can result in binge eating (BN) or to food restriction as a means of self-punishment (AN) later in life. **Behavioral theorists** also believe that this early experience with food is influential because children learn to model their parents' eating behaviors. So, parents who eat food as a means of comforting themselves are likely to unintentionally teach the same behavior to their children.

Sociocultural Factors

Historically, societies struggled with food scarcity, and low weight was due to inability to obtain sufficient amounts of food. In such societies, people of heavier weights were considered healthier, more attractive, and of higher social status than people of low weights. In our current society, the opposite is true. Exposure to media perpetuating this thin-ideal image is correlated with body dissatisfaction and disordered eating (Stice, Shupak-Neuberg, Shaw, & Stein, 1994; Thompson & Stice, 2001). Sociocultural influences, including media, family, and peers, may have a negative impact on body satisfaction, putting genetically vulnerable individuals at greater risk of developing an eating disorder.

Children of parents who exercise high levels of dietary restraint and emphasize weight loss are at increased risk of disordered eating (Baker, Whisman, & Brownell, 2000; Birch & Fisher, 2000). Further, children of *authoritarian* parents (parents who are controlling, set strict rules, and expect obedience) have a reduced ability to regulate calorie needs (Johnson & Birch, 1994) and are more likely to eat in the absence of hunger (Birch & Fisher, 2000). Girls are apparently more affected than boys by parental behaviors, especially by the mother's behaviors and attitudes. Daughters of mothers who are preoccupied with weight, restrict or limit foods, and/or encourage their daughters to lose weight are at a particularly increased risk for disordered eating (Francis & Birch, 2005). Parents who encourage healthy eating and explain the benefits of a healthy lifestyle, offer healthy options from which children can select their food, and eat together as a family have children with healthier lifelong eating habits (Patrick, Nicklas, Hughes, & Morales, 2005). It is important to note,

though, that the shared disordered eating between mothers and daughters or within families may be attributed to environment and learning, but it also may be due to shared genetics responsible for perfectionistic or obsessive personality types.

TREATMENTS

Only a small percentage of people with eating disorders receive treatment, and an even smaller percentage completes the recommended therapeutic phases (Halmi et al., 2005; Hudson et al., 2007; Noordenbos, Oldenhave, Muschter, & Terpstra, 2002). People with AN are particularly resistant to treatment and unlikely to initiate a search for help for several reasons—an individual's denial of the seriousness of the disorder, refusal to make changes in eating behaviors or gain weight, the expense of treatment, and under diagnosing of disordered eating by physicians (Walsh, Wheat, & Freund, 2000). However, recognition of symptoms, support, and treatment are critically important for recovery from eating disorders. Leading contemporary treatments involve individual, group, and family therapy; nutrition counseling; and often medication, especially when other psychological disorders are co-morbid with the eating disorder.

The first step in treating AN is helping the individual restore weight. This process is more challenging than it sounds, particularly in chronic cases. Digestion is slowed for these individuals, resulting in discomfort when they consume meals larger than what they have become accustomed to eating. Further, weight gain causes distress for people with AN, as this has been their fear. Behavioral tactics are usually the most effective methods for helping people with AN gain weight (Kaye, Klump, Frank, & Strober, 2000). Rewards, such as praise and computer or television time, are given when a person eats appropriately. This process can take place in an inpatient treatment center or at an individual's home, which often involves family supervision and support. Typically, a nutritionist or other trained professional creates a daily meal plan with gradual caloric increases over the span of several weeks (usually about 100 additional calories per week until weight is restored). This method, in contrast with force-feeding of a high-calorie diet in the first few days of treatment, is more tolerable to the person with AN both physiologically and psychologically. People with BN are able to begin psychological therapy and medication immediately on diagnosis as they are usually within a healthy weight range (Kaye et al., 2000). The most frequently prescribed medications for eating disorders are selective serotonin reuptake inhibitors (SSRIs), which are also antidepressants and work by elevating serotonin neurotransmission (Kaye, 2008).

Cognitive-behavioral therapy (CBT) is the leading type of psychological therapy for eating disorders (Bulik, Berkman, Brownley, Sedway, & Lohr, 2007; Walsh et al., 2000; Yager & Powers, 2007). CBT addresses an individual's maladaptive thoughts about food and body weight and also reinforces healthy eating behavior (Fairburn, 1995). **Dialectical behavior therapy,** a newer form of CBT, is used to train people to better regulate their emotions. This is particularly helpful for people who are prone to binge eating for emotional reasons (Telch, Argas, & Linehan, 2001).

Individual therapy is usually coupled with **family and group therapy**. Because family dynamics frequently contribute to the onset of disordered eating, it is important that the family members address their issues so that they can provide a supportive environment for the individual recovering from an eating disorder (Wilson, Grilo, & Vitousek, 2007). Group therapy can help sufferers realize that they are not alone. Because anorexics tend to isolate themselves and bulimics binge and purge secretly, sufferers are usually comforted by the realization that other people also suffer in similar ways. Additionally, in group therapy people can share tactics that they have found helpful and can support one another through the recovery process. Unfortunately, there are two main reasons for concern with group therapy—the sharing of unhealthy weight loss tactics and competition among group members to be the thinnest (this is particularly problematic among anorexics). Therapists work to ensure that the group therapy is beneficial and not harmful, as effective social and family support is important for long-term recovery.

Is Treatment Effective?

Simply stated, improvement from eating disorder symptoms is more likely with treatment than without it (Bulik et al., 2007; Shapiro et al., 2007; Walsh

This is an example of a group therapy session.

et al., 2000). Unfortunately, people with eating disorders often drop out of therapy or relapse after remission of symptoms, particularly in cases of chronic AN. However, the research on the effectiveness of therapy and specific forms of treatment is limited because of the small sample sizes and high dropout rates in most of the studies (Bulik et al., 2007). And, as discussed previously, people with eating disorders often have co-morbid psychological disorders and issues, which complicate the effectiveness of therapy.

Other problematic issues surrounding treatment are expense and accessibility. Recall Katie, discussed earlier in this chapter. She was in a treatment facility for 3 months—the length of time recommended by most therapists and psychiatrists. The average cost of inpatient treatment for eating disorders is $30,000 per month, and insurance companies do usually not cover it. Most people cannot afford to pay nearly $100,000 for the recommended 3 months of treatment. Taking such a long period of time away from work or school creates an additional challenge for people suffering with eating disorders.

ANIMAL MODELS OF ANOREXIA AND BULIMIA

Given the obstacles to therapy and high rates of relapse, there is hope that drug treatment will be possible in the treatment of eating disorders. To test potential therapeutic agents, animal models have been examined. You may wonder if animals could be feasible models of eating disorders. With the possible exception of non-human primates (in whom this type of research is essentially impossible for well-justified animal welfare considerations), animals are not thought to have a developed sense of self-awareness and in particular body image. So, the essential aspect of distorted body image, especially in AN, probably cannot be modeled. But other animal models have one key attribute of AN as it relates to eating: forgoing food when it is available despite substantial weight loss. These models fall into two categories: those that occur in nature, and those that are induced by a laboratory procedure.

Let's look first at the natural models. One of the most widely known is "incubation anorexia,"

which refers to the loss of appetite and weight loss (often 10% to 15%) observed in many species of birds while they have eggs in their nest (Mrosovsky, 1990), especially when only one sex does all the incubating. You might rightly point out that the bird is put into a conflict of keeping the eggs warm and protected versus leaving the nest to forage for food. However, this anorexia occurs in these birds even in a domesticated environment when abundant food is placed next to the nest. This observation leads to the conclusion that there are physiological changes (probably hormonal) during incubation that suppress appetite and, in a natural environment, will suppress hunger and keep the incubating bird "on task."

This model is not only task-related but, because birds are seasonal breeders, will be associated with specific day length (photoperiod) indicative of the season. If animals show physiological and behavioral changes in different seasons, they are said to be photoperiodic. There are other photoperiod-related changes in food intake. Many species eat less in the winter when days are short and lose substantial body weight (e.g., 20%; Iverson & Turner 1974), and, like the incubating birds, this occurs even in captivity when food is readily available. In the natural environment, food tends to be less abundant during the winter, and expending large amounts of energy in unsuccessful foraging is a poor survival strategy. The physiological suppression of hunger then has an adaptive function. Another example is in rutting deer (Yoccoz, Mysterud, Langvatn, & Stenseth, 2002): the males lose 10% to 15% of their body weight during rutting season, even though there is plenty of grass around; in contrast, females do not lose weight.

Unfortunately for the animal model perspective, humans are not photoperiodic with regard to mating or breeding behavior, but one could argue that some individuals such as those prone to seasonal affective disorder may exhibit some elements of photoperiodism. One established laboratory model that does not involve photoperiodism is called **activity-based anorexia** (ABA; Epling, Pierce, & Stefan, 1983). In this protocol, animals (usually rats or mice) are given food for a restricted time each day—often 2 to 4 hours.

Most species are able to adapt to this type of schedule quite well; although they don't eat as much as they would with 24-hour access, they do eat more than enough to maintain a healthy body weight. In fact, this type of time-restricted feeding regimen is common in zoos and for domestic pets. In ABA, the animals are additionally provided with a running wheel. As they lose weight, they tend to run more and so expend more energy, but their food intake does not rise commensurately (and may in fact be suppressed a bit). As a result, they are trapped in a spiral of progressively more negative energy balance and usually have to be removed from the experiment for humane reasons when weight loss exceeds a threshold (e.g., 15%).

Another model that does not involve ABA has recently been found using mice in one of the authors' labs (Atalayer & Rowland, 2012). In this case, food was also restricted to 160 minutes per day but spread out across the night into several meals or feeding opportunities (we used 4, 8, or 16 opportunities of 40, 20, or 10 minutes each). Additionally, the food was available as small pellets (20 mg) for which the mice had to work by emitting a fixed number of responses. After several days, the number of responses required (the price) was increased. Food intake was highly influenced by the condition: At 25 responses per pellet, the intake was <50% that at the lowest cost (2 responses), and the mice lost weight rapidly. You might question whether at 25 responses per pellet and only 160 minutes total access to food, the animals were simply running out of time to acquire more food. But analysis of when pellets were taken within an opportunity showed that even when weight was dropping, the mice ate progressively less within each window of opportunity

and eventually stopped eating, and overall ate less than half they could have consumed if they had used the time fully. One key feature of this procedure might be that the local rate of feeding is limited because responses need to be performed between each mouthful or pellet. (Slowing of eating by more chewing has been advocated as an appetite control device in humans and is discussed in other chapters.) This, or some other aspect of this situation, is leading to a "voluntary" failure to increase feeding duration within an opportunity.

In the case of bulimia nervosa, many animals (rats and mice in particular) are unable to vomit, and so that essential aspect (along with body image) of BN is not modeled. However, several protocols have been developed in which animals eat a large amount in a short time. In most of these protocols, using rats or mice, the relatively bland maintenance diet (chow) is available all the time and a preferred or palatable supplement is given occasionally. When the supplement is given every day, intake tends to be quite high and constant from day to day, and it is compensated by a reduction of chow intake over the rest of the day so that total caloric intake is not increased and no weight gain occurs. However, if the supplement is given every other day (or, in general, less predictably), the intake increases as the number of exposures increases and eventually greatly exceeds the intake of the supplement by the daily group (Corwin, 2004).

Are these useful models of AN or BN? We'll leave you to debate and think on this! Regardless, the relative absence of eating disorders among animals, infants, and young children supports that we are biologically driven to eat and survive, and eating disorders defy these innate motivations.

CONCLUDING REMARKS

Eating disorders are serious life-endangering psychiatric conditions. Biological, psychological, and sociocultural factors contribute to an individual's risk for the development and maintenance of disordered eating. Cognitive-behavioral therapy is the most effective and frequently used type of

psychotherapy for both AN and BN; however, access and affordability are hindrances to treatment for many sufferers. Early diagnosis and treatment yield the most optimistic outcomes, particularly when coupled with family and social support.

Let's review and apply your knowledge. Take some time to answer these chapter questions

1. What are the criteria for the diagnosis of AN? For BN?
2. Describe the personality types and behaviors most associated with AN and those most associated with BN.
3. What are the medical complications or problems associated with each eating disorder?
4. Provide several pieces of support for a biopsychosocial explanation for eating disorders.
5. What are the leading types of treatment? What are some of the issues surrounding treatment?
6. Discuss research involving animal models of eating disorders. What are the limitations of animal models when studying eating disorders?

Glossary

Activity-based anorexia   A laboratory model of weight loss involving exercise and reduced food intake.

Behavioral theorists   Researchers and practitioners focused on the effects of learning on behavior.

Biopsychosocial model   The theory that psychological problems are due to interactions of biological, psychological, and sociocultural factors.

Cognitive perspective   A psychological model focused on the content and process of human thinking.

Cognitive-behavioral therapy (CBT)   Psychological therapy that addresses maladaptive thoughts and dysfunctional behaviors.

Dialectical behavior therapy   A form of cognitive-behavioral therapy that emphasizes emotion regulation, mindful awareness, and acceptance.

Dopamine (DA)   A monoamine neurotransmitter associated with reward, motivation, and movement.

Family and group therapy   Formats in which the therapist meets with family members or groups of individuals with similar psychological issues.

Psychodynamic perspective   A theoretical model that attributes human functioning to interactions of forces and drives within the person, particularly in the unconscious mind. Childhood experiences are emphasized within this perspective.

Serotonin (5-HT)   A monoamine neurotransmitter involved with mood, appetite, and sleep. Some 14 receptor subtypes have been identified; the 2c receptor is most implicated in appetite and feeding.

References

American Psychiatric Association. (2000). *Diagnostic and statistical manual of mental disorders* (4th ed., text revision). Washington, DC: Author.

American Psychiatric Association. (2013). *Diagnostic and statistical manual of mental disorders* (5th ed.). Washington, DC: Author.

Atalayer, D., & Rowland, N. E. (2012). Effects of meal frequency and snacking on food demand in mice. *Appetite, 58,* 117–123.

Baker, C. W., Whisman, M. A., & Brownell, K. D. (2000). Studying intergenerational transmission of eating attitudes and behaviors: Methodological and conceptual questions. *Health Psychology, 19,* 376–381.

Becker, A. E., Burwell, R. A., Gilman, S. E., Herzog, D. B., & Hamburg, P. (2002). Eating behaviours and attitudes following prolonged television exposure among ethnic Fijian adolescent girls. *British Journal of Psychiatry, 180,* 509–514.

Birmingham, C. L., Su, J., Hlynsky, J. A., Goldner, E. M., & Gao, M. (2005). The mortality rate from anorexia nervosa. *International Journal of Eating Disorders*, *38*(2), 143–146.

Birch, L. L., & Fisher, J. O. (2000). Mothers' child-feeding practices influence daughters' eating and weight. *American Journal of Youth and Adolescence, 27*, 43–57.

Brown, J. M., Mehler, P. S., & Harris, R. H. (2000). Topics in review: Medical complications occurring in adolescents with anorexia nervosa. *Western Journal of Medicine, 172*(3), 189–193.

Bruch, H. (1973). *Eating disorders: Obesity, anorexia nervosa and the person within.* New York: Basic Books.

Bulik, C. M., Berkman, N. D., Brownley, K. A., Sedway, J. A., & Lohr, K. N. (2007). Anorexia nervosa treatment: A systematic review of randomized controlled trials. *International Journal of Eating Disorders, 40*(4), 310–320.

Bulick, C., Sullivan, P. F., Tozzi, F., Furberg, H., Lichtenstein, P., & Pedersen, N. L. (2006). Prevalence, heritability, and prospective risk factors for anorexia nervosa. *Archives of General Psychiatry, 63*(3), 305–312.

Corwin, R. L. (2004). Binge-type eating induced by limited access in rats does not require energy restriction on the previous day. *Appetite, 42,* 139–142.

DeBate, R. D., Tedesco, L. A., & Kerschbaum, W. E. (2005). Knowledge of oral and physical manifestations of anorexia and bulimia nervosa among dentists and dental hygienists. *Journal of Dental Education, 69*(3), 346–354.

Diaz-Marsá, M., Luis, J., & Sáiz, J. (2000). A study of temperament and personality in anorexia and bulimia nervosa. *Journal of Personality Disorders, 14*(4), 352–359.

Division of Nutrition, Physical Activity, and Obesity, National Center for Chronic Disease. (2011). Prevention and health promotion healthy weight—it's not a diet, it's a lifestyle. Retrieved from http://www.cdc.gov/healthyweight/assessing/bmi/adult_bmi/english_bmi_calculator

Drewnowski, A., Krahn, D. D., Demitrack, M. A., Nairn, K., & Gosnell, B. A. (1995). Naloxone, an opiate blocker, reduces the consumption of sweet high-fat foods in obese and lean female binge eaters. *American Journal of Clinical Nutrition, 61*(6), 1206–1212.

Epling, W. F., Pierce, W. D., & Stefan, L. (1983). A theory of activity-based anorexia. *International Journal of Eating Disorders, 3*(1), 27–46.

Fairburn C. G. (1995). *Overcoming binge eating.* New York: Guilford Press.

Farrell, C., Lee, M., & Shafran, R. (2005). Assessment of body size estimation: A review. *European Eating Disorders Review, 13,* 75–88.

Farrell, C., Shafran, R., & Lee, M. (2006). Empirically evaluated treatments for body image disturbance: A review. *European Eating Disorders Review, 14*(5), 289–300.

Ferguson, C. P., La Via, M. C., Crossan, P. J., & Kaye, W. H. (1999). Are serotonin selective reuptake inhibitors effective in underweight anorexia nervosa? *International Journal of Eating Disorders, 25*(1), 11–17.

Francis, L. A., & Birch, L. L. (2005). Maternal influences on daughters' restrained eating behavior. *Health Psychology, 24,* 548–554.

Gentile, K., Raghavan, C., Rajah, V., & Gates, K. (2007). It doesn't happen here: Eating disorders in an ethnically diverse sample of economically disadvantaged, urban college students. *Eating disorders, 15*(5), 405–425.

Haleem, D. J. (2012). Serotonin neurotransmission in anorexia nervosa. *Behavioural Pharmacology, 23*(5, 6), 478–495.

Halmi, K. A., Argas, W. S., Crow, S., Mitchell, J., Wilson, G. T., Bryson, S. W., & Kraemer, H. C. (2005). Predictors of treatment acceptance and completion in anorexia nervosa: Implications for future study designs. *Archives of General Psychiatry, 62*(7), 776–781.

Hayaki, J., Friedman, M. A., & Brownell, K. D. (2002). Shame and severity of bulimic symptoms. *Eating Behaviors, 3*(1), 73–83.

Herzog, D. B., Greenwood, D. N., Dorer, D. J., Flores, A. T., Ekeblad, E. R., Richards, A., … Keller, M. B. (2000). Mortality in eating disorders: A descriptive study. *International Journal of Eating Disorders, 28*(1), 20–26.

Hoek, H. W., & Van Hoeken, D. (2003). Review of the prevalence and incidence of eating disorders. *International Journal of Eating Disorders, 34*(4), 383–396.

Hudson, J. I., Hiripi, E., Pope, H. G., & Kessler, R. C. (2007). The prevalence and correlates of eating disorders in the National Comorbidity Survey Replication. *Biological Psychiatry, 61*(3), 348–358.

Johnson, S. L., & Birch, L. L. (1994). Parents' and children's adiposity and eating style. *Pediatrics, 94*(5), 653–661.

Iverson, S. L., & Turner, B. N. (1974). Winter weight dynamics in *microtus pennsylvanicus. Ecology, 55,* 1030–1041.

Katzman, D. K. (2005). Medical complications in adolescents with anorexia nervosa: A review of the literature. *International Journal of Eating Disorders, 37*(S1), S52–S59.

Kaye, W. (2008). Neurobiology of anorexia and bulimia nervosa Purdue ingestive behavior research center symposium influences on eating and body weight over the lifespan: Children and adolescents. *Physiology and Behavior, 94,* 121–135.

Kaye, W. H., Klump, K. L., Frank, G. K. W., & Strober, M. (2000). Anorexia and bulimia nervosa. *Annual Review of Medicine, 51*(1), 299–313.

Kaye, W. H., Frank, G. K., & McConaha, C. (1999). Altered dopamine activity after recovery from restricting-type anorexia nervosa. *Neuropsychopharmacology, 21,* 503–506.

Kaye, W. H., Fudge, J. L., & Paulus, M. (2009). New insights into symptoms and neurocircuit function of anorexia nervosa. *Nature Reviews Neuroscience, 10,* 573–584.

Kaye, W. H., Weltzin, T. E., McKee, M., McConaha, C., Hansen, D., & Hsu, L. K. (1992). Laboratory assessment of feeding behavior in bulimia nervosa and healthy women: Methods for developing a human-feeding laboratory. *American Journal of Clinical Nutrition, 55*(2), 372–380.

Kendler, K. S., MacLean, C., Neale, M., Kesler, R., Heath, A., & Eaves, L. (1991). The genetic epidemiology of bulimia nervosa. *American Journal of Psychiatry, 148*(12), 1627–1637.

Kendler, K. S., Walters, E. E., Neale, M. C., Kessler, R., Heath, A., & Eaves, L. (1995). The structure of genetic and environmental risk factors for six major psychiatric disorders in women. *Archives of General Psychiatry, 52,* 374–383.

Klibanski, A., Biller, B. M., Schoenfeld, D. A., Herzog, D. B., & Saxe, V. C. (1995). The effects of estrogen administration on trabecular bone loss in young women with anorexia nervosa. *Journal of Clinical Endocrinology & Metabolism, 80*(3), 898–904.

Klump, K. L., Miller, K. B., Keel, P. K., McGue, M., & Iacono, W. G. (2001). Genetic and environmental influences on anorexia nervosa syndromes in a population-based sample of twins. *Psychological Medicine, 31*(4), 737–740.

Klump, K. L., Suisman, J. L., Burt, S., McGue, M., & Iacono, W. G. (2009). Genetic and environmental

influences on disordered eating: An adoption study. *Journal of Abnormal Psychology, 118*(4), 797–805. doi:10.1037/a0017204.

Latner, J. D., & Wilson, G. T. (2000). Cognitive-behavioral therapy and nutritional counseling in the treatment of bulimia nervosa and binge eating. *Eating Behaviors, 1*(1), 3–21.

Lucas, A. R., Beard, M. C., O'Fallon, M. W., & Kurland, L. T. (1991). 50-year trends in the incidence of anorexia nervosa in Rochester, Minn.: A population-based study. *The American Journal of Psychiatry, 148*(7), 917–922.

Mathes, W. F., Brownley, K. A., Mo, X., & Bulik, C. M. (2009). The biology of binge eating. *Appetite, 52*(3), 545–553.

Miller, M. N., & Pumariega, A. J. (2001). Culture and eating disorders: A historical and cross-cultural review. *Psychiatry, 64*(2), 93–110.

Mrosovsky, N. (1990). *Rheostasis: The physiology of change.* New York: Oxford University Press.

Noordenbos, G., Oldenhave, A., Muschter, J., & Terpstra, N. (2002). Characteristics and treatment of patients with chronic eating disorders. *Eating Disorders, 10*(1), 15–29.

Patrick, H., Nicklas, T. A., Hughes, S. O., & Morales, M. (2005). The benefits of authoritative feeding style: Caregiver feeding styles and children's food consumption patterns. *Appetite, 44,* 243–249.

Pike, K. M., & Borovoy, A. (2004). The rise of eating disorders in Japan: Issues of culture and limitations of the model of "westernization." *Culture, Medicine and Psychiatry, 28,* 493–531.

Prouty, A. M., Protinsky, H. O., & Canady, D. (2002). College women: Eating behaviors and help-seeking preferences. *Adolescence, 37,* 353–363.

Root, T. L., Pinheiro, A. P., Thornton, L., Strober, M., Fernandez-Aranda, F., Brandt, H., … Bulik, C. M. (2010). Substance use disorders in women with anorexia nervosa. *International Journal of Eating Disorders, 43*(1), 14–21.

Shapiro, J. R., Berkman, N. D., Brownley, K. A., Sedway, J. A., Lohr, K. N., & Bulik, C. M. (2007). Bulimia nervosa treatment: A systematic review of randomized controlled trials. *International Journal of Eating Disorders, 40*(4), 321–336.

Silberg, J. L., & Bulik, C. M. (2005). The developmental association between eating disorders symptoms and symptoms of depression and anxiety in juvenile twin girls. *Journal of Child Psychology and Psychiatry, 46*(12), 1317–1326.

Shafran, R., & Fairburn, C. G. (2002). A new ecologically valid method to assess body size estimation and body size dissatisfaction. *International Journal of Eating Disorders, 32*(4), 458–465.

Smeltzer, D., Smeltzer, A., & Costin, C. (2006). *Andrea's voice—silenced by bulimia: Her story and her mother's journey through grief toward understanding.* Carlsbad, CA: Gürze Books.

Stice, E., Burton, E., & Shaw, H. (2004). Prospective relations between bulimic pathology, depression, and substance abuse: Unpacking comorbidity in adolescent girls. *Journal of Consulting and Clinical Psychology, 72*(1), 62.

Stice, E., Schupak-Neuberg, E., Shaw, H. E., & Stein, R. I. (1994). Relation of media exposure to eating disorder symptomatology: An examination of mediating mechanisms. *Journal of Abnormal Psychology, 103*(4), 836–840.

Sundgot-Borgen, J., & Torstveit, M. K. (2004). Prevalence of eating disorders in elite athletes is higher than in the general population. *Clinical Journal of Sport Medicine, 14*(1), 25–32.

Telch, C. F., Argas, W. S., & Linehan, M. M. (2001). Dialectical behavior therapy for binge eating disorder. *Journal of Consulting and Clinical Psychology, 69,* 1061–1065.

Thompson, J. K., & Stice, E. (2001). Thin-ideal internalization: Mounting evidence for a new risk factor for body-image disturbance and eating pathology. *Current Directions in Psychological Science, 10*(5), 181–183.

Turner, H., Bryant-Waugh, R., & Peveler, R. (2010). The clinical features of EDNOS: Relationship to mood, health status and general functioning. *Eating Behaviors, 11*(2), 127–130.

Tyrka, A. R., Waldron, I., Graber, J. A., & Brooks-Gunn, J. (2002). Prospective predictors of the onset of anorexic and bulimic syndromes. *International Journal of Eating Disorders, 32*(3), 282–290.

Walsh, J. M. E., Wheat, M. E., & Freund, K. (2000). Detection, evaluation, and treatment of eating disorders: The role of the primary care physician. *Journal of General Internal Medicine, 15,* 577–590.

Wilson, G. T., Grilo, C. M., & Vitousek, K. M. (2007). Psychological treatment of eating disorders. *American Psychologist, 62*(3), 199–216.

Yager, J., & Powers, P. S. (Eds.). (2007). *Clinical manual of eating disorders.* Washington, DC: American Psychiatric Publishing.

Yoccoz, N. G., Mysterud, A., Langvatn, R., & Stenseth, N. C. (2002). Age- and density-dependent reproductive effort in male red deer. *Proceedings of the Royal Society—Biological Sciences, 269,* 1523–1528.

Zerbe, K. J. (2008). *Integrated treatment of eating disorders beyond the body betrayed.* New York: W. W. Norton.

Zucker, N. L., Womble, L. G., Williamson, D. A., & Perrin, L. A. (1999). Protective factors for eating disorders in female college athletes. *Eating Disorders, 7,* 207–218.

11

Genes, Epigenetics, and Obesity

After reading this chapter, you will be able to

- Give examples of monogenic obesity and prevalence in human obesity
- Understand polygenic obesity, and challenges associated with identifying genes
- Define epigenetics and its implications for obesity
- Discuss the role of dietary factors in diet-induced obesity (and resistance)

Several neural mechanisms are thought to be involved in feeding, energy expenditure, and ultimately the observed level of body weight in an individual. Those neural mechanisms and the underlying physiology of digestion and metabolic processes have emerged through a process of natural selection that operates at the level of genes: Only the fittest survive to pass their genes to the next generation.

"My genes are making me fat" is an internal attribution that may be made by people whose BMI is higher than they would like. But is there any truth to this statement and, if so, is there anything that can be done about it? The purpose of this chapter is to discuss how genes map on to functional systems related to energy balance and modifications of these genes, and in a broader sense to discuss functional traits associated with genes. You don't have to be a geneticist to read and grasp the essentials of this chapter, but if you don't know anything about genes are or how

they operate, it's probably a good idea to refer to Appendix 2.

There are two main theoretical approaches to thinking about food intake and obesity, and these often and unfortunately compete for public attention and research funding. These two approaches are shown in Figure 11.1.

This distinction was recognized by early theorists of motivated behavior and embodied in the concepts of **drive**—a hypothetical internal propelling force, and **incentive**—an external attractive force (of food). Variations in genetic makeup could affect either physiology, for example, by causing a metabolic alteration that increases energy storage, or behavior, for example, via a change in a personality trait such as impulsiveness and hence the interaction with food objects. Thus, identifying a gene as linked to obesity does not tell us whether that gene has a *primary* effect on physiology or on behavior. Ultimately, however, one will affect the other because physiology and

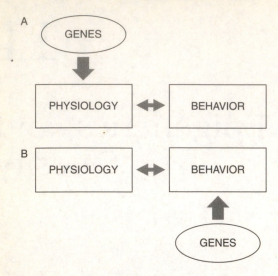

A

GENES

PHYSIOLOGY ⟷ BEHAVIOR

B

PHYSIOLOGY ⟷ BEHAVIOR

GENES

FIGURE 11.1   Two perspectives about how genes, and in particular obesity-linked genes, can affect food intake and obesity.
In panel A, the genes are having direct effects on physiological processes that secondarily cause reactive changes in feeding behavior. In panel B, the genes are having direct effects on feeding behavior that secondarily cause adaptive changes in physiology.

behavior are essential partners. At a descriptive level (e.g., body weight), you could argue that the distinction is not important, but if you planned to use that genetic information to devise interventions and treatments, then it matters a whole lot. As you read this chapter, repeatedly ask yourself this question: "physiology or behavior or both?"

MONOGENIC OBESITY

Monogenic (single gene) mutations that cause obesity are dramatic, and, although rare in humans, their study in animal models has led to significant advances in our understanding of food intake and obesity. The strength of animal models is that they allow us to study one factor in isolation, an ideal that can rarely be met in a human population. These models use genomic disruption, either by spontaneous or induced mutation, so the animal lives its entire life with the abnormal gene. It should be borne in mind that this type of mutation potentially allows for other systems to compensate for or adjust; as a result, the observed effect on food intake or obesity inevitably may be less than the independent or stand-alone contribution of the mutation.

The first well-studied genetically obese (and type 2 diabetic) model was the *ob/ob* mouse, a recessive mutation such that the mouse has to inherit two defective copies of the *ob* gene

(so-called because the offspring are obese) from its parents (Figure 6.2).

The *ob/ob* **phenotype** is caused by a point mutation at a single nucleotide base in DNA that results in premature termination of gene translation (i.e., the protein is short and nonfunctional). Jeffrey Friedman and his colleagues (Zhang et al., 1994) identified the protein—now called leptin from Greek *leptos* meaning thin—that was the normal product of this gene. Hence, this genetic mutation is now more correctly called *lep-/-*, indicating two defects (minus signs) of the leptin gene. These mice have normal birth weights but start to gain weight early in life; after they are weaned from their mothers, their weight gain is maintained by overeating and low activity. These animals also develop severe type 2 diabetes. In rats, different **point mutations** to the leptin gene are known—Zucker (*fa/fa*) and Koletsky (*f/f*)—and these also show early-life onset and severe obesity.

A second mouse mutation with a similar phenotype, called *db/db* for diabetes, was discovered at about the same time as *ob/ob*. Subsequent investigation showed that the genetic mutation caused a defect in one form of leptin receptor (LepRb). Like *ob/ob* mice, these mice start to become obese soon after weaning, by overeating as well as reduced activity, and their weights rapidly diverge from those of littermates that do not carry two copies of the defective gene (*lepR-/-*).

FIGURE 11.2 An adult *ob/ob* (or *lep-/-)* mouse weighs more than twice as much as littermates that are not homozygous for genetic defect.   http://www.montclair.edu/news/images/feature/sized/Mice-1.jpg.jpg

Are there examples of leptin-related mutations and obesity in humans? Yes, but they are quite rare. Montague et al. (1997) identified three very obese children who had undetectable blood levels of leptin; the obesity and other phenotypes exhibited by such children were reversed by chronic treatment with leptin. More commonly, but still relatively infrequently, mutations to the leptin receptor are found in up to 3% of individuals with severe obesity. These subjects have normal birth weights but start to gain weight abnormally fast within the first few months of life. They show increased food seeking and hyperphagia at least into adolescence (for a review, see Ramachandrappa & Farooqi, 2011). Thus, mutations with complete loss of functional leptin or its receptor produce phenotypes in humans very similar to those in *ob/ob* or *db/db* mice.

Another obese mouse mutation is the *agouti* mouse that produces too much agouti-related peptide (AgRP), an endogenous antagonist or blocker of **melanocortin (MC) receptors**. In the brain, one of the main MC signaling pathways involved in feeding is via MC4 receptors in the paraventricular nucleus of the hypothalamus that receive input from pro-opiomelanocortin (POMC) containing neurons in the arcuate nucleus. Consistent with the obesity phenotype of *agouti*, disruption of either the POMC gene or the MC4 receptor gene is also associated with severe (monogenic) obesity in mice. Again, equivalent loss-of-function mutations in humans are associated with overeating and early onset obesity (Ramachandrappa & Farooqi, 2011). Defects in the MC4 receptor are the most common, accounting for up to 5% of severe early-onset obesity. Another perhaps less optimistic way of looking at this is that leptin- and MC-related genetic defects together account for less than 10% of severe childhood obesity, which means these monogenic syndromes account for literally the tiniest tip of an immense iceberg of obesity.

BOX 11.1 What's the Evidence? Mutant Mice and the Lipostatic Hypothesis

When the *ob/ob* and *db/db* mutations were first discovered, their genetic basis was unknown. Instead, to investigate whether blood-borne factors might be responsible for the obese phenotype, parabiotic pairs were made and weight changes recorded over several weeks (Coleman & Hummel, 1969). In **parabiosis**, mice are joined surgically at the sides of their abdomens; small blood vessels grow across the union with a resultant slow sharing of blood. Combinations of adult (obese) *ob/ob*, *db/db*, and normal (non-obese) mice were produced with the following results (Figure 11.3):

- Pairing an *ob/ob* mouse with a normal mouse: The *ob/ob* mouse ate less and lost weight whereas the normal mouse was unaffected.
- Pairing a *db/db* mouse with a normal mouse: The normal mouse ate less and lost weight whereas the *db/db* mouse remained obese

These data support the classic **lipostatic** theory of body weight regulation and the concept that a circulating satiety molecule is inhibitory to food intake. In the top pair, the *ob/ob* mouse loses weight when paired with the normal partner. Although the *ob/ob* mouse does not produce its own leptin, it is able to respond to leptin received in blood from its normal partner. In the bottom pair, the *db/db* mouse produces leptin but does not respond to it because of a defective *LepRb* mutation. However, the extra leptin received from the *db/db* mouse exposes the normal mouse to a very high level of leptin, and this causes it to exhibit high satiety or loss of appetite.

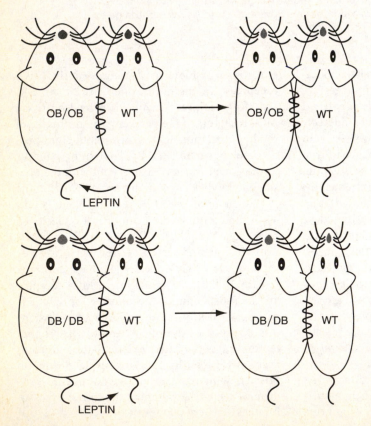

FIGURE 11.3 Parabiosis studies. The left side of each panel shows the state at the time of the surgical joining of either an *ob/ob* (top) or *db/db* (bottom) mouse with a lean littermate (wild type, WT). The right side shows the state after some weeks of union. The net transfer of leptin between the mice is shown.

Polygenic Obesity

Some human obesity-related genes have been discovered by screening the DNA of severely obese children for specific genes that were first identified as targets on the basis of animal or other studies. This is called a **candidate gene** approach, and the scientific hypothesis is that a pre-identified gene will differ in some way between obese and non-obese populations. A recent review of these findings (Walley, Asher, & Froguel, 2009, p. 434) stated "it is clear that candidate gene association studies have not provided unequivocal results, but the evidence is strong enough to suggest that many of these genes contain variants that have a modest effect on obesity."

An older and more traditional approach to human disease, including obesity, has been linkage studies based on clustering of a disorder within a family. By 2005, some 250 potential linkage sites in the human genome had been so identified (Rankinen et al., 2006), but replication of these results has often proven difficult and a **meta-analysis** (i.e., an analysis of several published studies) did not find strong evidence for linkage of BMI to any genetic locus (Saunders et al., 2007), suggesting that these gene variants have, at best, small effects on the predisposition to obesity.

Despite the failure of the candidate gene and linkage approaches to identify single-gene loss-of-function defects as a major contribution to human obesity, there is abundant evidence that both hereditary and experiential factors influence the prevalence of obesity. Another approach is to start with the idea that obesity is the result of several abnormal genes (i.e., polygenic), and

DO THE MATH: GENES AND OBESITY

Let's do a purely hypothetical exercise looking at how a polygenic disease relates to candidate gene studies. Suppose there are 100 possible genes for which an abnormality predisposes us to obesity (or metabolic efficiency, depending on how you look at it!). Further, suppose that each of these alleles is equally potent and independent, adding 1 unit to BMI. Assume that without any abnormal alleles, the default BMI is 22, the middle of the normal weight range. It follows that if an individual carries 10 "obesogenic" alleles, his or her BMI would be 32 (obese); if 20 alleles, the BMI would be 42 (extremely obese). Suppose that an individual with a BMI of 42 consents to DNA screening for a candidate gene study. Twenty of the obesogenic variants would show up, but 80 of them would not because this person carries only 20 of the 100 possible obesogenic alleles. Another person with BMI of 42 could have a completely different set of 20 obesity alleles. Thus, a screen of a large number of people with BMI 42 would reveal only 20% of them with any one *specific* obesity allele.

Question 1: If there are instead 200 possible obesity alleles, what is the probability of finding any one of them in this extremely obese population?

Question 2: Using the 200 allele example, what is this probability if instead the genetic screen used a less stringently selected population with an average BMI of 32?

Because (at least a few) obesity alleles could occur in non-obese individuals, scientists often express genetic data in terms of **odds ratio**, which is the probability of observing a specific genetic abnormality in an obese population compared with the probability of observing the same abnormality in a non-obese population.

Question 3: If the mean BMIs of normal weight (note: not the hypothetical "default" condition) and obese cohorts are 24 and 32, respectively, what is the odds ratio for a particular obesity gene?

(*Answers are at the end of this chapter.*)

that each allele or variant contributes only a small amount to obesity (see "Do the Math").

How does one go about looking for a lot of genes? Genome-wide association (GWA) studies in human populations are usually case-control designs in which large numbers of individuals with a particular trait and control subjects who do not have the trait (but are matched on other attributes such as sex, age, ethnicity, etc.) are tested to determine whether the allele frequencies of the target gene differ statistically between the two groups. The most common abnormality is a **single nucleotide polymorphism (SNP)**, in which a single base of the DNA coding strand is mutated. The cellular effect of the gene defect is not revealed by GWA, simply that the gene has an abnormal sequence. Some mutations produce complete loss of function (of the protein they encode, as in lep-/-, for example), whereas other mutations have minimal effect on function of the protein or even enhance its function. Thus, GWA studies by themselves are not mechanistic, although they do provide molecular leads for such studies.

At the present time, SNPs of at least 10 gene loci have been identified as risk factors for obesity (Walley et al., 2009). At least one of these is in the MC4R gene we have discussed before, but it accounts at best for 1% to 5% of human obesity. Put another way, 95% to 99% of obese humans do not carry an abnormality in this gene. A similar story is true for most of the other candidate genes considered in isolation, but together there could be an accumulated risk. As we cautioned, identifying a polymorphism does not in itself tell us whether that mutation produces a functional change in the protein product. This field is still in its infancy, so rather than describe individual results, we will illustrate how those results have been used to inform basic science.

The first example is from one of the loci identified in human populations, the *Fto* (human fat mass and obesity) gene. Approximately 16% of adults of European descent are homozygous for the at-risk allele of *Fto* and weigh on average 3 kg more than those without the at-risk allele (Church et al., 2010). FTO, the protein product of *Fto*, has a role in demethylation of DNA (i.e., is a potential epigenetic contributor, see later discussion). The odds ratio for the FTO gene is the highest found so far—1.67—or, put another way, for every five obese individuals with an abnormal FTO gene, there would be only three non-obese individuals in the matched population carrying that allele. One of the ways in which genes can be overexpressed is through the number of copies of the gene, so to investigate the role of *Fto*, transgenic mice were prepared with genomic overexpression of *Fto*, having 3 or 4 copies rather than the usual 2 copies. Both adult males and females showed increased body weight in proportion to the "dose" of the gene. Thus, by 20 weeks of age (the lifespan equivalent of ~15 years in humans), the mean body weights of mice with 2, 3, and 4 copies were 23, 26, and 29 g, respectively (Church et al., 2010). The 4-copy mice also ate more and had a threefold increase in expression of AgRP in the hypothalamus. Unlike the *ob/ob* and MC4R-/- models, this is not massive obesity, but if you consider these relative body weight differences in mice (i.e., ~25% increase for 4 versus 2 copies) as translating directly to BMI of humans, this would be a substantial effect.

A second example comes from the MC4R-/- model, mentioned earlier, although the odds ratio is only 1.12 for adults and 1.30 for children (Loos et al., 2008). There are MC4 receptors in the hypothalamus, including the PVN, but there are also MC3 receptors made from a different gene but sharing the natural ligand α-MSH. If the MC3 receptor gene is embryonically disrupted in mice (MC3R-/-), they grow with near-normal weight but have slightly higher body fat content and correspondingly less lean body mass (Butler & Cone, 2001). So even though their "mouse BMI" is the same as controls, they have more body fat. However, when MC3R gene deletion is introduced together with the obesity-producing MC4R-/- deletion (a so-called double knockout), the result is more extreme obesity than MC4R-/- alone (Chen et al., 2000). This is an example that adding two at-risk genes can have an additive or a more than additive effect and supports the notion that combinations of multiple small gene vulnerabilities could in principle produce a large susceptibility to obesity.

FIGURE 11.4 Obesity will occur, even in a genetically predisposed organism, only if the environment provides the food resources necessary to become obese.

Other genes identified in GWAs include a gene involved in neuronal growth (brain-derived neurotrophic factor, odds ratio 1.11), as well as other factors that may be particularly important during early development (Walley et al., 2009), in part consistent with the current rise in childhood obesity. But obesity will occur only if the environment is conducive (Figure 11.4).

For example, the overeating and obesity in MC4R-/- mice was prevented completely by giving them access to running wheels from an early age before they could become obese (Haskell-Luevano et al., 2009). This activity was entirely voluntary and accounts for only a small fraction (<10%) of the total energy expenditure. This is an example of when a small amount of exercise does have a preventative effect on obesity. (It would be more difficult to examine whether exercise will reverse existing obesity in rodents, because most of them become "couch mice" that don't run much in a wheel at higher BMIs.)

One of the questions you might be asking is, "How can we use this type of genetic information to devise new treatment strategies for humans?" In the case of the monogenic leptin deficiency described earlier, by knowing that the gene product—a blood-borne hormone—is missing, replacement via leptin infusions is a viable strategy and has had some success. But this is a rather unique and rare condition. If instead, the monogenic obesity were due to a leptin receptor defect, could we introduce viable leptin receptors in cells that are supposed to express leptin receptors, and only in those cells? In general, this is the ambitious and technically difficult goal of gene therapy. Even if the technical problems can be overcome, ethical issues remain (Box 11.2).

BOX 11.2   Gene Therapy

The objective of gene therapy is to introduce a "healthy" gene (or additional copies of the gene) and have it incorporated into the DNA of the recipient. Viruses are natural agents that penetrate cells, and so viral vectors (carriers) are the most promising gene delivery devices. In the 2012 movie *The Bourne Legacy*, the lead character (Aaron Cross) receives a viral vector injection that will make permanent cognitive enhancements that previously were maintained by a drug. He (and other "subjects") had also received viral treatments to enhance mitochondrial respiration by a few percentage points, with the objective of increasing physical endurance. There are artistic extensions of scientific reality in this plot, but we may not be very far removed from some of this reality. These fictional interventions are not "gene fixes" in the previously mentioned sense but are "gene enhancers" designed to create "superhumans." However, the distinction between the two usages can become fuzzy. For example, the same increased mitochondrial respiration could burn calories and produce weight loss (provided you weren't also engaged in physical endurance events!). More importantly, what would be the criteria (e.g., having a specific mutation) to be eligible for gene therapy, and would it be covered by insurance or would it be available only to a privileged few?

To return to a more realistic example, there is evidence that leptin receptors are involved in many brain functions, so it is likely that even a perfect "gene fix" for demonstrably defective leptin receptors would have multiple effects. Further, because the mutation would have been present from birth until the age of the gene fix, it may have had permanent developmental effects on the brain, and these would not necessarily be reversed by the procedure.

EPIGENETICS AND DEVELOPMENTAL PROGRAMMING

Epigenetics is the study of heritable changes in gene expression or phenotype caused by mechanisms other than alterations in the nucleotide base sequence of DNA. Such changes would not show up in the genetic screens discussed so far. The two well-established epigenetic mechanisms are methylation and histone modification.

Methylation occurs when a methyl group is added to a DNA base, most usually cytosine (to make 5-methylcytosine), which interferes with the transcriptional activity of the gene within which the methylated site occurs (Figure 11.5).

Different positions of methylation cause an imbalance in the ratio of transcribed genes and of their protein products. This would cause the overall function of a cell to "lean" more in one direction than another. One of the functions of FTO, mentioned earlier, is to remove methyl groups at specific sites, so altering the transcription of other genes in a cell.

A more recent addition to epigenetic mechanism research concerns the role of non-coding RNA molecules (i.e., they don't lead to production of specific proteins). It is now appreciated that the amount of the genome devoted to non-coding RNAs tends to increase with evolutionary complexity, and given that the brain is a highly transcriptionally active tissue, these will be of particular importance in the human brain (see Qureshi & Mehler, 2012, for a recent review). These non-coding molecules have diverse roles in modifying the transcription of coding genes. We are unaware of specific examples relating to food intake or obesity at this time, but there is expanding evidence for their role in neurodevelopment and plasticity.

An early observation that triggered the idea for epigenetic influences on obesity comes from Dutch health records: Children born during an intense famine during early 1940s (World War II) showed up in middle age as several kilograms heavier than those who had not experienced severe food restriction in early life (Eckel, 2008).

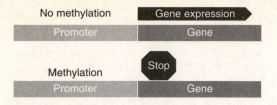

FIGURE 11.5 Repression of gene transcription by methylation.

This led to controlled animal experiments to test the hypothesis that calorie restriction in early life leads to adults who are vulnerable to eat more or gain excess weight when food is plentiful. This is consistent with the broader concept of **developmental programming**, that the early environment has long-lasting or permanent effects on gene expression to affect behavior and health (Remmers & Delemarre-van de Waal, 2011). One of the mechanisms by which this programming might affect feeding circuits is in the development and ultimate number of neurons projecting from the arcuate nucleus to the paraventricular nucleus (regions within the hypothalamus). The converse of this, and more relevant to modern Western society, is that fetal over-nutrition (e.g., overweight mothers) might have deleterious consequences (Chen, Simar, & Morris, 2009). In rodent studies, early life over-nutrition has either had no effect or increased body weight of offspring as they grow—that is, both over- and under-nutrition may have the same direction of epigenetic influence on body weight. This is an area of intense inquiry, and the conclusions will almost certainly change as more results are obtained, but the crucial take-home message is that abnormal infant nutrition in either direction may have permanent effects on brain development, gene expression, and ultimately health and longevity.

DIETARY OBESITY

Long before the obesity epidemic, genetically obese rodent models, and the concept of reward systems, it was well known that overeating

could lead to obesity in both humans and animals (Figure 11.6). Veterinarians now report an obesity epidemic in our domestic pets that rivals or even exceeds that in humans. Because the lifestyles that we impose on our pets often emulate our own, this parallel "obesification" sheds insight into the human condition (Klimentidis et al., 2010). Although people may attribute genetic misfortune to their own obesity, they do not commonly apply the same argument to their pets!

The fact that highly palatable and/or energy-rich diets produce increased body weight was one of the key underpinnings for favoring a settling point or allostatic approach to body weight over fixed set point models. High-fat diets do lead to obesity, and a large number of junk food animal diets have been devised to emulate one or more aspects of a human Western-style diet.

For most preclinical (animal) studies of obesity, food is freely available so the subjects can eat as much as they want whenever they feel like it. This is called *ad libitum* feeding and, you could argue, is in fact how most of us live. For the control condition in laboratory studies, rats and mice are typically fed a diet that contains only ~10% calories from fat, and they have no choice—it's the same old relatively bland food all the time. Relative to this rather impoverished dietary condition, it is not surprising that animals with more palatable, dense, or varied diets eat more and become relatively fatter, even within a few weeks. But that hardly emulates the human obesity problem, which often evolves slowly over decades.

Most humans do not, of course, live in a world with a single bland food. We have a variety of foods, many of which are palatable or high in fat content. Not surprisingly, even in rats and mice, having such a choice leads to much higher daily intakes and weight gain than animals fed chow. Figure 11.7 shows the results from a study in which one group of mice was fed chow and another group received a high-fat diet *ad libitum* for 4–5 months (the lifespan equivalent of about

FIGURE 11.6   Junk food diets that have variety and high-fat content promote excess weight gain in humans and laboratory animals.

20 years in humans); the high-fat–fed group weighed 50% more than chow-fed controls, and selected fat pads (dissected out after sacrifice) showed an even larger fractional increase.

At least in the home, most Americans have a variety of foods available *ad libitum* and eat a diet that on average has about 30% calories as fat. In mice, which do not have additional social or commercial pressures to eat, we see that *ad libitum* access to a high-fat diet is sufficient to produce an obesity epidemic in which weight gain takes them from normal to obese

categories as they move from young adults to middle age.

Genetically different strains of mice or rats show different susceptibilities to diet-induced obesity (West, Boozer, Moody, & Atkinson,1992). For example, the C57BL/6 (B6) strain, commonly used in genetic studies, is quite prone to diet-induced obesity. However, within an ostensibly identical cohort of B6 mice, Koza et al. (2006) noted substantial individual variability in their propensity to high-fat-diet–induced obesity. They reasoned this must be because of individual epigenetically

TALKING POINT 11.1

To what extent do you have *ad libitum* access to food? When do you not have access to food? How often, when you feel hungry, do you immediately seek food, rather than put up with hunger for a while? Why do you think

that many people find it so difficult to adhere to a diet for an extended period of time? If you agree that *ad libitum* food can produce inappropriately high intake, how would you try to prevent it?

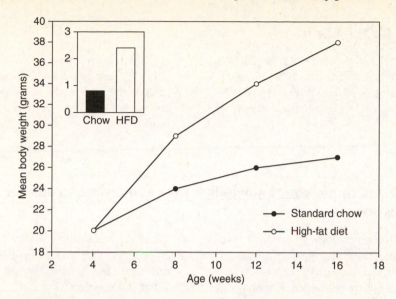

FIGURE 11.7 **Typical growth of mice fed either a low-fat or a high-fat diet from 4 to 16 weeks of age.**

The inset shows the mean weight (in grams) of a major subcutaneous fat pad dissected out from chow and high-fat groups at 16 weeks of age.

programmed differences and went on to show that expression of certain genes in fat tissue and in the brain differed among individuals in relation to their vulnerability to obesity. In rats, it has been shown that propensity to obesity on a high-fat diet is a heritable characteristic: Starting with a commonly used outbred stock strain (Sprague-Dawley), Levin and his colleagues noticed that some individuals gained more weight than others when fed a moderate fat diet. By then breeding high-gaining males with high-gaining females, within a few generations most of the offspring showed propensity to diet-induced obesity (obesity prone). Conversely, by breeding low-gaining males and females for several generations, most of the offspring did not gain much weight on the same diet, so were termed *obesity resistant* (Levin, Dunn-Meynell, Balkan, & Keesey, 1997).

The concept of *dietary resistance* provides a new perspective on genes and obesity. All of the single gene and GWA approaches referred to earlier are looking for alleles or mutations that are associated with human or animal obesity and/ or vulnerability to obesity. This assumes that the "default" is not obese. But what if obesity is in fact a normal biological response to our food environment, and that it is resistance to obesity that is abnormal. Thus, the focus on obesity-resistant rodents mentioned earlier might be particularly useful. (In addition to Levin's obesity-prone and obesity-resistant lines, many inbred strains of rats or mice have different propensities to become obese on a high-fat diet.) Animals that are resistant to developing obesity must either not find a high-fat diet particularly palatable and/ or burn more energy via metabolic processes or behavioral adjustments (i.e., activity). Humans potentially have additional cognitive resistance available, including body image and deliberate dietary restraint.

Answers to Do the Math

1. With 100 alleles, the chance is 20% (20/100); with 200 alleles, the chance is 10% (20/200).
2. For mean BMI = 32, on average 10 (32−22) obesity alleles will be present; the chance is 5% (10/200).
3. For the control population, on average 2 (24−22) obesity alleles will be present for a 1% (2/200) chance. For the obese population, the chance is 5% (as in question 2), so the odds ratio is 5.

Let's review and apply your knowledge. Take some time to answer these chapter questions

1. Do genes affect physiology, behavior, or both? Why does understanding this matter in thinking about genes and obesity?
2. What is the difference between monogenic and polygenic obesity: Is one any easier to treat than the other? Give example(s).
3. What are GWA studies and what do they tell us?
4. What do you understand by the concept of *epigenetics*; give an example of how this is relevant to feeding, metabolism, or obesity.
5. What is dietary obesity? List reasons why you think some people and animals apparently are resistant to an obesifying environment.

Glossary

Candidate gene   An approach to genetic analysis in which it is hypothesized that a pre-identified gene will differ between individuals with and without a particular trait such as obesity.

Developmental programming   The concept that events (including over- or under-nutrition) early in life, either before and/or after birth, can have permanent effects on development of the brain and behavior.

Drive   The hypothetical internal forces that motivate behavior.

Epigenetics   Changes in gene expression of a cell that are not caused by changes in the underlying DNA sequence. Examples include chemical modification (methylation and acetylation) of specific nucleotides that alter the rate of gene expression. Some of these epigenetic changes are heritable.

Incentive   The ability of external cues to elicit approach and consummatory behaviors.

Lipostatic theory   An early theory of weight regulation emphasizing the role of body fat and signals derived from fat to affect food intake.

Melanocortin (MC) receptors   A family of receptors whose ligands are peptides derived from pro-opiomelanocortin (POMC). For energy regulation, MC type 3 and 4 receptors in brain are involved.

Meta-analysis   A study in which the results of several other published studies are considered together for consistency of overall effect across studies that are comparable along specified dimensions.

Monogenic   A trait such as obesity that is caused by an abnormality in a single gene.

Odds ratio   The probability of finding an abnormal gene in a population with a specific trait divided by the probability of finding the same gene abnormality in a population that does not have that trait.

Parabiosis   A technique by which two animals are surgically joined, often by joining their abdominal cavities, and share hormonal (blood-borne) or other physiological signals.

Phenotype An observed trait of an individual (e.g., obesity or resistance to obesity).

Point mutation A single nucleotide mutation or substitution in a DNA or RNA sequence.

Single nucleotide polymorphism (SNP) A DNA sequence variation occurring when a single nucleotide in the genome differs between members of a biological species or between paired chromosomes.

References

Butler, A. A., & Cone, R. D. (2001). Knockout models resulting in the development of obesity. *Trends in Genetics, 17,* S50–S54.

Chen, A.S., Marsh, D.J., Trumbauer, M.E., Frazier, E. G., Guan, X. M., Yu, H., ... Van der Ploeg, L. H. (2000). Inactivation of the mouse melanocortin-3 receptor results in increased fat mass and reduced lean body mass. *Nature Genetics, 26,* 97–102.

Chen, H., Simar, D., & Morris, M. J. (2009). Hypothalamic neuroendocrine circuitry is programmed by maternal obesity: interaction with postnatal nutritional environment. *PLoS ONE, 4,* e6529.

Church, C., Moir, L., McMurray, F., Girard, C., Banks, G. T., Teboul, L., ... Cox, R. D. (2010). Overexpression of *Fto* leads to increased food intake and results in obesity. *Nature Genetics, 42,* 1086–1092.

Coleman, D. L., & Hummel, K. P. (1969). Effects of parabiosis of normal with genetically diabetic mice. *American Journal of Physiology, 217,* 1298–1304.

Eckel, R. H. (2008). Obesity research in the next decade. *International Journal of Obesity, 32,* S143–S151.

Haskell-Luevano, C., Schaub, J. W., Andreasen, A., Haskell, K. R., Moore, M. C., Koerper, L. M., ... Xiang, Z. (2009). Voluntary exercise prevents the obese and diabetic metabolic syndrome of the melanocortin-4 receptor knockout mouse. *FASEB Journal, 23,* 642–655.

Klimentisis, Y.C., Beasley, T.M., Lin, H.Y., Murati, G., Glass, G. E., Guyton, M., ... Allison, D. B. (2010). Canaries in the coal mine: A cross-species analysis of the plurality of obesity epidemics. *Proceeding of the Royal Society series B, 278,* 1626–1632.

Koza, R.A., Nikonova, L., Hogan, J., Rim, J.-S., Mendoza, T., Faulk, C., ... Kozak, L. P. (2006). Changes in gene expression foreshadow diet-induced obesity in genetically identical mice. *PLoS Genetics, 2,* e81.

Levin, B. E., Dunn-Meynell, A. A., Balkan, B., & Keesey, R. E. (1997). Selective breeding for diet-induced obesity and resistance in Sprague-Dawley rats. *American Journal of Physiology: Regulatory, Integrative and Comparative Physiology, 273,* R725–R730.

Loos, R. J., Lindgren, C. M., Li, S., Wheeler, E., Zhao, J. H., Prokopenko, I., ... Mohlke, K. L. (2008). Common variants near MC4R are associated with fat mass, weight, and risk of obesity. *Nature Genetics, 40,* 768–775.

Montague, C.T., Farooqi, I. S., Whitehead, J. P., Soos, M. A., Rau, H., Wareham, N. J., ... O'Rahilly, S. (1997). Congenital leptin deficiency is associated with severe early onset obesity in humans. *Nature, 387,* 903–908.

Qureshi, I. A., & Mehler, M. R. (2012). Emerging roles of non-coding RNAs in brain evolution, development, plasticity, and disease. *Nature Reviews Neuroscience, 13,* 528–541.

Ramachandrappa, S., & Farooqi, I. S. (2011). Genetic approaches to understanding human obesity. *Journal of Clinical Investigation, 121,* 2080–2086.

Rankinen, T., Zuberi, A., Chagnon, Y.C., Weisnagel, S. J., Argyropoulos, G., Walts, B., ... Bouchard, C. (2006). The human obesity gene map: The 2005 update. *Obesity, 14,* 529–644.

Remmers, F., & Delemarre-van de Waal (2011). Developmental programming of energy balance and its hypothalamic regulation. *Endocrine Reviews, 32,* 272–311.

Saunders, C. L., Chiodini, B. D., Sham, P., Lewis, C. M., Abkevich, V., Adeyemo, A. A., ... Collier, D. A. (2007). Meta-analysis of genome-wide linkage studies in BMI and obesity. *Obesity, 15,* 2263–2275.

Walley, A. J., Asher, J. E., & Froguel, P. (2009). The genetic contribution to non-syndromic human obesity. *Nature Reviews Genetics, 10,* 431–442.

West, D. B., Boozer, C. N., Moody, D. L., & Atkinson, R. L. (1992). Dietary obesity in nine inbred mouse strains. *American Journal of Physiology: Regulatory, Integrative and Comparative Physiology, 262,* R1025–R1032.

Zhang, Y., Proenca, R., Maffei, M., Barone, M., Leopold, L., & Friedman, J. M. (1994). Positional cloning of the mouse obese gene and its human homologue. *Nature, 372,* 425–432.

12

Treatments for Obesity

After reading this chapter, you will be able to

- Identify anti-obesity drugs and their mechanism of action
- Recognize and critically consider the difference between "approved" or "controlled" drugs and over-the-counter "supplements"

- Appreciate the leading types of weight-loss surgeries, their potential health benefits and factors to consider
- Know the leading types of behavioral therapies used for weight loss and maintenance of a healthy weight

The obesity epidemic has been discussed throughout this book. Obesity is not simply a cosmetic problem; it is associated with decreased quality of life; psychological distress; and numerous health problems, including cardiovascular disease and stroke, type 2 diabetes, cancer, and premature death. Further, overweight and obesity have a devastating economic impact in direct (e.g., health care) and indirect (e.g., lost work days) costs, estimated in 2008 to be $147 billion in the United States (Finkelstein, Trogden, Cohen, & Dietz, 2009), or about $500 per year for every man, woman, and child. By now, that cost is probably nearer $1,000. Thus, obesity is problematic for an individual's health and also for a society's economic health. In this chapter, we will explore the leading methods for treating obesity: drugs, surgery, and behavior therapy.

ANTI-OBESITY DRUGS

Anti-obesity drugs generally work in one of two ways: by reducing energy intake or by increasing energy expenditure. To date, there is no "magic bullet"; the most effective medications result in weight loss of about 5% to 10% (usually 10 to 15 lbs. more than placebo), which is helpful, but certainly not a "cure" for obese people whose weights may be 50% to 100% over their healthy weight. Further, drug therapy can be expensive and is associated with health risks and side effects. Anti-obesity drugs work centrally (in the brain) and peripherally (e.g., in gastrointestinal tract) and have varied mechanisms of action.

Drugs That Reduce Energy Intake

Drugs can reduce energy intake by either suppressing appetite or disrupting the absorption of food consumed. One of the first documented uses of a natural compound to blunt appetite was chewing of coca leaves by South American natives. Cocaine is an effective appetite suppressant but is also highly addictive. So, too, is the synthetic compound, amphetamine, and a host of structurally related compounds, which were widely prescribed in the 20th century until about 1960 when addiction became a recognized problem. These drugs act primarily at **dopamine** nerve terminals in the brain to increase the amount of dopamine signaling. Dopamine, as discussed in other chapters, is associated with reward; so, these drugs seem to act like food as a reinforcer, and to substitute for food at a practical level.

Drug companies looked for compounds similar to amphetamine but without abuse potential, and in around 1970 researchers developed **fenfluramine**, a drug that increases brain levels of **serotonin** (Colman, 2005). This was used quite widely, but the weight loss was not dramatic (around 10 to 20 pounds over 6 months), and the weight was often regained when use of the drug was stopped. In the 1990s, an "off-label" use of fenfluramine (a slight sedative) with **phentermine** (an amphetamine-like stimulant), a mixture called *fen-phen*, became popular. After several cases of pulmonary hypertension (a potentially fatal illness) and heart valve problems were linked to this drug combination, fenfluramine was pulled from the market in the late 1990s.

In 1997, the U.S. Food and Drug Administration (FDA) approved **sibutramine** (sold as Meridia). This drug has a dual chemical action, increasing serotonin (like fenfluramine) and norepinephrine (Campfield, Smith, & Burn, 1998). The drug was withdrawn from the market in 2010 when studies indicated that the risk of heart attack and stroke outweighed the benefit of the modest weight loss associated with the drug.

The increased concern over risk versus benefit of prescription anti-obesity drugs prevented the FDA from approving other centrally acting weight loss drugs until 2012 (that's 15 years later!). **Qsymia**, which was called Qnexa until its approval, is a combination of phentermine and topiramate (Cooke & Bloom, 2006). Topiramate (sold as Topomax), an anticonvulsant drug prescribed for seizures and migraines, carries risks for side effects, drug interactions, and birth defects. **Lorcaserin** (marketed as Belviq) was also approved by the FDA in 2012. Lorcaserin, like fenfluramine, increases serotonin levels resulting in feelings of satiety; lorcaserin works specifically at the serotonin 2C receptors. Both Qsymia and lorcaserin were initially rejected by the FDA in 2010 due to concerns about health risks. These new drugs are to be prescribed only to obese patients or patients with BMI over 27 who also have additional health issues (e.g., hypertension or type 2 diabetes).

The only peripherally acting prescription drug is **orlistat** (called Xenical), approved by the FDA in 1999. Orlistat partially prevents the absorption of fat by inhibiting the intestinal enzymes that break fat down for absorption (Campfield et al., 1998; Cooke & Bloom, 2006). So you can in principle eat fatty food have it run right through you! Actually, people taking this tend to eat low-fat foods because of the unpleasant effects if they eat a lot of fat (e.g., gas and fecal incontinence), and so they actually reduce caloric intake by this "indirect" method. Because there are no known serious health risks of orlistat, it has been given over-the-counter (nonprescription) status in a lower dose formulation called Alli. Neither drug is particularly popular or widely used because of only modest weight loss efficacy and unpleasant side effects.

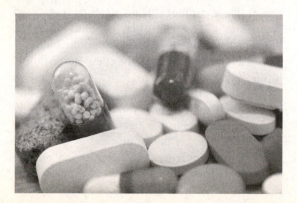

TABLE 12.1	Overview of Anti-obesity Drugs		
Drug	**Effect**	**Neurotransmitter Action**	**FDA Status**
Amphetamine	Stimulant and appetite suppressant	Dopamine agonist	Controlled substance
Fenfluramine	Appetite suppressant	Serotonin agonist	Withdrawn
Phentermine	Stimulant and appetite suppressant	Norepinephrine agonist	Approved
Sibutramine	Appetite suppressant	Serotonin and norepinephrine agonist	Withdrawn
Qsymia (phentermine + topiramate)	Stimulant and appetite suppressant	Norepinephrine agonist	Approved
Lorcaserin	Appetite suppressant	Serotonin agonist	Approved
Rimonabant	Appetite suppressant	Cannabinoid antagonist	Not approved
Orlistat	Inhibits fat absorption	Acts in the periphery	Approved

Cannabinoid receptor blockers, with actions in the brain and the periphery, have been studied as possible anti-obesity drugs. Activation of the cannabinoid system (e.g., by smoking marijuana) is known to stimulate hunger (Kirkham, 2009), so the reverse (antagonism) should prevent hunger (Xie et al., 2007). However, it is now known that reward is mediated in part by the cannabinoid system. What "side effects" of a drug that antagonizes this system would you be on the lookout for? Did you guess alterations of mood? If so, you are on the right track. Companies that were in the process of researching cannabinoid antagonists for weight loss have since halted their investigations because of risks of psychiatric disturbances including depression and suicidal thoughts (Le Foll, Gorelick, & Goldberg, 2009).

Drugs and Supplements That Increase Energy Expenditure

No FDA-approved weight loss medications work primarily by increasing energy expenditure, although drugs such as phentermine do stimulate metabolism in addition to suppressing appetite. However, many products sold as diet or herbal **supplements** are marketed with claims that they increase energy expenditure and result in weight loss. Substances labeled as supplements are neither subject to Drug Enforcement Administration (DEA) registration requirements of safety and proof of efficacy (which are required of controlled substances) nor pre-approval by the FDA. The FDA regulates the safety of a supplement and accuracy of its marketing *after* it reaches the market. So, supplements and their constituents often change over time. For example, the over-the-counter diet supplement Dexatrim today contains different ingredients than in past formulations because the FDA has now banned the compounds in the original formulations.

Most herbal weight loss remedies have not been tested scientifically for efficacy compared with placebo, have not been tested for safety, and are not regulated for amount or quality of the main ingredients (i.e., what it says on the label doesn't have to meet strict pharmaceutical standards of accuracy). For example, a recent fad weight loss supplement is an extract of the South African cactus, *Hoodia Gordonii*. Hoodia was allegedly chewed to suppress hunger by Kalahari Bushmen while out hunting. What is the active chemical in Hoodia, how does it work (brain, periphery, etc.), and more importantly does it actually work to suppress appetite? Even if chewing the cactus made the hunters less hungry when food was not available, does that necessarily mean it will help overweight people eat less when food is available, particularly when the food is particularly palatable? To date, there has been only one scientific study of the effectiveness of Hoodia for weight loss in humans. The researchers found that consumption of Hoodia had no significant effects on energy intake, weight, or body fat compared with placebo; further, the participants on the drug had more complaints and adverse effects (e.g., headache, nausea) than those on placebo (Blom et al., 2011). Buyer beware!!

CALORIE SUBSTITUTES

Calorie substitutes theoretically provide a drug- or supplement-free method of reducing energy intake without reducing the quantity of food consumed. **Saccharin** (frequently marketed as Sweet 'N Low) was the first true no-calorie artificial sweetener, and hopes were that it would reduce people's caloric intake. Unfortunately, it has not (Slavin, 2012; Swithers & Davidson, 2008)—it also has a slight bitter aftertaste, so its use has been sporadic.

Aspartame (often called Equal or NutraSweet) was introduced about 30 years ago and is found in a wide variety of foods and low-calorie beverages and has replaced most applications of saccharin. However, despite its widespread use, calorie intake continues to increase. You've seen it: super-sized fast food with a diet coke—people use the low-calorie label as a license to load up on something else. Interestingly, some research indicates that physiological responses to sugar substitutes (e.g., increased insulin release) may also explain the failure of these products to yield weight loss (Swithers & Davidson, 2008).

Sucralose (marketed as Splenda) is a more recent arrival. It is derived from sucrose and probably has the most authentic sugar flavor of the three sweeteners (Quinlan & Jenner, 2006), but we doubt whether it will effectively cut caloric intake for the same reason that aspartame has been ineffective.

Olestra is a fat substitute; its chemical structure is similar to the fat molecule but cannot be broken down and so is not absorbed. It gives food the satisfying "mouth feel" of fatty food and is used mainly in cooking. In a lab study of olestra, human participants were fed either a high-calorie breakfast made with real fat or an otherwise identical low-calorie breakfast made with the "fake fat" (Rolls, Pirraglia, Jones, & Peters, 1992). Their food intake was then monitored for the rest of the day. The people in the fake-fat group reported being hungrier in the evening and ate larger dinners, resulting in no net difference in daily caloric intake. It seems that compensation for our "norm" energy levels can blunt the effectiveness of any of the calorie substitutes. This partially explains the difficulty of maintaining weight loss through dieting or the use of calorie substitutes.

TALKING POINT 12.1

Have you tried any of the calorie substitutes, perhaps in diet soda or yogurt? Could you detect a difference in taste compared with the same product sweetened with sugar? Did you notice any difference in appetite or weight as a result of your use of calorie substitutes?

SURGERY FOR OBESITY (BARIATRIC SURGERY)

Because of the limited efficacy of even approved drugs, some people have looked for surgical treatments. Bariatric, or weight-loss, surgery can be extremely beneficial for some people, particularly those who are extremely obese and have been unable to lose weight with diet and exercise. Surgery results in average loss of about 100 lbs. (Higa, Boone, Ho, 2000) and can eliminate symptoms of type 2 diabetes and hypertension (Sugerman, Wolfe, Sica, & Clore, 2003) and improve quality of life (Dymek, le Grange, Neven, & Alverdy, 2002).

Surgery for obesity is generally allowed only for individuals who have a body mass index (BMI) of 40 or higher (this is referred to as extreme or morbid obesity) or have a BMI of 35 to 39.9 (obesity), and a serious weight-related health problem, such as type 2 diabetes or high blood pressure. Additional psychological and physical assessments are conducted to ensure that potential candidates are fit for surgery.

Types of Surgery

Gastric bypass and gastric banding are the two most frequently performed types of weight-loss surgery. Both can now be performed laparoscopically, allowing minimal invasiveness and reduced risks of complications and death compared with open surgery (mortality rates are now less than 1%; Bushwald, Estok, Fahrbach, Banel, & Sledge, 2007). Gastric bypass, also called Roux-en-Y surgery, actually reduces the size of the functional stomach. A small stomach pouch is created by stapling and sealing off the lower part of the stomach; the pouch is then connected with the upper portion of the small intestine. The reduction in stomach size results in feelings of fullness (and sometimes pain) after eating only small amounts of food.

Gastric banding surgery involves the placement of a prosthetic band around the entrance to the stomach, functionally reducing the amount of food that can pass through. This procedure is less invasive and more easily reversed or modified if desired or needed. Both procedures are considered effective and safe, especially now that they are typically performed laparoscopically. However, with both, the reduced stomach size requires the consumption of only small amounts of food at a time and the inclusion of vitamin supplements in the diet (the reduced stomach and intestinal tract interfere with the absorption

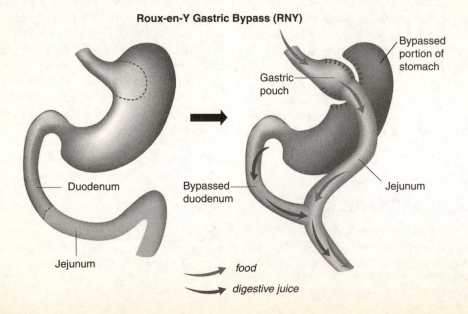

Roux-en-Y Gastric Bypass (RNY)

Bypassed portion of stomach

Gastric pouch

Duodenum

Bypassed duodenum

Jejunum

Jejunum

food

digestive juice

Adjustable Gastric Band (Lap Band)

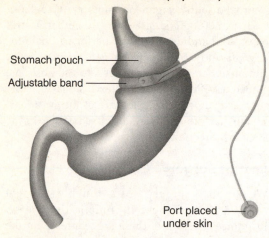

Stomach pouch

Adjustable band

Port placed
under skin

of vitamins, so higher-than-normal amounts need to be consumed). Research indicates that patients have fewer complaints and problems postoperatively with gastric banding but that gastric bypass yields better long-term success (Nguyen, Slone, Nguyen, Harman, & Hoyt, 2009).

Physiological Effects of Surgery

As noted previously, about 70% of a patient's weight above ideal is generally lost after surgery. As expected, as most of this weight loss is in the form of fat, it is accompanied by a lowered plasma concentration of **leptin**, the satiety hormone released from fat cells (discussed in other chapters). But what about **ghrelin**, the appetite-enhancing peptide secreted by the stomach? Findings indicate that obese people who have not had an operation have lower ghrelin levels than normal weight controls, and these levels are reduced further by gastric banding and a bit more by Roux-en-Y bypass but still less than in patients whose stomach has been completely removed (for reasons other than bariatric surgery; Cummings et al., 2002; Leonetti et al., 2003). And ghrelin levels are lower in patients following surgery than in patients who lost comparable weight by dieting (Leonetti et al., 2003). Ghrelin release, normally coinciding with onset of meals, is greatly reduced by the banding or bypass procedures. Whether

these hormonal changes are of functional significance is not clear. However, this may help explain the reduced appetite and long-term maintenance of weight loss after surgery in contrast with dieting.

A significant health benefit associated with weight loss surgery is the remittance of symptoms of type 2 diabetes in most cases (Cummings, Overduin, & Foster-Schubert, 2004). Many diabetic patients are able to discontinue their medications on leaving the hospital following surgery, which precedes much of the weight loss; so, something other than weight loss facilitates the improvement in glucose metabolism. As discussed elsewhere, obesity-related type 2 diabetes is most often due to insulin resistance. Weight-loss surgery seems to restore sensitivity to insulin, quickly allowing adequate regulation of glucose. Further, the post-surgical reduction in ghrelin levels facilitates the action of insulin (Cummings et al., 2004).

Factors to Consider Regarding Surgery

One of the critical factors that is now recognized is the need for intensive medical and psychological support for surgical patients, both before and after surgery. In particular, selection of patients is important: It is unethical to do such a surgery on people whose profile suggests they will not attempt to maintain the weight lost or be able to understand the limitations of their new condition. Patients must be prepared for the changes they must make to their eating behaviors and the psychological effects of body changes. Social support (family, peers, or support group) is a critical component of long-term success and increased quality of life after surgery. A standardized interview has been developed by the Medical Psychology Service at the VA Boston Healthcare System to ensure thorough assessment of patient readiness for surgery and to facilitate patient education about the procedure and behavioral changes that are needed afterward (Sogg & Mori, 2004). The focus is on seven areas:

1. Weight, diet, and nutritional history: Does the patient have a history of unsuccessful dieting?

2. Current eating behaviors: What is eaten? Is there bingeing behavior? Etc.

3. Medical history: Are there other medical conditions or recent surgeries?

4. Understanding of surgical procedures and risks: Does the patient show a "minimum understanding"?

5. Motivation and expectations: Does the patient understand realistic goals and is he/she willing to work for them?

6. Relationships and social support: Is the family willing to help/deal with weight loss?

7. Psychiatric complications: Are there any mitigating mental disorders that need treatment?

Adolescents and Surgery

The number of extremely overweight teenagers has risen dramatically over the past two decades, and they can have all of the adverse health symptoms of adults and a reduced quality of life and self-esteem. These issues can potentially be improved with weight-loss surgery (Capella & Capella, 2003). The question is whether gastric bypass or banding should be performed on adolescents and, if so, at what age or under what circumstances. There is a need to establish age guidelines, BMI criteria, and exclusionary factors such as drug use and the type of motivational/support factors that were discussed earlier in the Sogg & Mori checklist.

Cost of Surgery

Weight loss surgery costs roughly $20,000 to $30,000, and more if complications arise. Insurance coverage of these procedures is on the rise because, despite the high cost, analyses overwhelmingly indicate that the risks and expenses associated with obesity outweigh those associated with surgery (Salem, Devlin, Sullivan & Flum, 2008). However, many employers do not purchase insurance with weight-loss surgery provisions, and

---

BOX 12.1   **A Celebrity's Experience with Weight and Surgery**

Singer Carnie Wilson has been outspoken about her lifelong battle with weight. She underwent gastric bypass in 1999 and lost over half of her body weight, going from 300 lbs. to 150 lbs. in a year and a half. However, after two pregnancies and an admitted lack of adherence to healthy lifestyle changes, she gradually regained most of the weight. She underwent a second bariatric surgery (a lap band procedure) in 2012 and renewed her resolve to maintain a healthier eating and exercise habits.

Well-known television personality and weatherman, Al Roker, also has struggled with food and weight for most of his life. In his new book *Never Goin' Back* (2012), Roker reveals that he gained nearly half of the weight he lost after gastric bypass. He has since lost that weight; he now maintains a healthy weight by adhering to a strict diet and healthy exercise routine. Roker and Wilson both consider bariatric surgery an aid, not cure-all, in the treatment of obesity.

most insurance companies including Medicaid/Medicare provide coverage only at certain facilities, typically in urban settings, and often do not cover all of the medications and follow-up care.

Although obesity is found among all socioeconomic status (SES) groups in Western society, morbidly obese people are overrepresented in low-SES populations and in rural communities (Livingston & Ko, 2004). The expense of surgery and the scarcity of surgical hospitals in rural compared with urban areas make weight loss surgery inaccessible for many people at the highest risk for health problems associated with obesity.

Weight Regain After Surgery

Most weight lost occurs within 18 months following the bariatric surgery (Buchwald et al., 2007; Magro et al., 2007). However, some weight gain after that is quite common. Patients with extremely high BMIs (>40), binge-eating disorder, and/or a lack of social support seem to be at the highest risk for weight regain after surgery, particularly if they do not adhere to sufficient follow-up visits and support group meetings (Magro et al., 2007).

DIET, EXERCISE, AND BEHAVIORAL THERAPY

All types of weight loss discussed thus far are most successful when coupled with the behavior changes of diet and exercise. Many people pursue behavior changes in lieu of medications, supplements, or surgery to avoid side effects and expense. We suspect you are familiar with television shows such as "The Biggest Loser" in which obese individuals lose significant weight through intense workouts and changes to their diets. Many fitness trainers, nutritionists, physicians, and other weight loss experts promote varied versions of diet and exercise plans, often depicting theirs as the most effective. In fact, no one weight loss plan has been scientifically proven superior over others, and results are typically modest

(Tsai & Wadden, 2005). Essentially, they all work to reduce calorie intake, increase activity, and modify behavior. Further, as with the problems surrounding accessibility of surgery for low-SES individuals, many commercial weight loss programs and fitness training sessions are not financially feasible for many obese individuals.

Weight loss is the primary goal of **behavioral therapy (BT)**, but other psychological issues may be addressed with BT (e.g., depression). The goal here is to arm subjects with a new set of eating habits that they can keep with them the rest of their lives (i.e., relearn what and when to eat). Unfortunately, most BT programs are not tremendously effective in the long term. According to Wing and Phelan (2005), participants in behavioral weight loss programs lose an average of 7% to 10% of their body weight within 6 months of standard treatment, but gain back almost 50% of the lost weight after 1 year. Their research indicates that approximately 20% of dieters are successful at maintaining long-term weight loss. They also report six strategies for long-term success: "(1) engaging in high levels of physical activity; (2) eating a diet that is low in calories and fat; (3) eating breakfast; (4) self-monitoring weight on a regular basis; (5) maintaining a consistent eating pattern; and (6) catching 'slips' before they turn into larger regains" (p. 225S).

In an attempt to improve the long-term prognosis, Perri et al. (2001) compared two types of 1-year extended BT, relapse prevention training (RPT) and problem-solving therapy (PST), with a standard BT group without extended therapy sessions. With RPT participants are taught methods to anticipate issues that could trigger relapse (i.e., overeating) and to plan alternate coping mechanisms or behaviors. PST involves problem-solving efforts by a health care provider to help the person manage issues on the completion of therapy. In their study, all groups received weekly 2-hour group sessions for 5 months, including self-monitoring, goal setting, low calorie/fat diet, and home-walking program. At the end of this, all had lost (the expected) ~9% initial weight.

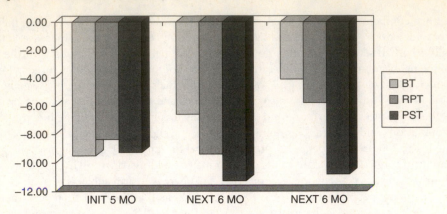

FIGURE 12.1 Average percentage of weight loss of patients in three behavioral therapy treatments for obesity during the first 5 months of treatment, and at 6 months and 1 year later.

The standard BT-only group had no additional treatment but had follow-up visits at 6 and 12 months. The RPT group had biweekly sessions for the next 12 months. Therapy included risk identification, cognitive coping, long-term planning, and so on. The PST group also had group discussions of specific problems that arose since last session and guided solutions over the 12 months.

Their results are represented by Figure 12.1. The graph shows the percentage of weight loss at the end of the different phases of the study. The standard BT-only group slowly regained about half their lost weight over the next year, as expected based on previous research. The RPT group did not seem to have much advantage over standard BT. The PST group did best in terms of maintaining the weight loss. The elements of peer group support and discussion involved in this therapy seem particularly beneficial.

CONCLUDING REMARKS

Obesity carries many risks to physical and psychological well-being. At present, the leading treatments also carry risks and are quite costly. Because losing weight once it has been gained in excess is challenging and often unsuccessful long term, the best course is prevention. The concept of preventive care has received increased attention among health care professionals, insurance companies, and in the political arena (as it relates to health care expenses). Despite the growing obesity problem in many countries around the world, there is no established evidence-based national obesity prevention or weight loss program (Swinburn, Gill, & Kumanyika, 2005). Does this matter? Is obesity treatment or prevention an issue of national or global concern? Evidence overwhelmingly supports that there is a need to address the problem; the health benefits (e.g., better quality of life, increased work productivity, reduced health expenses) outweigh the expenses of preventive or weight loss programs. However, remaining questions around such a program include who should fund it, who should be targeted, and what should be done. Several studies targeting school-age children and adolescents have found prevention programs successful at reducing obesity rates and cost effective in the long term (Taylor et al., 2007; Wang, Yang, Lowry, & Wechsler, 2003). We remain optimistic that heightened awareness and concern about obesity, coupled with empirical data supporting the effectiveness of prevention programs, will yield increased proactive efforts to improve the health of current and future generations.

Let's review and apply your knowledge. Take some time to answer these chapter questions

1. What are the leading anti-obesity medications? Briefly describe how each works. What side effects are associated with each medication?

2. What are some over-the-counter (i.e., nonprescription) supplements for weight loss? What are some concerns with these?

3. Name and discuss four calorie substitutes. Are these effective for weight loss?

4. Name and briefly describe the two leading types of weight loss surgeries. Are these effective? What are some issues or reasons for concern surrounding surgery?

5. Describe behavioral therapy for weight loss or maintenance. What factors seem particularly beneficial?

6. Why is obesity prevention a good idea? Think of some ways this could be done on a local, national, or global level.

Glossary

Aspartame   Non-caloric artificial sweetener.

Behavioral therapy   A form of psychological therapy in which problematic behaviors are identified and improvements are learned.

Cannabinoid receptor blockers   Drugs that are antagonists or blockers of action of cannabinoid transmitters.

Dopamine (DA)   A monoamine neurotransmitter associated with reward, motivation, and movement.

Fenfluramine   Structural analog of amphetamine that was developed in the 1960s to have appetite suppressant effects without stimulant or abuse potential. It works primarily by increasing serotonin transmission in brain. Withdrawn from the clinical market due to side effect of pulmonary hypertension.

Ghrelin   Peptide released from enteroendocrine cells, primarily in the stomach, during fasting. Injection of ghrelin to animals stimulates food intake.

Leptin   Peptide released from adipose (fat) cells in approximate relation to their fat content. Thus, blood concentrations of leptin are a rough measure of the amount of body fat. Several cells in the brain involved in feeding have receptors for and respond to circulating leptin.

Lorcaserin   Potential appetite suppressant drug that works primarily as an agonist or stimulant at serotonin (5HT) type 2c receptors.

Olestra   A fat substitute in which fatty acid chains are bonded to a sucrose molecule, with a resultant molecule that has the "mouth feel" of fat but cannot be broken down and absorbed in the intestine. It was originally developed as a drug to lower cholesterol levels but was instead approved as a food additive.

Orlistat   An inhibitor of intestinal lipase: blocks or attenuates the absorption of triglycerides from the gastrointestinal tract.

Phentermine   A structural analog of amphetamine that is both a stimulant and appetite suppressant

Qsymia   Newly approved combination drug treatment consisting of phentermine and topiramate that acts centrally to reduce appetite and promote weight loss and improvement of type 2 diabetes.

Saccharin   Non-caloric artificial sweetener.

Serotonin (5-HT)   A monoamine neurotransmitter involved with mood, appetite, and sleep. Some 14 receptor subtypes have been identified; the 2c receptor is most implicated in appetite and feeding.

Sibutramine   Centrally acting appetite suppressant drug, structurally related to amphetamine, and having a dual neurochemical action that increases the amounts of norepinephrine and serotonin in active synapses.

Sucralose It is a structural analog of sucrose, but is non-caloric because it is not metabolized; it tastes sweeter than aspartame or saccharin.

Supplements Additives to a natural food or foods; because many of these are regulated only loosely (if at all), it is sometimes difficult to assess their safety and efficacy.

References

Blom, W. A., Abrahamse, S. L., Bradford, R., Duchateau, G. S., Theis, W., Orsi, A., … Mela, D. J. (2011). Effects of 15-d repeated consumption of Hoodia gordonii purified extract on safety, ad libitum energy intake, and body weight in healthy, overweight women: A randomized controlled trial. *The American Journal of Clinical Nutrition, 94*(5), 1171–1181.

Buchwald, H., Estok, R., Fahrbach, K., Banel, D., & Sledge, I. (2007). Trends in mortality in bariatric surgery: A systematic review and meta-analysis. *Surgery, 142*(4), 621–635.

Campfield, L., Smith, F. J., & Burn, P. (1998). Strategies and potential molecular targets for obesity treatment. *Science, 280*(5368), 1383–1387.

Capella, J. F., & Capella, R. F. (2003). Bariatric surgery in adolescence. Is this the best age to operate? *Obesity Surgery, 13,* 826–832.

Colman, E. (2005). Anorectics on trial: A half century of federal regulation of prescription appetite suppressants. *Annals of Internal Medicine, 143*(5), 380–385.

Cooke, D., & Bloom, S. (2006). The obesity pipeline: Current strategies in the development of anti-obesity drugs. *Nature Reviews Drug Discovery, 5,* 919–931.

Cummings, D. E., Overduin, J., & Foster-Schubert, K. E. (2004). Gastric bypass for obesity: Mechanisms of weight loss and diabetes resolution. *The Journal of Clinical Endocrinology & Metabolism, 89*(6), 2608–2615.

Cummings, D. E., Weigle, D. S., Frayo, R. S., Breen, P. A., Ma, M. K., Dellinger, E. P., & Purnell, J. Q. (2002). Plasma ghrelin levels after diet-induced weight loss or gastric bypass surgery. *The New England Journal of Medicine, 346*(21), 1623–1630.

Dymek, M. P., le Grange, D., Neven, K., & Alverdy, J. (2002). Quality of life after gastric bypass surgery: A cross-sectional study. *Obesity Research, 10*(11), 1135–1142.

Finkelstein, E. A., Trogden, J. G., Cohen, J. W., & Dietz, W. (2009). Annual medical spending attributable to obesity: Payer- and service-specific estimates. *Health Affairs, 28,* w822–w831.

Higa, K. D., Boone, K. B., & Ho, T. (2000). Complications of the laparoscopic Roux-en-Y gastric bypass: 1,040 patients—What have we learned? *Obesity Surgery, 10,* 509–513.

Kirkham, T. C. (2009). Cannabinoids and appetite: Food craving and food pleasure. *International Review of Psychiatry, 21,* 163–171.

Le Foll, B., Gorelick, D. A., & Goldberg, S. R. (2009). The future of endocannabinoid-oriented clinical research after CB1 antagonists. *Psychopharmacology, 205,* 171–174.

Leonetti, F., Silecchia, G., Iacobellis, G., Ribaudo, M. C., Zapaterreno, A., Tiberti, C., … Di Mario, U. (2003). Different plasma ghrelin levels after laparoscopic gastric bypass and adjustable gastric banding in morbid obese subjects. *The Journal of Clinical Endocrinology & Metabolism, 88*(9), 4227–4231.

Livingston, E. H., & Ko, C. Y. (2004). Socioeconomic characteristics of the population eligible for obesity surgery. *Surgery, 135,* 288–296.

Magro, D. O., Geloneze, B., Delfini, R., Pareja, B. C., Callejas, F., & Pareja, J. C. (2008). Long-term weight regain after gastric bypass: A 5-year prospective study. *Obesity Surgery, 18*(6), 648–651.

Nguyen, N. T., Slone, J. A., Nguyen, X. M., Hartman, J. S., & Hoyt, D. B. (2009). A prospective randomized trial of laparoscopic gastric bypass versus laparoscopic adjustable gastric banding for the treatment of morbid obesity: Outcomes, quality of life, and costs. *Annals of Surgery, 250*(4), 631–641.

Perri, M. G., Nezu, A. M., McKelvey, W. F., Shermer, R. L., Renjilian, D. A., & Viegener, B. J. (2001). Relapse prevention training and problem-solving therapy in the long-term management of obesity. *Journal of Consulting and Clinical Psychology, 69*(4), 722–726.

Quinlan, M. E., & Jenner, M. F. (2006). Analysis and stability of the sweetener sucralose in beverages. *Journal of Food Science, 55*(1), 244–246.

Rolls, B. J., Pirraglia, P. A., Jones, M. B., & Peters, J. C. (1992). Effects of olestra, a noncaloric fat substitute on daily energy and fat intakes in lean men. *American Journal of Clinical Nutrition, 56*, 84–92.

Salem, L., Devlin, A., Sullivan, S. D., & Flum, D. R. (2008). Cost-effectiveness analysis of laparoscopic gastric bypass, adjustable gastric banding, and nonoperative weight loss interventions. *Surgery for Obesity and Related Diseases 4*(1), 26–32.

Slavin, J. (2012). Beverages and body weight: Challenges in the evidence-based review process of the Carbohydrate Subcommittee from the 2010 Dietary Guidelines Advisory Committee. *Nutrition Reviews, 70*(s2), S111–S120.

Sogg, S., & Mori, D. L. (2004). The Boston interview for gastric bypass: Determining the psychological suitability of surgical candidates. *Obesity Surgery, 14* (3), 370–380.

Sugerman, H. J., Wolfe, L. G., Sica, D. A., & Clore, J. N. (2003). Diabetes and hypertension in severe obesity and effects of gastric bypass-induced weight loss. *Annals of Surgery, 237*(6), 751–758.

Swinburn, B. B., Gill, T. T., & Kumanyika, S. S. (2005). Obesity prevention: A proposed framework for translating evidence into action. *Obesity Reviews, 6*(1), 23–33.

Swithers, S. E., & Davidson, T. L. (2008). A role for sweet taste: Calorie predictive relations in energy regulation by rats. *Behavioral Neuroscience, 122*(1), 161–173.

Taylor, R. W., McAuley, K. A., Barbezat, W., Strong, A., Williams, S. M., & Mann, J. I. (2007). APPLE Project: 2-y findings of a community-based obesity prevention program in primary school–age children. *American Journal of Clinical Nutrition, 86*, 735–742.

Tsai, A., & Wadden, T. A. (2005). Systematic review: An evaluation of major commercial weight loss programs in the United States. *Annals of Internal Medicine, 142*(1), 56–66.

Wang, L. Y., Yang, Q., Lowry, R., & Wechsler, H. (2003). Economic analysis of a school-based obesity prevention program. *Obesity Research, 11*, 1313–1324.

Wing, R. R., & Phelan, S. (2005). Long-term weight loss maintenance. *American Journal of Clinical Nutrition, 8*, 222S–225S.

Xie, S. S., Furjanic, M. A., Ferrara, J. J., McAndrew, N. R., Ardino, E. L., Ngondara, A. A., … Raffa, R. B. (2007). The endocannabinoid system and rimonabant: A new drug with a novel mechanism of action involving cannabinoid CB1 receptor antagonism—or inverse agonism—as potential obesity treatment and other therapeutic use. *Journal of Clinical Pharmacy & Therapeutics, 32*(3), 209–231.

13

Where Do We Go From Here?

After reading this chapter, you will be able to

- Evaluate the distinction between normal and abnormal eating
- Discuss the relative roles of industry, government, and individuals in addressing obesity
- Quantify the relative contributions of exercise versus diet in combating obesity
- Evaluate the potential of educational programs, including improved use of food labels

OBESITY, THE DISEASE

Not everyone agrees that obesity is either a disease or something that should be treated. Unlike some cancers or cardiovascular-related diseases or stroke, obesity is not a direct cause of death, although it is strongly associated with increased incidence of these life-shortening afflictions. Throughout this book, we have emphasized that obesity is caused by intake that exceeds expenditures over a sustained period. Eating behavior, and therefore obesity, is under some degree of volitional control—as seen, for example, in the concept of dietary restraint. It has become popular to suggest that eating, or overeating, shares features of addiction or substance abuse. In the coming revision of the American Psychological Association's *Diagnostic and Statistical Manual* (DSM-V), the diagnosis of Substance Abuse Disorder requires that an individual meet a

minimum of 2 from a list of 11 criteria. Following, for 5 of these criteria, we inserted a term such as *food* or *food consumption* in place of substance or substance use:

1. Craving or a strong desire or urge to consume food.
2. A great deal of time is spent in activities to obtain food, consume food, or recover from its effects.
3. Food is often consumed in larger amounts or over a longer period than was intended.
4. Food consumption is continued despite knowledge of having a persistent or recurrent physical or psychological problem that is likely to have been caused or exacerbated by food.
5. There is a persistent desire or unsuccessful efforts to cut down or control food consumption.

TALKING POINT 13.1

Most of you have probably experienced two or more of the listed items within the past year, so by that definition, you have a food abuse disorder! What do you think about this characterization? If you don't agree with it, how would you change or qualify these definitions? How would our ancestral hunter-gatherers have come out relative to these definitions?

These definitions raise a more difficult question: "When does normal use (of drugs or food) become abnormal?" Although drugs are not biologically essential as is food, it is true to say that almost everyone tries one or more drugs but relatively few continue to use these drugs at a damagingly high level despite easy availability—at least for alcohol and tobacco. Likewise for food: Not everyone overeats or becomes obese, perhaps because they exhibit some aspect of restraint. Is the "disease" of obesity primarily a failure to exhibit restraint and may be more accurately categorized as a disorder of impulsivity (Best et al., 2012; Schag, Schonleber, Teufel, Zipfel, & Giel, 2013)? It is important to make a distinction between overeating as an affliction of the systems that normally control energy balance compared with viewing it a problem of impulsivity that happens to be directed toward food: These alternative views could and should greatly affect the types of interventions considered.

Regardless of the diagnosis and intervention, payment for professional treatment is the next issue. Table 13.1 documents recent health care expenditures and life expectancy at birth as one index of the effectiveness of that health investment. Whereas obesity and its related illnesses—diabetes, heart disease, stroke, osteoarthritis—account for only some of these total costs, together they account for a significant and growing portion. The nations of the world self-sort into three main groups. The bottom tier has a median expenditure of <$1,000 and life expectancy 72 years. The middle tier has a median expenditure of about $3,500 (8%–10% of GDP) and life expectancy of 81 years. Comparing the lower and middle tiers, one could conclude that

Impulsivity—related to thrill-seeking?

the more you spend the longer the life expectancy. But then there's the United States: expenditures >$7,000, almost twice the percentage of GDP of the middle tier, yet lower life expectancy. You need not be a trained economist to realize there's something very troublesome here. This trajectory (Garber & Skinner 2008) means that within 10 years, health care in the United States (regardless of the ratio of public to private funding) will

TABLE 13.1	Health Care Expenditure and Longevity Around the World		
Country	Health expenditure per person per year ($)[a]	Health expenditure as percentage of GDP[a]	Overall life expectancy (yr)[b]
United States	7,164	15.2	78.0
Norway	5,207	8.5	80.4
Canada	3,867	9.8	80.5
Germany	3,922	10.5	79.4
Sweden	3,622	9.4	80.9
United Kingdom	3,222	8.7	79.5
Australia	3,365	8.5	81.4
Israel	2,093	8.0	80.6
Russia	985	4.8	67.8
Brazil	875	8.4	72.4
Saudi Arabia	831	3.6	73.3
China	265	4.3	72.8
India	122	4.2	64.2

[a] Data from the *World Health Report, 2008*—after correction for purchasing power parity.
[b] Life expectancy at birth, averaged for males and females, from United Nations World Population prospects, 2010.

account for 20% of GDP; other nations are projecting rapid increases as well. This trajectory is, in a word, unsustainable.

EXERCISE, THE CURE (?)

Every professional anti-obesity intervention we have mentioned to date, including diet, drugs, or surgery, comes along with the qualifier "and exercise." Although reduction of intake is certainly helpful, it is more effective in a context of increased energy expenditure. Starting with the automobile, then to elevators, automatic doors, remote controls, and more, every aspect of modern life is replete with devices that decrease our personal energy expenditure. Not only is our food itself obesogenic, but it is presented within an environment that often is deliberately engineered to minimize energy expenditure.

Let's look at the energy that is expended in exercise. The energy cost of exercise increases with body weight and with the intensity and duration of the activity. To compensate for differences in body weight, energy output is often expressed in **metabolic equivalent of task (MET)** units, where 1 MET is defined as 1 kcal/kg body weight/hour.

TABLE 13.2	Met Values Associated with Various Physical Activities	
Physical activity		**MET range**
Sleeping, watching television		0.9–1.0
Typical desk work, light housework, slow walking		1.5–2.5
Brisk walking, heavy housework, golf (walking)		3.0–5.0
Fast walking/jogging (5 mph), exercise/flat bicycle, casual sports		5.5–7.5
High intensity or uphill exercise, heavy manual labor		8–11
Trained athlete at maximum exertion		>20

Thus, for a 70 kg (154 lb.) person, 1 MET equals 70 kcal/hour and for a 140 kg (308 lb.) individual, 1 MET equals 140 kcal/hr. Resting metabolic rate (BMR) is only slightly less than 1 MET so, to a good approximation, the MET value of an activity reflects the fold-increase above BMR. Table 13.2 shows the approximate MET values associated with a number of activities.

You might recall that calculations on foraging cost that we presented earlier in the book are somewhat similar to those in Table 13.2, but now we have brought them into the terminology of exercise science. You should note several points in your answers. First, it takes a long duration of exercise at low intensity to significantly increase metabolic expenditure over the 24-hour period. Second, even if an individual exercises at a level that for most people is quite intense, one average caloric snack or beverage can completely undo the energy benefit. Exercise is a good idea because it has other benefits besides calorie burning, but it is not a good idea to think that exercise alone can solve obesity. It is also important to note that even small movements over a long period of time can have beneficial effects, which is why there is contemporary interest in promoting workplace strategies such as stand-at desks, exercise ball chairs, or simply stretching or standing from time to time. Sitting still, as on the couch, is definitely the worst! One recent study showed that just by standing and either walking or stepping in place during just the advertisements while watching TV almost doubled energy expenditure during the viewing period (Steeves, Thompson, & Bassett, 2012).

DO THE MATH

Suppose your BMR is 1 MET and you spend an entire 24 hour period doing absolutely nothing. What is your total energy expenditure in MET-hours? (1 MET-hour = 1 kcal/kg). The next day, you decide to get up and go for a brisk walk (@ 4 MET) for 1 hour, and then collapse back on the couch for the remaining 23 hours. What is your total energy expenditure? Another day, you increase the duration of your brisk walk to 2 hours. What is your expenditure? And another day you get up off the couch for just 1 hour and run at 7 mph @ 8 MET. What is your expenditure now? Then you get a job: routine office work (8 hours @ 2 MET) and commuting by public transportation (1 hour @ 2 MET), with the remaining 15 hours at home doing nothing; again, your expenditure? Next, you still have your job, but on the way home, you stop at the gym for a 1-hour moderate to vigorous workout @ 8 MET: your expenditure now? Last, you weigh about 150 lbs. and for simplicity assume that 1 MET = 75 kcal/hour. Your gym has a "juice bar" and sells a 300-kcal, 20-ounce smoothie (this is a fairly typical size) that you just can't resist. For how much *extra time* would you have to do your gym workout to offset the calories in the smoothie? *(Answers at end of chapter.)*

TALKING POINT 13.2

Many people agree that exercise would be a good idea but seem to be unable or unwilling to put that belief into action. Why is this so difficult? How many resolutions to walk or jog regularly are broken? How many pieces of home exercise equipment lie unused? How many gym memberships are allowed to lapse? Can you find any data on these or cite personal experience?

One possible problem is that exercise has immediate features that are functional barriers, such as time investment, breathlessness or aching, sweatiness or other cosmetic concerns compounded with the fact that there is minimal immediately tangible benefit or reward. Ideally, exercise should be self-reinforcing, and that is true for a relatively small number of avid exercisers. But most people require external reinforcers such as accolades from family or friends, social reinforcement by belonging to a group, or institutional reinforcement for meeting specific goals. In a recent yearlong study, financial incentives were associated with sustained weight loss over the course of a year. Weight loss was most significant for the participants who could earn money for meeting weight-loss goals but had to pay into a bonus pool of money if they failed to meet these goals (Mayo Clinic, 2013).

Group belongingness is another powerful motivator and social reinforcer, from the group that walks or jogs around the neighborhood every day to organized nonprofit sports clubs or teams to for-profit organizations such as fitness clubs and gyms. If you aren't there on any given day, someone will most likely contact you and urge you to come the next time. However, some individuals (often including the most obese) believe they don't live in enabling environments and/or have the financial means to participate in organized activities: This behavior is called **self-handicapping**. For these people or groups in particular, it behooves society to encourage ways to exercise, including low-cost shoes or clothes and community security. On a longer-term basis, built environments should encourage exercise, for example, by making stairs rather than elevators the focal point of an entranceway or by including spaces for group activities. Commercial gyms have a vested interest in increasing retention of members, and this might best be done with incentives based on attendance and/or reaching attainable fitness targets. Businesses have an interest in employee exercise, because that often translates into fewer sick days and increased productivity. Large businesses can do this by creating times and places for employee exercise, but for small businesses this presents a more challenging proposition. In the next sections, we will consider ways that private and public sectors can address both exercise and food intake.

ROLES FOR GOVERNMENT AND/OR INDUSTRY

The earliest healers in human culture were shamans who generally used a mixture of herbal remedies and spirituality to guide sick people. The shaman, like other learned people, was revered and at least in part materially supported by a tribe—perhaps the first form of community health care cost or expenditure. Translated to modern societies, a decision has to be made about priorities in spending, and this is often wrapped up in politics. How much can we spend on health care without harming other critical functions including national security, infrastructure, and education to name but a few? Does a government choose to guarantee health to all, or to none, or only to those who themselves can afford it? The countries shown in Table 13.2 represent a fair cross-section of different approaches to the general problem. Regardless of the total expenditures and politics, it is in the best interests of governments and other payers such as insurance companies to enable or even promote health and well-being.

It is generally agreed that prevention is far more cost effective than treatment, although most of the expenditures continue to be on treatment. Arguably, obesity is an easily preventable condition, and this would net huge savings in treatment, not to mention reduced hardship for the obese individual (e.g., increased mobility, improved physical and mental health). In a broader context of public health, some of the points made by the World Health Organization (2008) included the following:

- The ultimate responsibility for shaping national health systems rests with governments.
- The legitimacy of state intervention (should include) economic actors—the medical equipment industry, the pharmaceutical industry, and the professions.
- Relative to all other affluent nations, the U.S. health sector underperforms consistently across domains of health outcomes, quality, access, efficiency, and equity.

One of the points here is that over the past 100 years, governments have increasingly taken on a larger role in protecting their citizens from harm, and that cannot be achieved without the involvement of many stakeholders. Governments and businesses have two principal ways in which

they can influence health in general and obesity in particular: education and incentive.

Let's first consider education. What are the causes of obesity, how can the public become informed of the risks, and is it possible to use this information to change behavior? Many countries, including the United States, have quite good public information and education programs sponsored by government, schools, or private businesses and corporations (Wakefield, Loken, & Hornik, 2010). The challenge is to get more individuals actively engaged in programs of behavior change or maintenance, including eating less or eating better and exercising more. Most models of behavior change emphasize the need to adapt health messages to specific populations. For young people, we need to help them never become overweight. A different approach is needed for people who are already obese and are seeking to lose weight, and that message will have age-sensitive variants. Cutting across categories is an issue of culturally appropriate interventions: Many ethnic groups have strongly entrenched cuisines or social cultures surrounding eating and to modify or change behavior in these contexts will require culturally sensitive approaches.

Aside from education about an individual's health, it is also important to offer information about the foods themselves. There are many excellent public and commercial sources of information about the content and calories in particular foods, and we talked about nutritional content and food labels earlier in this book. Typical food labels in the United States are shown in Figure 13.1.

Although there is a lot of information, it is not always presented in a way that will provide the time-pressed customer with a quick summary. First, the print is small and so those with less acute vision may not even try to read it. Second, even if they can read the label, do individuals add up the relevant categories (calories, salt etc.,) across all the foods that they buy in the store on that occasion, or even put together at home into a single meal? We think not: These labels are not used by most of the people most of the time. A creative solution called **traffic light labeling** is being tried

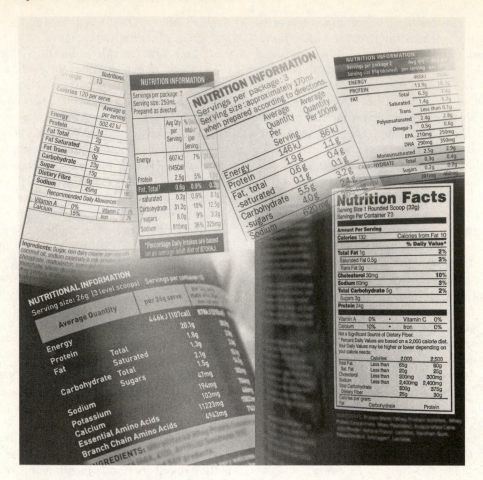

FIGURE 13.1   Traditional food labels.

in several European countries (Sacks, Veerman, Moodie & Swinburn, 2011): The color of the label (red, amber, or green) reflects a composite of the various dimensions (Figure 13.2).

For a nutritionist, such categories may not be as scientifically rigorous as desired, but they do impart a message that is understandable to shoppers. Additionally, exactly why certain constituents make a food "less healthy" than another can be controversial—who sets the category boundaries, and on the basis of what data? Consumer friendliness may outweigh any downside to simplification, but a dual or hybrid label that incorporates both traditional details and the color summary might be satisfactory!

A second principal mode of influence is via monetary or other tangible incentive, such as in the Mayo Clinic study cited previously. This could be achieved in several ways. The first would be through health insurance premiums or other direct health cost. Recall from an earlier chapter that the weight and height table compiled by the Metropolitan Life Insurance Company established premium payments on the basis of perceived health risks: Obesity was regarded as a preexisting condition. Although imposing a penalty on the basis of preexisting conditions is politically controversial, the converse may not be: For example, analogous to automobile insurance, if an individual establishes a sustained record of

Each 1/2 pack serving contains

of your guideline daily amount

FIGURE 13.2   Traffic light food label.   *Source:* Food
Standards Agency and bbc.co.uk.

TALKING POINT 13.3

Is portion size more of a dietary hazard than
the constituents themselves? For example, the
label on a typical can of soup in the United
States says that it contains two servings, but
once you have opened the can, what do you do
with the other serving? What other foods (or
beverages) can you find that present similar
problems? Do you think it would be useful
to reduce package size to equal one portion,
even if it means that the cost per portion
might be higher? What are some advantages
and disadvantages or limitations of this type
of approach to the problem? And, who might
"impose" this change?

healthy BMI (or other agreed-upon index), might
their health insurance cost be reduced? Larger
employers, many of whom pay health insurance
for their employees, might then be incentivized to
address obesity by improving cafeteria offerings
and/or employee exercise opportunities.

At the level of food consumption, there
are also creative ways in which buying patterns
could be influenced. For example, each food item
or category (e.g., using the traffic light scheme)
could be coded at checkout to yield an overall
"healthy shopping score" (or percentage), and target levels could be associated with rebates or other
incentives. To implement these schemes would
require the cooperation of the food manufacturing and retail industries (Chandon & Wansink,
2012). Another way of achieving this would be
altering relative prices of healthy compared with
unhealthy food options. Currently, most reduced-
calorie versions of a food cost the same or more
than the high-calorie versions—driven in part
by consumer demand—but that is not the only
principle on which absolute cost could be based.
Such change would require a major and industry-
wide agreement, and that might require government incentives to business. At the present time, a
small number of countries or municipalities have
enacted a sales tax on foods or beverages that are
seen to contribute to obesity and metabolic disease,
including fat and sugar. But, in tax-averse societies
such as the United States, these strategies provoke
vigorous public resistance rather than compliance.
Nonetheless, for tobacco and alcohol—the two
most widely used drugs—a significant portion of
their purchase price is in taxes; major laws prohibit
exposure of our youth to these drugs; and there
are sustained health-related media messages on
the dangers of overuse, including from the manufacturers. Together, these environmental strategies
have been successful in reducing, but by no means
eliminating, excessive alcohol and tobacco consumption in the United States.

EATING IN, EATING OUT, AND EATING ALL ABOUT

Throughout this book, we have included examples relevant to eating at home (e.g., food shopping) or eating out (e.g., portion size in restaurants). The average American eats at a restaurant about 200 times per year, and the fraction of food expenditures outside the home rose steadily until about 2006 and has been stable at about 49% (Economic Research Service, 2011). There are certainly great differences between individuals of different ages and socioeconomic means both in the frequency and the type of restaurant visited, but the gross statistic means that some 20% of all meals (assuming 3 per day) are prepared by someone other than either the consumer or a dining companion. And an increasing amount of food consumption occurs as snacks (e.g., in children; Ford, Slining, & Popkin, 2013), implying a lack of structure or, as the title of this section calls it, "eating all about."

Ultimately, to allow individuals to exert greater and informed control over what and how much they eat, all three of these aspects of eating need to be addressed in a coherent manner. Let's talk first about snacks because in some ways, they might be the easiest to examine. We will distinguish four types of occasions for snacking, although there is certainly some degree of overlap:

- Planned snacking, such as a midmorning snack you might take to work or school
- Social snacking, as visiting someone's home or at a business meeting

- Impulsive snacking, such as happening to pass a vending machine or shop
- Idle snacking, usually at home such as when you are watching TV or studying

Insofar as snacking is not well compensated by reductions in the size of subsequent meals, almost everything we consume as snacks increases our caloric intake above what it would have been. It would be difficult or unproductive to initiate an intervention to reduce frequency of snacking; it is relatively easy (for government and industry) to influence the number of calories associated with snacks. Earlier in the book we presented data showing that the number of calories in many portions including snack foods has doubled over the past 20 years. This could just as easily be reversed, provided that all parties "buy into" such a change. Further, the type of food offered as snacks could be changed, and already we see some grassroots efforts to promote more fruits as snacks (Wansink, Shimizu, & Brumberg, 2013). However, to become a successful strategy to address obesity, fruits would have to become a snack frequently or most demanded by consumers—that is, become the social norm. Snacking often introduces variety, which itself may promote intake (Epstein et al., 2013). Snack providers, ranging all the way from corporations that stock vending machines to friends making snack food for visitors need to embrace the concept that these items should contain more fruit or other healthful content. Functionally, caloric beverages are snacks: Again, it may be important that zero or low-calorie options become the norm rather than the exception.

What about eating out and portion size? Although it is true that many restaurants now offer low-calorie or reduced-size portions, these do not account for a majority of the meals that are ordered. Thus, to be an effective strategy, consumers need to be persuaded to choose smaller options more frequently. This could be accomplished by education as well as restructuring of prices, but this will be ineffective unless we can reach a "tipping point" at which reduced-calorie

TALKING POINT 13.4

Snacks

Can you think of ways in which food manufacturers and vendors could be incentivized to sell only (or mostly) low-calorie snack options, and how the consuming public might be incentivized to buy or demand primarily those alternatives?

or otherwise healthful meals become the industry and consumer norm. Also, it is not very helpful if an individual eats a healthy entrée simply to justify a high-calorie dessert—dessert portions in restaurants, as well as shops that sell desserts only, need to be encouraged to promote reduced-portion sizes or lower fat content. This will require a radical overhaul of industry pricing strategies—which doesn't seem to be on the horizon.

What about eating in? Individuals can be encouraged to buy lower-calorie or healthier foods, but there is no guarantee that what is prepared or consumed in the home reflects what is purchased—for example, fresh fruit or vegetables that are not eaten are eventually discarded. Some traditional cuisines use high levels of fat in preparation, and to adhere to "grandma's recipe" is an emotional rather than a rational choice. To effect change in such choices is an educational rather than an economic matter. One way to educate is via simple food labeling on retail goods as discussed earlier, as well as on restaurant menus (Ellison, Lusk, & Davis, 2013).

TO THE FUTURE

We have now finished our exploration of the psychology of eating. As educators, we hope that you have a much better understanding of the many factors that shape healthy and unhealthy eating behaviors. We also hope that we have raised questions that you seek to answer for yourselves. Perhaps you have learned some facts about eating that will help you in your own lives, or perhaps you have been inspired to apply some of this knowledge to help the lives of others. We may have given you new ideas about helping others, especially in the realm of controlling intakes and body weight, in a world replete with influences that make that difficult. The solution to the contemporary eating-related problems that we have addressed lies not just in genes, or development, or society, or politics, or business: The solution is in all of them working together.

Answers to problems in Do the Math

Condition 1: 24 hours at rest = 24 × 1 = 24 METs/day

Condition 2: 23 hours @ 1 MET plus 1 hour @ 4 MET = 27 METs/day (12.5% increase)

Condition 3: 22 hours @ 1 MET plus 2 hours @ 4 MET (8 total) = 30 METs/day (25% increase)

Condition 4: 23 hours @ 1 MET plus 1 hour @ 8 MET = 31 MET/day (29% increase)

Condition 5: 15 hours @ 1 MET plus 9 hours @ 2 MET (18 total) = 33 MET/day (37.5% increase)

Condition 6: 14 hours @ 1 MET plus 9 hours @ 2 MET plus 1 hour @ 8 MET = 40 MET/day (67% increase)

Condition 7: Smoothie contains 300 kcal = 300/75 = 4 METs. At 8 MET (per hour) for your moderately vigorous workout, you would need 30 minutes more in the gym to offset the smoothie.

Glossary

Metabolic equivalent of task (MET)   One MET is defined as 1 kcal/kg body weight/hour. Resting metabolic rate is just under 1 MET, so to a good approximation the MET value of a specific activity reflects the fold-increase above basal energy expenditure doing that activity.

Self-handicapping   A psychological mechanism through which individuals believe that a particular goal is not within their reach, and as a result they don't strive to attain that goal.

Traffic light labeling   A class of labels placed on food products that instead of listing detailed numerical information about nutrient content, gives an easy-to-read categorical summary often in the three colors used in traffic lights where red = not healthful, amber = intermediate, green = most healthful category.

References

Best, J. R., Theim, K. R., Gredsya, D. M., Stein, R. I., Welch, R. R., Saelens, B. E., … Wilfley, D. E. (2012). Behavioral economic predictors of overweight children's weight loss. *Journal of Consulting and Clinical Psychology, 80,* 1086–1096.

Chandon P., & Wansink, B. (2012). Does food marketing need to make us fat? A review and solutions. *Nutrition Reviews, 70,* 571–593.

Economic Research Service. (2011). *Food CPI and expenditures.* Unites States Department of Agriculture. Retrieved from http://www.ers.usda.gov/data-products/food-expenditures.aspx (table 10).

Ellison B., Lusk J. L., & Davis, D. (2013). Looking at the label and beyond: The effects of calorie labels, health consciousness, and demographics on caloric intake in restaurants. *International Journal of behavioral Nutrition and Physical Activity, 10,* 21.

Epstein L. H., Fletcher K. D., O'Neill J., Roemmich, J. N., Raynor, H., & Bouton, M. E. (2013). Food characteristics, long-term habituation and energy intake: Laboratory and field studies. *Appetite, 60,* 40–50.

Ford C. N., Slining M. M., & Popkin B. M. (2013). Trends in dietary intake among U.S. 2- to 6-year old children, 1989–2008. *Journal of the Academy of Nutrition and Dietetics, 113,* 35–42.

Garber, A. M., & Skinner, J. (2008). Is American health care uniquely inefficient? *Journal of Economic Perspectives, 22,* 27–50.

Mayo Clinic. (2013, March 7). *Money talks when it comes to losing weight, Mayo Clinic study finds.* Retrieved from http://www.mayoclinic.org/news2013-rst/7357.html

Sacks G., Veerman, J. L., Moodie, M., & Swinburn B. (2011). "Traffic light" nutrition labelling and "junk-food" tax: A modelled comparison of cost-effectiveness for obesity prevention. *International Journal of Obesity, 35,* 1001–1009.

Schag, K., Schonleber, J., Teufel, M., Zipfel, S., & Giel, K. E. (2013). Food-related impulsivity in obesity and Binge Eating Disorder—a systematic review. *Obesity Reviews* (in press: doi 10.1111/obr.12017).

Steeves, J. A., Thompson, D. L., & Bassett, D. R., Jr. (2012). Energy cost of stepping in place while watching television commercials. *Medicine and Science in Sports and Exercise, 44,* 330–335.

Wakefield, M.A., Loken, B., & Hornik, R. C. (2010). Use of mass media campaigns to change health behaviour. *Lancet, 376,* 1261–1271.

Wansink, B., Shimizu, M., & Brumberg, A. (2013). Association of nutrient-dense snack combinations with calories and vegetable intake. *Pediatrics, 131,* 22–29.

World Health Organization. (2008). *World Health report 2008—Primary health care.* New York: Author.

APPENDIX 1

Overview of Neurons and Brain Architecture

The purpose of this appendix is to provide a very brief introduction and/or review of how the brain works. The brain, like other organs, is composed of cells, and the two main cell classes are **neurons** and **glia**. Glia are often (but probably erroneously) thought of as "servants" to the neurons, and so we will not discuss them further. The brain has an extensive network of blood vessels (the main input arteries are the carotid and vertebral) that provides the brain with a continuous supply of nutrients and oxygen (bound to hemoglobin). In adult humans, the brain accounts for almost 20% of the fuels and oxygen used by the entire body despite weighing only about 2% of the mass. Additionally, the brain is cushioned within and without by cerebrospinal fluid (CSF); this is made in four fluid-filled cavities inside the brain called ventricles (Figure A1.1). In addition to acting as a shock absorber, the CSF contains and transports certain chemical signal molecules.

A human brain contains about 100 billion (10^{11}) neurons with about 100 trillion (10^{14}) **synapses** or connections between them. Neurons are cells that integrate information at one point in the brain and transmit signals to cells in another part of the brain or body. They interface with other neurons via synapses and on average (from the previous estimate), each neuron has a thousand synapses. But neurons are by no means all the same, so "the typical neuron" is a fictional construct. With that disclaimer, a cartoon of a typical neuron is shown in Figure A1.2!

It consists of the cell body that contains the nucleus, which in turn contains chromosomes (see Appendix 2). The entire neuron is filled with a fluid called cytoplasm (*cyto-* means of a cell). Branching off of the cell body is one axon and (typically) many dendrites. The dendrites are often highly branched, like a tree, and contain **receptors** to receive information from other cells. The length of an axon is usually many thousands of times the tiny diameter of the cell body (unlike the cartoon!) and depends on the anatomical locations and functions of the neuron: It may range from very short to tens of centimeters long. Long axons are usually covered

Human Brain

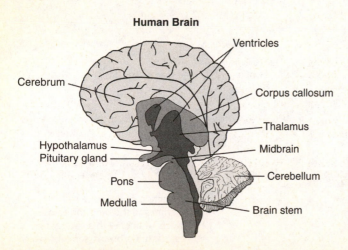

Cerebrum

Ventricles

Corpus callosum

Thalamus

Hypothalamus
Pituitary gland

Midbrain

Pons

Cerebellum

Medulla

Brain stem

FIGURE A1.1 A midsagittal (down the middle) sketch of the human brain. The front or rostral end is at the left of the figure. In humans, the brain is "bent" because we are bipeds, so the caudal (back) part—the brainstem—orients down.

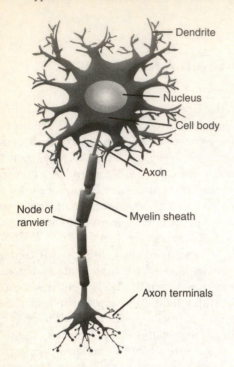

FIGURE A1.2   Cartoon of a typical neuron.
The various parts are not drawn to scale.

in a sheath of myelin, a sort of "insulator" that speeds up conduction of action potentials (see later discussion). At the end distal or farthest part from the cell body, an axon typically branches into several terminal zones or buttons. Most or all of these terminals form a synapse with another cell, often the dendrites of that next cell. Most synapses are unidirectional and are chemical: **Neurotransmitters** carry a signal from presynaptic to postsynaptic neurons.

In much the same way that our skin makes each of us physically separate, all cells including neurons are separated from the extracellular fluid in which they are suspended by a skin that is composed of a thin double-layered lipid or fatty membrane. This membrane is punctuated by many proteins that have specialized functions (Figure A1.3).

One such family of proteins, found most abundantly on dendrites, is neurotransmitter receptors. Specific transmitters are released, mostly at synapses, from terminals of the presynaptic neuron and activate corresponding receptors on postsynaptic cells. One of the goals of behavioral

Plasma Membrane Structure

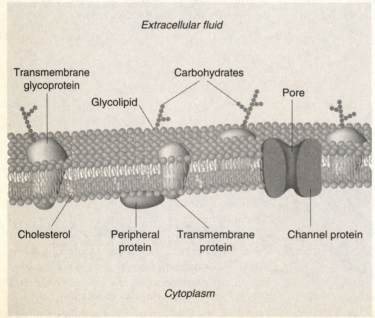

FIGURE A1.3   Plasma membrane structure.
Depiction of part of a cell membrane showing the two layers of lipid with a variety of associated proteins, some of which pass through the membrane.

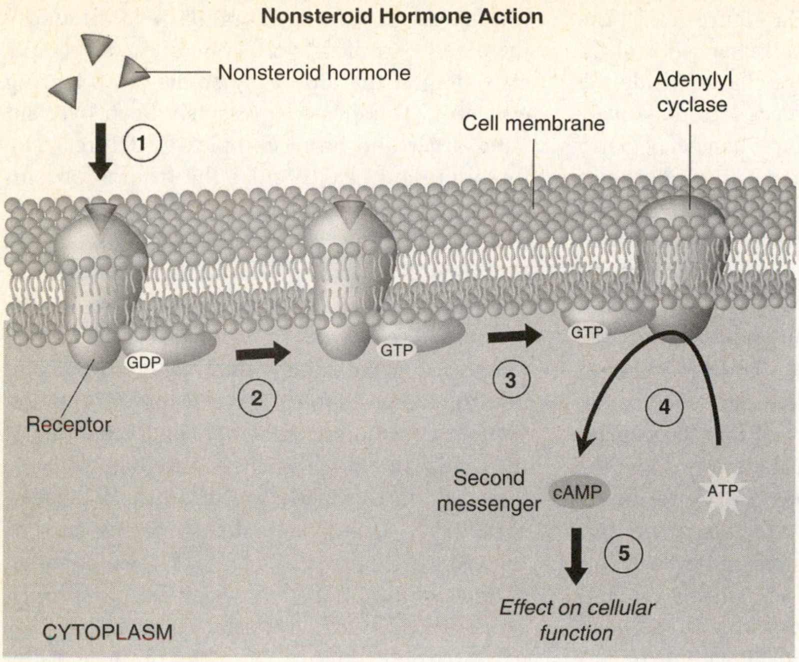

Nonsteroid Hormone Action

FIGURE A1.4 **Nonsteroid hormone action.** Transmitters (or hormones) interact with receptors of appropriate shape (in this cartoon, triangles). The receptor shown is a G-protein coupled receptor (GPCR) that sets in motion a series of reactions inside the cell.

neurobiology is to understand which transmitters and synapses control particular behaviors, such as foraging or feeding.

Transmitters are released as stored packets or vesicles from terminals and bind to and activate receptors by virtue of complementary shapes, much like a key fits in a lock (Figure A1.4). The part of the receptor on the outside surface of a neuron is the equivalent of the lock: It has to form a three-dimensional binding pocket that is more or less unique for the particular transmitter at that synapse. This is the same as the principle of different odorants binding to different receptors. Each neurotransmitter (or hormone) has at least one unique receptor. Many transmitters have several receptors, called *receptor subtypes*, but the binding pockets of each subtype have to be of similar shape because they all have to bind the same endogenous transmitter.

Receptors are primary input devices for a neuron as well as other types of cells. Once a receptor is occupied by a transmitter, which is a very brief event after which the transmitter leaves, the receptor initiates a local effect on the postsynaptic cell. This effect can be of two main types. The first,

ionotropic effect, is a direct and rapid mechanism that briefly opens a small channel in the membrane to allow charged particles (ions) to flow, like the pore shown in Figure A1.3. The second, **metabotropic** action, is a slower but longer-lasting cascade of reactions inside the cell initiated by a second (intracellular) messenger. Most metabotropic receptors are of the GCPR family, one type of which is sketched in Figure A1.4. At any given instant in time, a neuron will be bombarded with many chemical inputs, and the next instant with a potentially different set of inputs. Some of these inputs are **excitatory**, some are **inhibitory**, depending on the way each particular receptor works (details of which are beyond the present text). What do we mean by excitatory and inhibitory?

Cells such as neurons, by virtue of their membrane and channels, are **polarized**—they have a different electrical charge inside the cell relative to the outside. This charge difference is the membrane potential, which in neurons at rest is about −70 millivolts (mV), with "minus" meaning the inside is negative relative to the outside. When neurotransmitters act at receptors and cause ions to flow across the membrane through channels (such as the pore in Figure A1.3), the **resting membrane potential** is changed slightly. Excitation adds a net positive charge inside the cell, which as a result becomes less negatively charged. Conversely, inhibition adds a net negative charge inside the cell, which as a result becomes even more negatively charged. When enough net excitation builds through adding up many small excitatory events, a neuron reaches a **threshold** and generates an **action potential**, which is a brief (often less than one-thousandth of a second) but quite large electrical disturbance (~100 mV) that normally starts at the first part of the axon where it leaves the cell body and then propagates by a process of self-renewal all the way down the axon to the terminal buttons. At the terminal, the action potential initiates a sequence of events that ends with the release of transmitter, which is normally prepackaged in vesicles inside the buttons. The transmitter diffuses across the synapse and has either excitatory or inhibitory effects at its postsynaptic receptors. Thus, the action potential is a digital all-or-none signal that ends by sending a brief chemical signal to the next cell.

The brain is organized, from back to front, as hindbrain/brainstem, midbrain, and forebrain (Figure A1.1). The hindbrain is evolutionarily the oldest part of the vertebrate brain, essentially a swelling at the top of the spinal cord. During evolution, this has progressively been overlaid with larger and more complex structures. The forebrain and in particular the frontal lobes of the cortex are more highly developed in humans than in any other terrestrial mammal. Incoming sensory signals enter the brain through the cranial nerves, most of which enter the brainstem, including the nerves that carry taste and visceral information. We cannot reasonably understand how the forebrain integrates sensory information without considering structures and functions of the hindbrain, and how these articulate with the forebrain. In this book, we introduce brainstem, hypothalamic, and cerebral cortical mechanisms for feeding; for pragmatic reasons, these are often studied in isolation, but their functions must articulate seamlessly. Evolution (of mammals) has basically built upward from the brainstem, but that does not mean that a newer structure took over the function of an older structure; instead, we should think of more recently evolved structures as adding to whatever analysis is done at more caudal levels of the brain.

Glossary

Action potential   A brief but large (~100 mV) positive-going electrical potential that normally starts where the axon leaves the cell body and propagates by self-renewal to the terminal end of the axon. The number of action potentials in a given neuron per unit of time is often referred to as its "firing rate."

Excitatory   Refers to membrane events that produce net positive charge to flow into a cell. The most common of these are very small in amplitude and are called *excitatory postsynaptic potentials* (EPSP).

Glia   Glia provide critical service and support functions for neurons, including metabolic and structural support (astroglia) or forming myelin sheaths to speed axonal conduction (oligodendroglia).

Inhibitory   Refers to membrane events that produce net negative charge to flow into a cell. The most common of these are very small in amplitude and are called *inhibitory postsynaptic potentials* (IPSP).

Ionotropic   An ionotropic receptor is an aggregation of protein subunits passing through a membrane to form a channel or pore. Particular subunits have specific chemical binding and/or electrical properties that cause them to change shape and so open (or close) the channel and regulate the flow of ions. The action of these channels is brief and localized and directly gives rise to either an EPSP or IPSP.

Metabotropic   A metabotropic receptor consists of one or more proteins passing through a membrane. Binding of a hormone or transmitter on the outside surface causes the inside part of the protein to initiate chemical cascade(s) inside the cell. Whereas the chemical interaction on the outside is brief, the events initiated inside the cell have a relatively long and widespread sphere of influence.

Neurons   Neurons are cells that are specialized to transmit electrical information (mediated by flow of ions across the membrane) quickly and over relatively large distances. Most neurons are thus highly structured and have a long axon and elaborate "trees" of dendrites projecting from small cell bodies.

Neurotransmitters   Small molecules that are used for neuron-to-neuron communication, most usually via synapses and synchronized with arrival of action potentials at nerve terminals. There are several chemically distinct classes of neurotransmitters; the most numerous class is neuropeptides.

Polarized   A cell membrane is polarized when normally (at rest) there is an electrical charge difference between the two sides. Depolarization and hyperpolarization refer, respectively, to a decrease or increase in the resting charge difference.

Receptor   One or more protein molecules, often in the cell membrane, with a binding site that interacts with a hormone or transmitter by virtue of shape complementarity (e.g., lock and key). This binding normally activates the receptor and produces either ionotropic or metabotropic action.

Resting membrane potential   The electrical charge difference observed between the inside and outside of a neuron under steady-state conditions (no chemical or electrical disturbance).

Synapse   Narrow gap between the terminal of a presynaptic neuron and part of a postsynaptic neuron (most usually a dendrite). The membranes on the pre- and postsynaptic side of the synapse are highly specialized to enable, for example, neurotransmitter release and receptor function, respectively.

Threshold   The exact level of depolarization at which an action potential is initiated. For a given neuron, this threshold is constant, determined by the spatial density and type of ion channels that are regulated by the initial depolarization.

APPENDIX 2

Genetics

Genes are a set of instructions that are passed from parent to offspring. They are made of helical strands of deoxyribonucleic acid (DNA) that are wound together in pairs (double helix) and are located in serial fashion along chromosomes. Humans have 23 chromosomes arranged in paired or diploid structures; a gene may or may not be identical on these two chromosomal strands. These diploid genes are called *alleles* and may code for visible phenotypic (expressed) traits such as eye color or pigmentation. With two possible alleles, A and B, there are three possible combinations (AA, AB, and BB). AA and BB are called **homozygous** and show the phenotypic traits of A or B, respectively. AB is called **heterozygous** and will show the trait that is dominant (e.g., A if A is dominant over B). In order for the phenotype of a non-dominant (recessive) gene to be exhibited, the individual has to be homozygous for the recessive trait.

Each of these paired chromosomes contains hundreds of genes that together constitute an individual's **genome**. Despite this large number of genes, each strand of DNA is composed of only four building blocks called **nucleotide bases**: It is essentially a four-letter alphabet (A = adenine, G = guanosine, T = thymidine, C = cytosine). When these molecular letters are joined head-to-tail in different and very long sequences, we get far more possible sequences than there are genes actually present (just as there are many more ways we could arrange sequences of 26 letters than there are actual words in languages using Latin-based alphabets). A functional or complete piece of DNA-encoded information is called a **gene**, perhaps analogous to a paragraph. In addition to the coding region, each gene also has a regulatory region that allows it to be switched on or off (e.g., if you're in bed, then a light or e-reader is the "switch" that enables you to read this text). These coding genes are then joined together (along with what is called non-coding DNA, which in fact comprises the vast majority of all human DNA) into chromosomes (analogous to chapters or sections). Thus, each chromosome contains many genes, and these are often referred to by their location on a chromosome. Chromosomes aggregate as pairs: Humans normally have 23 pairs of chromosomes. These chromosomes are packaged in the nucleus and are wound around ball-like proteins called **histones**.

DNA actually exists as two strands that are wound together in a double helix configuration (Figure A2.1). One strand of DNA is the coding strand, effectively what we have mentioned earlier. The other strand is complementary and, among other things, can be used to repair or recreate the coding strand if necessary. Complementary in this case refers to the fact that the two strands of the helix are held together by weak chemical bonds, and specifically A always binds or bridges to T, and G always binds to C. Primed with this rule, if you knew a coding strand sequence (say ATTTGCTCGA) you could write the complementary sequence (TAAACGAGCT).

Transcription is the process by which double-stranded DNA in a gene is copied into single-stranded messenger ribonucleic acid (mRNA). The double helix of a gene is "unzipped" a bit at a time by an enzyme (DNA polymerase) that "walks" along the helix, and a single strand copy is made of the primary or coding strand of DNA of the segments as they unzip. This single-strand copy is composed of ribonucleic acid (RNA) using a four-letter or nucleotide alphabet similar to DNA, except that uracil (U) substitutes for thymidine (Figure A2.2).

What controls which genes are being transcribed and in what amount? As mentioned earlier, genes have two main regions, regulatory

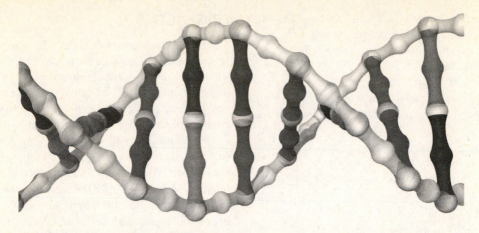

FIGURE A2.1 Double helix structure of DNA.
Bridges between the two strands in this model represent linking of complementary base pairs.

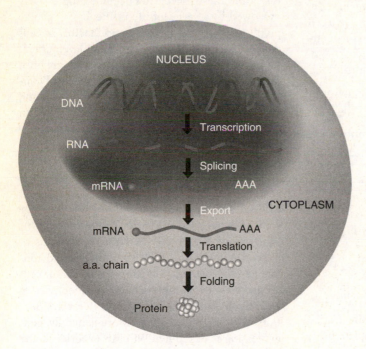

FIGURE A2.2 Transcription and translation.
A gene's double-stranded DNA is "copied" into a single-stranded RNA molecule, which then can undergo "editing" to form a strand of messenger RNA (mRNA). This then leaves the cell nucleus; in the surrounding cytoplasm, it attaches to ribosomes and is "translated" into a chain of amino acids (a.a.). That chain may then be folded to form a 3-D protein.

and coding. What we have talked about so far is the coding region. The regulatory region is a lot like a switch and occurs "upstream" of the coding region—just as this book has a start and an end, so a gene has directionality. Numerous chemical signals called **transcription factors** can bind to regulatory regions of genes and cause them to turn on or turn off. The more of a transcription factor that is present, the more or longer is the transcriptional activity. In short, genes can be turned on and off and the amount of a particular mRNA present is one indicator of how much transcription is occurring at that particular time.

The transcript is then cut and edited—much like our initial drafts of this book have been sliced and diced extensively! Once a final messenger RNA (mRNA) is made, it moves from inside the nucleus to a nearby part of the cell where **ribosomes** direct the translation of blocks of 3 bases in the mRNA code into a particular amino acid. These amino acids are then joined into a chain. There are 64 possible three-letter blocks, **codons**, that can be made from four letters (AAA, AAU, etc., through UUU), and there are 20 naturally occurring amino acids. Relatively short chains of amino acids are called *peptides* and include hormones such as insulin or leptin and neurotransmitters such as NPY and orexin. Long chains of amino acids are critical proteins in a cell. Some of these proteins are embedded in the membrane, like receptors for transmitters, and some proteins are enzymes that direct chemical reactions inside the cell.

Mutations are "mistakes" that occur in the process of transcription or translation of a gene that lead to a change in the amino acid sequence of the protein specified by that gene. The term *mutation* often has a negative connotation, but that is not always the case. Proteins are long chains of amino acids that adopt three-dimensional shapes that allow them to recognize and perform specific tasks, such as the "lock" function of a neurotransmitter or odor receptor. But the entire protein is not part of the critical part of the lock. By analogy, suppose you get a copy of your front door key and somehow the machine operator added an extra notch; whether that mistake would render your key dysfunctional will depend on where the extra notch was placed. For example, if it were in the handle, it would be inconsequential; on the other hand, it might turn your key into a master key that in a biological sense would improve its fitness. Thus, only some genetic variations or **polymorphisms** have adverse or loss-of-function outcomes.

EPIGENETICS

The DNA sequence of a cell is not the whole story. In fact, all of our cells contain identical chromosomal DNA, yet we are composed of lots of quite different and specialized cell types, for example, skin, brain, gastrointestinal tract. And within these categories are many different types; for example, neurons reside in different brain regions (e.g., NTS, arcuate, cortex) and thus have different connectivity and different neurotransmitters (e.g., POMC, NPY/AgRP). An embryonic cell is totipotent (can become anything); what it does become depends on a series of events or choice points that collectively are called *differentiation* (Figure A2.3).

By analogy, a newborn human might have an almost infinite number of possible life trajectories, but these trajectories become progressively narrowed by a series of life influences or choice points. Many of the differentiation factors in cells depend on when during embryonic development they are formed and where precisely they are born in the developing embryo. That is, the local context into which a cell is born exerts a profound effect on which parts of the genome actually can be expressed as the cell matures (e.g., a gastrointestinal cell cannot ask for a "do-over" to become a brain cell; the differentiation choices, once made, are more or less irrevocable). In addition to local chemical and tissue-related factors, it is apparent that external or environmental factors may play some role, perhaps in fine-tuning the system. One well-known example is that raising animals or people in environments with limited social contact or other stimulation causes fewer brain cells to survive and/or more limited connectivity in parts of the brain, as well as behavioral dysfunctions that are hard to treat. More generally, gene expression is dependent on both experience and environment: This is the field of **epigenetics**.

Transcription of a gene is determined in part by its local chemical milieu. The chromosomes that we described earlier do not simply float around: They are wrapped tightly around proteins in the cell nucleus called histones. Both DNA and the histones may be chemically modified to

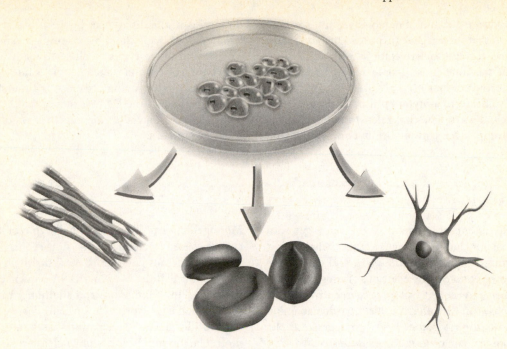

FIGURE A2.3 Differentiation of totipotent cells to become (in this case) muscle, blood, or brain cells.

influence the tightness of this wrapping and thus the ease with which a gene can be unzipped and copied by DNA polymerase. Genes can be modified by addition of methyl groups (methylation), especially at C (cytosine) residues in the promoter region and decrease gene availability for transcription. Likewise, the histones may be chemically modified by acetylation or methylation; adding acetyl groups (acetylation) in general loosens the wrap around the histones and so increases gene expression. Several food components have effects on these epigenetic regulators. For example, green tea contains compounds called polyphenols that decrease DNA methylation. Grapes contain a compound called resveratrol that affects histone acetylation. Food restriction also has this effect. Importantly, these epigenetic changes do not involve changing the gene or gene product but nonetheless are heritable across generations.

Heredity of traits

Our genes are inherited from our parents: For a given gene, each parent contributes one **allele**

or alternative form. As we noted earlier, if both alleles are the same, you are homozygous for that gene and the functions or traits that it encodes (the expressed **phenotype**). If the alleles are not the same, you are heterozygous for that gene, and only the autosomal dominant form is expressed. Familial hypercholesterolemia (high blood cholesterol level that increases the risk of cardiovascular disease) is caused by a dominant mutation in a gene that normally removes low-density lipoproteins (LDL) from the blood; this occurs in about 1 in 500 individuals. Sickle cell disease (mutation in hemoglobin resulting in various symptoms, ultimately reducing life span) is caused by an autosomal recessive gene; originally prevalent in people indigenous to Africa, global migration now has this occurring in as many as 1 in 2,000 people in European and American countries.

These are examples of **monogenic** or single gene phenotypes or traits. But most traits are **polygenic**, arising from several genes. Eye color is a good example. Originally, brown was thought to be dominant and blue recessive, but it is now known that several genes expressed in and around the iris account for eye color inheritance, as well as the fact that most people do *not* have either pure brown or blue eyes!

The term **polymorphism** is used in two principal ways. The first refers to two (or more) phenotypes coexisting within a species: Sexual dimorphism, the differences between males and females, is perhaps the most common example. The second usage refers to alternative forms of **genotype**. For example, a single nucleotide polymorphism (SNP, pronounced *snip*) is a mutation of a single base in the DNA sequence that, if in a coding region, may alter the effectiveness of the translated protein.

Glossary

Allele   Alternate form(s) of the same gene. In animals including humans, genetic material is organized in chromosome pairs, and each chromosome contains one allele of a given gene.

Codons   A sequence of three consecutive nucleotide bases on RNA that specifies a particular amino acid. As the ribosome "reads" consecutive triplet codons, a chain of amino acids is constructed.

Epigenetics   Changes in gene expression of a cell that are *not* caused by changes in the underlying DNA sequence. Examples include chemical modification (methylation and acetylation) of specific nucleotides that alter the rate of gene expression. Some of these epigenetic changes are heritable.

Gene   The smallest unit of heredity in organisms. A gene is made of a double strand of DNA, the base sequence of which determines the particular (protein) product encoded by that gene.

Genome   The complete set of inherited chromosomes and DNA. It contains both the genes (coding and regulatory regions) as well as apparently non-coding regions.

Genotype   The genetic makeup of a specific individual (rather than a species), including allele variations, and most usually referring to a specific trait.

Heterozygous   The two alleles of a gene in an individual are different.

Histones   Proteins found in cell nuclei around which the chromosomal DNA strands are wound.

Homozygous   The two alleles of a gene in an individual are the same.

Monogenic   An observable phenotypic or trait change caused by alteration of a single gene.

Mutations   Molecular "mistakes" in which one or more nucleotide bases in a DNA sequence are substituted (also omissions and additions) and so the functional gene product is usually changed.

Nucleotide bases   Nucleotide bases are the molecular building blocks of nucleic acids. For DNA, they are adenine (A), thymidine (T), guanosine (G), and cytosine (C). These are joined head-to-tail via chemical bonds to form a long strand.

Phenotype   The aggregate observed characteristics of an individual, including physiology and behavior.

Polygenic   An observable phenotypic or trait change caused by alteration of several genes.

Polymorphism   When two or more distinct phenotypes for a trait exist in the same population; the most common example is sexual dimorphism.

Ribosomes   Specialized structures just outside the nucleus of cells at which mRNA (chain of nucleotide bases) is translated into a protein (chain of amino acids); see also **codons**.

Transcription   The process by which the information contained in the nucleotide base sequence of a gene (DNA) is copied or translated into a single strand of ribonucleic acid (RNA).

Transcription factors   Chemical factors that engage upstream or regulatory regions of genes to initiate transcription.

CREDITS

Chapter 1: p. 3, Stasys Eidiejus/Fotolia; p. 5 (top), ZINQ Stock/Fotolia; p. 5 (bottom), Adrian Hillman/Fotolia.

Chapter 2: p. 13 (left), LHF Graphics/Fotolia; p. 13 (right), Leonid Andronov/Fotolia; p. 15 (top), Altin Osmanaj/Fotolia; p. 15 (bottom), Leonid Andronov/Fotolia; p. 16, Alila Medical Images/Fotolia; p. 17, Alila Medical Images/Fotolia; p. 18, o.meerson/Fotolia; p. 19, Steve Cukrov/Fotolia; p. 20, gozzoli/Fotolia.

Chapter 3: p. 29, p6m5/Fotolia; p. 31, oigro/Fotolia; p. 33, OOZ/Fotolia.

Chapter 4: p. 46, aratum/Fotolia; p. 47, Morphart/Fotolia; p. 51, Natalia Merzlyakova/Fotolia; p. 55, Scott Griessel/Fotolia; p. 57, Minerva Studio/Fotolia.

Chapter 5: p. 61, Everett Collection Inc/Alamy; p. 63, Ilia Shcherbakov/Fotolia; p. 64, Elenathewise/Fotolia; p. 65, matka_Wariatka/Fotolia; p. 67, Renata Osinska/Fotolia; p. 68, JLV Image Works/Fotolia; p. 70, erwinova/Fotolia.

Chapter 6: p. 77, Piotr Marcinski/Fotolia; p. 80, Odua Images/Fotolia; p. 81, Sergiy Bykhunenko/Fotolia; p. 82, Emily Splane; p. 84, ChantalS/Fotolia; p. 88 (top) spotmatikphoto/Fotolia; p. 88 (bottom) matka_Wariatka/Fotolia.

Chapter 7: p. 97 (top), Emily Splane; p. 97 (bottom), stocksolutions/Fotolia; p. 99 (top), Pressmaster/Fotolia; p. 99 (bottom) ksena32/Fotolia; p. 100, Wellford Tiller/Fotolia; p. 102 (top first) Hinochika/Shutterstock; p. 102 (left column top), Hinochika/Shutterstock; p. 102 (left column bottom), JJAVA/Fotolia; p. 102 (right column bottom), Monkey Business/Fotolia; p. 104, WavebreakMediaMicro/Fotolia.

Chapter 8: p. 108 (top), Brent Hofacker/Fotolia; p. 108 (bottom), Brenda Carson/Fotolia; p. 109, creative soul/Fotolia; p. 110, sherstobitov/Fotolia; p. 111, Jiri Hera/Fotolia; p. 113, Jasmin Merdan/Fotolia; p. 114, Cathy Keifer/Shutterstock; p. 117, G.Nicolson/Fotolia.

Chapter 9: p. 127, Rudie/Fotolia; p. 129, valdis torms/Fotolia.

Chapter 10: p. 140, Randall Reed/Fotolia; p. 141, Alberto Pellaschiar/AP Photo; p. 145, Angelo Giampiccolo/Fotolia; p. 148; Yuri Arcurs/Fotolia.

Chapter 11: p. 157, John Sholtis/AP Photo; p. 161, julien tromeur/Fotolia; p. 164, Gennadiy Poznyakov/Fotolia.

Chapter 12: p. 169, mady70/Fotolia; p. 172, Alila Medical Images/Fotolia; p. 173, Alila Medical Images/Fotolia; p. 174, Allison Leach/Getty Images.

Chapter 13: p. 181, Entropia/Fotolia; p. 182 (right column top), Minerva Studio/Fotolia; p. 182 (right column bottom), Tracy King/Fotolia; p. 184, kojikoji/Fotolia; p. 186, Les Cunliffe/Fotolia; p. 188, Yuri Arcurs/Fotolia.

Appendix 1: p. 191, Balint Radu; p. 192 (top) Balint Radu/Fotolia; p. 192 (bottom), Alila Medical Images/Fotolia; p. 193, Alila Medical Images/Fotolia.

Appendix 2: p. 197 (top) korni007/Fotolia; p. 197 (bottom), Alila Medical Images/Fotolia; p. 199, Andrea Danti/Fotolia.

INDEX